THORSTEIN VEBLEN

THORSTEIN VEBLEN

David Riesman

with a new introduction by

Stjepan G.Meštrović

Transaction Publishers
New Brunswick (U.S.A.) and London (U.K.)

New material this edition copyright © 1995 by Transaction Publishers, New Brunswick, New Jersey 08903. Originally published in 1953 by Charles Scribner's Sons. "Preface to the 1960 Edition" originally published by Charles Scribner's Sons, 1960.

This book is printed on acid-free paper that meets the American National Standard for Permanence of Paper for Printed Library Materials.

Library of Congress Catalog Number: 94-31537
ISBN: 1-56000-776-1
Printed in the United States of America

Library of Congress Cataloging-in-Publication Data

Riesman, David, 1909–
    Thorstein Veblen / David Riesman ; with a new introduction by Stjepan G. Meštrović.
        p. cm.
    Originally published : New York : Scribner's, 1953.
    Includes bibliographical references and index.
    ISBN 1-56000-776-1 (pbk.) : $21.95
    1. Veblen, Thorstein, 1857–1929. 2. Economics—United States—History. 3. Sociology—United States—History. I. Title.
HB119.V4R5   1994
330\.092—dc20   94-31537
                                                                                CIP

To REUEL DENNEY
Friend and Fellow-Student
of Vebleniana

CONTENTS

INTRODUCTION TO THE
TRANSACTION EDITION

W HY should a reader living in the 1990s be interested in this reissue of David Riesman's 1953 book on Thorstein, Veblen who wrote in the spirit of the previous *fin de siècle*?[1] According to David Riesman, "to the very considerable extent that his country is still our country, what he had to say in *The Theory of the Leisure Class* remains applicable; to the extent that we are living in a new country, we must make new mirrors, new selections, though often based on his models of analysis, to help us understand it" (p. 191). I agree that these are compelling reasons to read Veblen, but why read Riesman's analysis of Veblen, as opposed to books by Joseph Dorfman,[2] John Diggins, or Rick Tilman, among the other analysts of Veblen? The primary difference between Riesman and most other analysts of Veblen seems to be that Riesman uses Veblen as a vehicle for his own social criticism of American society. Riesman's book is not just another scholarly treatise on Veblen (though it is that to some extent), but constitutes the rare opportunity to read a leading American social critic on, and *through,* another leading American social critic.

David Riesman is one of those rare and gifted writers whose thought remains forever young. Though he was born in 1909, Riesman's opinions and arguments have always struck me as being fresh, more exciting and contemporary than discussions that I have had with any colleague or student. I would urge the college or university student who has picked up this book, in particular, to finish reading it for another reason. David Riesman is the teacher that students dream of: interesting, generous with his time, kind, non-elitist, and frankly exhilarating. While these qualities in a teacher are rare at any university, they stood out especially strongly in the snobbish atmosphere at Harvard University. It was David Riesman's example as a teacher that inspired me to pursue both sociology and teaching. I believe that some of the qualities that make Riesman an outstanding teacher, and have earned him the American Sociological Association teaching award, come through in this book as well. Riesman's students as well as colleagues know him as almost fanatical in his sense of responsibility to them, and to the institutions that he serves (from Harvard to sociology and teaching as institutions). Thus, this book should be read as an analysis written by one of America's supreme educators who has devoted himself to issues in education.[3]

Riesman never comes across as lecturing even when he lectures. Rather, his arguments always come across as discussions. Similarly, Riesman makes it clear that the interpretations in this book are "tentative and hypothetical: they are offered as contributions to the stream of discourse on Veblen" (p. xlix). The best way to read this book is to undertake to enter a discussion with David Riesman on Veblen for the sake of "idle curiosity" as well as with a careful eye on making sense of the present. I have written this introduction with the aim of stimulating such a discussion, and, curiously enough, wrote it as part of an ongoing discussion with David Riesman.

A final reason for appreciating this particular book on Veblen is Riesman's ability to be critical of persons, ideas, and institutions in ways that most of the rest of us find startling. David Riesman is the social critic *par excellence*. He asserts early in this book that in contrast to some other analysts of Veblen, Riesman has a "less sympathetic opinion of Veblen's permanent intellectual achievement" (p. xlviii). I shall confess to one self-conscious bias: I am sympathetic to both Veblen and Riesman, the two great American social critics that begin and end the strange and often bloody twentieth century.

HOW SHOULD VEBLEN BE READ?

I agree with David Riesman that "It is a measure of Veblen's strength as a social critic that no rounded judgment of his work can be made that is not also a judgment of American society, now as well as then" (p. xxxvi). Several distinct aspects of this assessment need to be distinguished. First, Riesman's approach needs to be understood as an aspect of his career-long interest in American "social character" expressed in *The Lonely Crowd,* a number of other books, and his course at Harvard University, Social Sciences 136, "Character and Social Structure in America." In this regard, one should pay close attention to Riesman's discussion of the affinities and differences among Veblen, Mark Twain, Henry Ford, Henry Adams, particularly in the concluding chapter.[4] Second, Riesman analyzes Veblen as a Norwegian-American, which is an approach that is commensurate with contemporary sensitivity to the multicultural nature of American society, but is decidedly out of sync with most other studies of Veblen (and of the other founders of sociology!).[5] Riesman would have us think of Veblen as the *Norskie* who was not completely Americanized. Riesman claims that Veblen "never sought to escape his Norwegian identity and affiliations" yet "it was hard for him to feel at home in Norway or in little Norway" (p. 5). Third, and closely related, Riesman is sensitive to the interplay of individual with national or social character in general. Throughout his study of Veblen, Riesman never lets us forget that Veblen was a member of a minority in American society, and behaved as such. Minority members are always aware of their marginal status, and they tend to write in code when they criticize the majority (Veblen's satiric style may be considered part of that code, a defense mechanism by which Veblen could always claim he did not mean to be taken seriously). The pity is that Veblen's defense mechanism worked all too well: He is still dismissed as just a satirist. According to Riesman, "marginality is often constructive." He makes some fascinating analogies between Veblen and the social status of being Jewish in the sense that both were marginal: "Veblen saw in the Jews something of his own career and fate" (p. 132n).[6] Zygmunt Bauman has observed that in the previous *fin de siècle* especially, Jews—who were marginal to the European societies in which they lived and worked—contributed greatly to the Western culture that ultimately rejected them.[7]

Yet contemporary sociology has been tardy in acknowledging how some of its founders had to write in code due to the social status of living as a Jew of German descent in France (Durkheim), or a German Jew living in Berlin (Simmel), for example.[8] Fourth, Riesman's elaboration of the Veblen-America connection needs to be compared and contrasted with Jean Baudrillard's exposition of the same connection.

It is amazing how often America is rediscovered by authors such as Veblen, Kafka, Baudrillard, Freud, Twain, H.G. Wells and others.[9] Baudrillard, frequently hailed as *the* spokesperson for postmodernism, changes slightly Veblen's portrait of America as the barbaric land of leisure and infinite consumption.[10] He keeps Veblen's celebrated concepts of conspicuous waste, conspicuous leisure, conspicuous consumption, vicarious conspicuous waste, vicarious conspicuous leisure and vicarious conspicuous consumption.[11] The minor adjustment consists of the claim that images and fictions, not material goods, are consumed, and that the rapidly aging Me-generation former Yuppies are today's leisure class.[12] The obvious difference between Baudrillard and Riesman is that Riesman does not concern himself with the term *postmodernism.* That is just as well, because many have concluded that the word *postmodernism* is a contemporary buzzword that obscures more than it illuminates.[13] Besides, Baudrillard denies that he is a postmodernist at the same time that he obviously relishes this title.[14] (Here one should note an interesting similarity between Baudrillard and Veblen as somewhat irritating and provocative thinkers who do not allow themselves to be pinned down, and with whom, as an intellectual or a reader, one is practically compelled to form a love-hate relationship.) The more important point for comparison is that in his *America,* Baudrillard extrapolates from Veblen to conclude that America is the dawning of the future, albeit an inauthentic future, and the cultural center of a Disney-like world.[15] This claim has produced a hailstorm of protest and criticism that center on the questions: Why aren't Japan and Germany considered as legitimate rivals to America's role as cultural leader? Does Baudrillard really "mean it," or is he just being satirical, like Veblen is alleged to have been in *The Theory of the Leisure Class*?[16]

In the pages that follow, I depict David Riesman's reading of Thorstein Veblen as an important alternative to the postmodernist reading. For those who suspect that postmodernism is just a fad that will pass away, Riesman's analysis will come across as the discussion for all seasons, not just our *fin de siècle*. And for those who wish to cling to the postmodernist absorption of Veblen, Riesman's version of Veblen will offer an interesting point of departure for further discussion.

WHO IS THE REAL BARBARIAN?

The 1990s have been developing along the post-Cold War trajectory captured by the American philosopher and former State Department employee, Francis Fukuyama, who put into circulation again Hegel's phrase, the "end of history."[17] But in Fukuyama's version it is the United States of America, not Germany, that serves as the focal point of this endgame. Those who refuse to take Fukuyama seriously claim, perhaps correctly, that he bastardizes Hegel. Using George Ritzer's vocabulary of the "McDonaldization of Society,"[18] one might paraphrase this criticism as the assertion that Fukuyama offers us a fast-food McHegel sandwich instead of the elaborate and heavy German meal that can really be found in Hegelianism. But this criticism is beside the point when one considers that in the present *fin de siècle,* Americans desire to have all their insights in fast, bite-sized morsels, and that philosophers have been arguing for many years as to what Hegel really meant, with no resolution on the horizon. The more important point is that Riesman challenges the glib assertions found in the Fukuyama craze: that the Allies (France, Britain, and the United States) are superior to Germany and other nations mired in history, that democracies do not go to war with other democracies, and that the Allies have reached the end point of democratic development envisaged by Hegel (albeit, let me repeat that Hegel reserved this mystical state for Germany). One of Riesman's most devastating criticisms of Veblen concerns

Veblen's dramatic about-face regarding which nation is truly barbaric: "Before the [Great] war, Veblen plainly regarded American capitalists as latter-day barbarians; how is it that he suddenly sees the Germans as the real barbarians?" (p. xxxviii).

Riesman notes that one of the Allies in the First World War was czarist Russia, hardly a democracy. Riesman elaborates: "It is curious that Veblen associated both America and England with democracy during the First World War, when he had so much more critical a view, both before and after the War."[19] It is worth pondering why "Veblen's identification of the Allies and the US with democracy seems curious" (p. xxxviii). Nowadays, no one seriously questions these linkages. Baudrillard lampoons this assumption by equating America with Disneyland and pure democracy for the leisure class while the rest of the world must exit. Allan Bloom's best-seller, *The Closing of the American Mind,* argues that many of America's twentieth century ills stem from an over-absorption of Germany philosophy and social thought, especially Nietzsche.[20] (We should not forget that Bloom was one of Fukuyama's most important mentors).

As illustration of the automatic assumption that Germany is still barbaric compared to the Allies, consider the June 1994 celebration of the fiftieth anniversary of D-Day. The ceremonies in Europe centered on the United States, England, France, and Italy. One might wonder why Italy was invited, given that Italy fought on the side of fascists for most of World War II. Similarly, France's Nazi collaboration remains one of the most unexplored chapters of World War II. And why were the Russians not invited? After all, the Russians took twenty times the casualties of the Western Allies, and three-quarters of all German losses came on the Russian front. In any case, the American media seemed to take it for granted that the Germans did not belong at the D-Day events.[21] Susan Eisenhower, the granddaughter of General Dwight Eisenhower, noted that "Keeping the Germans at arm's length, especially after a tentative invitation had been extended, 'implies that we harbor some belief that the Germans have a kind of ethnic original sin'" (*New York Times,* 5 June 1994, p. E4).

Worried that a reunified Germany would dominate Europe, the leaders of Britain and France took tentative steps in December 1989 and January 1990 to create a British-French entente to "check the German juggernaut," former British Prime Minister Margaret Thatcher has written in her memoirs, adding, "I produced from my handbag a map showing [Mr. Mitterand] the various configurations of Germany in the past, which were not altogether reassuring for the future."[22] Lady Thatcher seemed particularly concerned over German expansionism into Eastern Europe and the Balkans. Given these indicators of anti-German sentiments, it cannot be a coincidence that the Allies blamed Germany for the war in the Balkans that Serbia began in 1991.[23] Along these lines, one should also consider the fact that many American opinion makers routinely compare the Serbian fascism of the 1990s with German Nazism, a comparison that may or may not be fair to the Germans, but is certainly worth discussing.[24] The negotiators for the European Community in the current Balkan War were Lord Carrington and Lord Owen, both British. Germany was deliberately excluded from shaping the destiny of the Balkan nations recently freed from the yoke of communism. It is not far-fetched to suspect that Britain's geopolitical interests, which traditionally stressed the isolation and containment of Germany, are operative despite all the ostentatious talk of a United States of Europe.

In sum, there is much to be learned and debated in David Riesman's forceful exposition of a typically Allied anti-German bias found in Veblen's work that has erupted again in the present *fin de siècle*. I find the following somewhat long passage by Riesman, taken from a letter,[25] particularly thought-provoking:

"The Kaiser did not preside over a totalitarian society. Erich Fromm told me a remarkable story. At the end of his school term in the spring of 1914, a teacher had told the students that, in the fall, they would have to know how to sing the British national anthem. When the students returned after the war had broken out, he asked them to sing it, and they responded that of course, with the coming of the war, they had not needed to learn it. He felt free enough to chastise them, to say that there would surely be a Britain after the war, which the British were likely to win in any case, and he insisted that they sing the British national anthem then. The Kaiser's Germany did not prevent such independence. Yet, in the First World War, I lived through anti-Hun ferocity far greater than the anti-Nazi feeling during the Second World War. My counter-factual dream was that Wilson could have brokered a peace between the exhausted French and the Germans whose Social Democratic party was resistant to further war credits, and then we would have had neither Nazism nor Stalinism. This would not have been appeasement, because I do not attribute to Germany the responsibility for the outbreak of the war.... The Austrians, the Russians, the French, all bear responsibility for the outbreak of the First World War. Thus, dealing with the Germans in that war would not have been appeasement, unlike the situation in the Balkans today. Wilson, the Southerner, was eager to support the British."

NATIONALISM

Regarding the issue of nationalism, Riesman uncovers yet another fruitful contradiction in Veblen's writings: Veblen was against nationalism because it involves wasteful, honorific, and hence barbaric rituals, ceremonies, and related phenomena, while, on the other hand, Veblen sometimes came across as an American nationalist and ethnocentric defender of the Allies against the German barbarians. Thus, Veblen thought that "national ambitions are inconsistent with the world economy" and that the nation itself "is as out of date as the priesthood" (p. 128). Riesman seems to agree with Veblen's anti-nationalism, as indicated by Riesman's self-revealing phrase concerning "the extent that we have succeeded in overcoming the contamination of nationalism within ourselves" (p. xl). Since writing that statement in 1960, Riesman claims that he has learned "not to regard nationalism as necessarily evil; it depends."[26] Leah Greenfeld and others have written in recent years on the need to distinguish good from evil nationalism.[27]

Nevertheless, it is interesting to think, in Veblen's terms, of "pride of tribe and nation" as "wasteful," hence barbaric. Was Veblen right that "the fewer governments the better" (p. 128)?[28] One ought to connect this aspect of Veblen's thought with Robert N. Bellah's controversial concept of "American civil religion," and civil religion in general as a luxurious and seemingly unnecessary blend of religion and politics.[29] There is no doubt that American civil religion is alive and well in the 1990s, as evidenced by the furious celebration of Americanism following the victory in the Gulf War and, more recently, the controversy surrounding the Alamo in Texas as a "shrine" to American democracy. But the civil religions of Russia, the Ukraine, Serbia, Norway, and a host of other nations seem also to be getting noisier in the 1990s. Is it possible to transcend this wasteful habit of nationalism mingled with religious ceremonialism? At times, Veblen wrote as if it were possible. Let us try to imagine such a purely rational society, completely efficient and lacking useless nationalism. Who would fight for such a society if it were attacked? Who would pay taxes to support a wasteful government (for by Veblen's standards, all governments are wasteful)? In general, who would make sacrifices for one's nation, soil, and tribe in a purely rational society? It is impossible to imagine such a society.

Ironically, even the Bolsheviks, whom Veblen admired, failed to overcome nationalism or civil religion. It is important to note Riesman's observation that despite his skepticism, Veblen fell in readily with the pro-Bolshevik propaganda in the United States. The Bolsheviks espoused a transnational, ascetic ideology that must have appealed to Veblen because of his own disdain for wastefulness in general and the wastefulness of barbaric capitalism in particular. Yet it is nothing less than shocking that a thinker as astute as Veblen failed to recognize Bolshevism in particular as disguised Russian nationalism and communism in general as the disguised nationalism of the dominant group in a given country (for example, Serbian domination of Yugoslav communism).[30] Finally, one has to take into account both Stalin's and Tito's "success" in locating different parts of the economy in different units in the former So-

xviii INTRODUCTION TO THE TRANSACTION EDITION

viet Union and the former Yugoslavia, so that they would have to cooperate and are in deep trouble now because they are separate "nations." Both Stalin and Tito took account in some measure of ethnic and nationalist differences, both to oppose and to support, despite the different brands of communism that each adopted.

Riesman is probably right that "Veblen's hovering image of a world society purged of all friction based on history, association, and culture seems a Technocrat's illusion" (p. 96). It is alarming that in the 1990s, one finds vestiges of this Technocratic illusion in the writings of Bloom, Fukuyama, some postmodernists, and the Clinton administration. President Clinton's speech to the French National Assembly on 7 June 1994—the second speech to the assembly by an American president since Woodrow Wilson promoted the League of Nations there in 1919—criticized the idea of nationalism as inherently dangerous (*New York Times,* 8 June 1994, p. A4). Thus far, the Clinton presidency has sought to make the United States act as one nation among many joined in the vision of the end of history, far removed from Tocqueville's portrait of America as the beacon of democracy set upon the world's hill. While one can sympathize with Clinton's alarm at the shot of militant nationalism fired by Serbia in 1991, and heard around the world, hardly any attention is being paid to how a good and healthy form of nationalism might be recognized, or nurtured.

But Riesman is right to point out that what irked Veblen the most about nationalism was its power to "defeat and delay socialism" (p. 127). One might argue that this is precisely what happened in the fall of communism: The nationalism that the communists and socialists sought to eradicate survived their efforts to eradicate it, and returned with a vengeance. Arguably, nationalism is the strongest social force in the world today, and there is serious reason to worry that Serbian "ethnic cleansing" is the wave of the future in many nations. The citizens of the United States should not be complacent in this regard: The "white flight" into American suburbs is an unofficial "ethnic cleansing" in its own right, and whites, females, and gays have practically taken on the status of ethnic groups. Is gay bashing in the United States fundamentally different from the hate crimes being committed by the Serbs in the 1990s? Veblen's and Riesman's concept of nationalism ought to be expanded to account for these related phenomena such that, for example, American men and women at times behave as if they belonged to different nations. Furthermore, it seems to be a "paradox that nationalism has erupted all over the world even while there have been some moderately successful efforts to reduce tariffs and barriers to trade among nations"[31] such as the North American Free Trade Agreement.

FEMINISM AND FEMININITY

Riesman observes that Veblen defended "the 'feminine' as against the 'masculine' elements in civilization" (p. 2). In general, Veblen felt that modernity involves the evolution from peaceable, productive, matriarchal, savage societies to barbaric, warlike, wasteful, and patriarchal societies. Nowadays one will get into fierce conflict if one associates the "feminine" with anything that is non-aggressive and not sufficiently ruthless, at least in some, though not all, university departments. Feminists are decidedly split on the issue whether feminism ought to involve emulation of patriarchal power or the shift to a softer and fundamentally different feminine source of "power."[32] Veblen, an early feminist, has much to offer to this discussion.

Veblen takes seriously women's roles in society and in history, starting with matriarchy and the role of the mother. Riesman takes Veblen's mother, and father, seriously. "Much of Veblen's work may be read as an internalized colloquy between his parents" (p. 6). Perhaps it is true that much of Riesman's work may be read similarly, and in general, it is worth pondering how all great sociologists might be understood differently if one took their upbringing into account. Typically, contemporary sociologists trace the influences of positivism, Kantianism, utilitarianism and a host of other "isms" upon the adult theorists that concern them, but fail to investigate what might turn out to be the most decisive influence of all, the parents. Riesman jars the complacent sociologist by his focus on Veblen's mother and father. Like Sigmund Freud,

Veblen was his mother's favorite. Veblen's mother was softer than his father, whimsical and imaginative; she "enjoyed folktales and the Bible" (p. 6). I agree with Riesman that "Veblen is at his best when he takes the side of the one who is maternal, and is destructive when he tries to be 'hard'" (p. 7). How might his work have turned out differently had the roles been reversed such that his father was the "maternal" one, and his mother "hard"? Or if both were soft or hard? Generalizing further, one might wonder what one should expect from the so-called Generation X, many of whom were raised within minimal parenting?

Riesman links the contradictions found in Veblen's life and work—his detachment, voyeurism, and perhaps even cruel indifference contrasted with his maternal aspects such as his high regard for workmanship, generosity, and other non-barbaric traits—with the tension he felt between a father's hardness bordering on cruelty with a mother who embodied maternal values. Thus, Veblen is someone who forces the reader to enter into a love-hate relationship with him intellectually. (As I have suggested earlier, Baudrillard evokes a similar love-hate reaction.) Perhaps this is why Riesman makes it clear that he does not sympathize with Veblen overall, yet he finds many sympathetic aspects in Veblen's work. It is Veblen who evokes the ambivalence, and Riesman who exposes it.

In this way we may appreciate Riesman's exposition of the "buried sadism" in Veblen as evidenced by his cruel pranks and his heartless treatment of students. But there is a buried compassion in Veblen as well, for Veblen clearly sympathizes with the women who are "kept" for display by the men in the leisure class, and likewise with children and all others who fall into the domain of maternal values. I agree with Riesman that "much of his [Veblen's] work may be seen as a passionate defense of women" (p. 41). Yet a balanced discussion of this point might involve taking issue with Riesman's claim that women are "intrinsically freer than men of such superstitions as nationalism" (ibid.). One noteworthy contemporary counter-example would be the widespread support by Serbian women for the suspected war criminal, Slobodan Milošević.[33] This is a complex issue, and requires careful analysis.

Marx and Veblen are both severe critics of capitalism, yet Veblen keeps Marx at a distance.[34] Perhaps Veblen could not identify with Marx and Marxism because of the optimism and unilateral pro-Enlightenment assumptions found in Marxism, and its philosophical bedrock, Hegelianism.[35] Veblen was a pessimist, after all, and despite the overlap between his and Marx's contempt for capitalism and affection for social engineering, Veblen's pessimism proved to be the overriding factor, and Riesman may be right that "it is his [Veblen's] pessimism which attracts many people to him today".[36]

Thus, Veblen presents a "picture of modern capitalism as the demonic disguise of earlier more open brutalities" (p. 46). Riesman tries to give Veblen the benefit of the doubt by noting that "in reading Veblen we must never forget that he lived and wrote at a time when Americans, both on the land and in the cities, could and did starve to death; when homeless men wandered the roads without hope of public succor" (p. xxxvii). But ultimately, Riesman disagrees with this one-sided assessment of capitalism by Veblen because Riesman sees conspicuous *production* as well as conspicuous consumption in capitalism.

On the other hand, Veblen's assessment of capitalism seems to still ring true when one considers its effects in postcommunist Russia and Eastern Europe. The West exported the most mean-spirited version of capitalism to these nations, one without safety nets or regulatory mechanisms that are taken for granted in the West. Russia and other Eastern European nations paid huge sums for money to Western consultants to teach them capitalism, but are beginning to find out that these lessons primarily benefit the West, not Russia and Eastern Europe. To add insult to injury, the West has erected stiff trade barriers that make it difficult, if not impossible, for the postcommunist nations to compete. One might retort that it is hubris, not viciousness, on the part of Professor Jeffrey

Sachs of the Harvard Economics Department, and other consultants like him, to think that the Russians could shift easily to capitalism and free markets, an assumption that has led already to disastrous consequences. But Veblen's point seems to be that the viciousness lies in the capitalist dogma, not its high priests, such as Jeffrey Sachs. Especially in his relatively neglected essay, "Christian Morals and the Competitive System,"[37] Veblen argues that capitalism, at its best, is a blend of patriarchal, selfish barbarism and matriarchal, humanistic production, but that the barbaric component has gained the upper hand. I think this assessment still stands in the 1990s, especially with regard to the export of capitalism to formerly communist nations.

Moreover, and in line with Veblen's devastating criticism of American capitalism that it cannot sustain production without war, one could point out that his critique still applies in this, our post-Cold War era. The United States does not really have the capability to sustain a peacetime economy, and periodic new wars will undoubtedly have to be found to keep the dual economy going.

With regard to the general cultural milieu of the leisure class, Riesman is undoubtedly right that "in Veblen's view, hardly any American is so poor and benighted as to escape participation in the leisure class in his mode of life as well as in his dreams" (p. 171). American capitalism is based on the consumption of material goods as well as on consumerism for consumerism's sake, of ideas, slogans, images—whatever. This is a theme that can be traced from Veblen's *Theory of the Leisure Class* through Riesman's *Abundance for What?*[38] to Baudrillard's previously mentioned *America*. On the other hand, Riesman is right to criticize Veblen (and by extension, Baudrillard) for overlooking what he terms *conspicuous production* (p. 191) the fact that Americans like to display their very workmanship. It is a fascinating question which contributed most to the fall of communism in the late 1980s and early 1990s: conspicuous consumption or conspicuous production? A compelling argument can be made for both scenarios.

For example, the Iron Curtain failed to keep out televised *images* of Western decadence, anomie, consumerism, and the imaginary life of the leisure class that Veblen so brilliantly prophesied. Thus, the American television soap opera "Santa Barbara" mesmerized *babushkas* as well as young women in the former Soviet Union and Eastern Europe. Riesman was right to suggest during the height of the Cold War, "with all the seriousness of satire, that the United States undertake to bring down the Soviet Union without war by an uninterrupted bombing of its people with consumer goods, from nylons to refrigerators, canned goods, and jeeps" (p. 193).[39] On the other hand, Riesman argued that "the most important conspicuous production is that of armaments, in which a jet bomber becomes a symbol of national emulative propensity" (ibid.). Without a doubt, the U.S. military amazed even many Americans with its weaponry during the Gulf War. However, it is still an open question whether this is the sort of "production" that Veblen had in mind.

Riesman is also right to chastise Veblen for failing to note that "puritanical asceticism, though it has greatly changed its forms, is by no means dead in America" (p. 179). Examples of this persistent puritanism abound, the most recent being the virulent anti-smoking campaign in the United States, regarded by most Europeans as fanatical. (One should keep in mind that Veblen specifically cites the smoking of cigarettes as a barbaric, wasteful habit of the leisure class.) Along these lines, Veblen failed to appreciate the norm of thriftiness in the United States, which co-exists, awkwardly, with conspicuous consumption. Thus, Veblen would have been amazed, had he lived long enough, by the fanatical coupon-clipping, bargain-shopping ethos of the contemporary United States. The awesome power of Madison Avenue and other sources of advertising in the United States is offset by the equally awesome power of American mothers who "train" their children to shop wisely and to see through advertisements. Perhaps it is true that "lack of such 'training' in Eastern Europe must be one of the reasons for bitter resentment against the exploiters of capitalism who have come in to make a killing."[40]

Another dimension to Veblen's critique of capitalism is his contempt for lawyers as the high priests of the pecuniary culture that he regarded as barbaric. Bashing lawyers has become popular in the 1990s, with lawyers taking the brunt of hostile jokes that depict them as selfish, vicious, and parasitical on the rest of society. This attitude is due in some measure to the oversupply of lawyers in the United States, the fantastic rate of lawsuits, and the doubling of the prison population just since 1980. It is also not helpful to the image of lawyers that the often unpopular Clinton administration is packed full of lawyers (including the president and first lady, of course), reportedly more than any previous administration. David Riesman seems to regard Watergate as a watershed event regarding the social function of lawyers:

> "What is striking in the Watergate story, as many observed at the time, is how large a proportion of those involved in the shady doings and then the attempt to cover these up, were lawyers. Of course, these begin with Nixon himself. Then there is the unscrupulous former Attorney General, Mitchell, and his successor, Richard Kleindienst. There were lawyers all around, including John Dean, the President's Counsel, and then Earl Krogh, Jr., Colson, and (outside the government) Herbert Kalmbach, and ever so many others.... When Tocqueville was here, he thought of the lawyers as forming a kind of aristocracy, a reserve against populist demagoguery, just as he thought of the jury system as training in citizenship. Alas, for these ideals! What our proliferation of lawyers has done is rather to turn us into a litigous society and one that is inclined to think in terms of yes/no answers to difficult questions, rather than the answers that might be given by a scholar or a scientist—answers of 'more or less' or 'maybe'."[41]

Arguably, lawyers put a huge burden on social institutions such that, for example, "It is lawyers who enforce Affirmative Action, which removes incentives from those it supposedly tries to help, and puts them in positions where it is thought that they got there through Affirmative Action and not on merit."[42] Nevertheless, against Veblen's and the current popular prejudice, Riesman believes that major responsible law firms try to keep their business clients honest. In general, current American society is not only packed full of lawyers, but is susceptible to them, which means that many of them try to keep their clients—and each other—honorable.[43]

Riesman observes that Veblen "made a decisive Satan out of Wilson," in part because "Veblen maintained that the peace [at Versailles] had not been vindictive enough" (p. 123). In his typically thought-provoking manner, Riesman elaborates on the implications of Veblen's attitude toward Wilson:

"I fault Woodrow Wilson for creating a situation which brought us both Hitler and Stalin. But he brought us Hitler in part by agreeing to French terms, where the Germans did pay for war reparations and helped create a situation into which Hitler could come. Thus, Wilson was wrong in making war and also in making peace. Veblen criticized him only for making an insufficiently harsh peace."[44]

Regarding the contemporary relevance of this discussion, one might note the striking line of continuity from Wilson through Jimmy Carter to Bill Clinton, all of them Southern Democrats and moral idealists who ran afoul of their respective Congresses. All of them pretended to be humble but were not (and President Clinton is not) humble. But Veblen's perspective enriches our understanding of two other dimensions of what might be termed idealism in American foreign policy (in contradistinction to the realpolitik practiced by Henry Kissinger and his disciples): peacemaking itself has become the new leisure class, and peacemaking often hides a hostile intent.

Regarding the first point, any serious reader of Veblen will spot the huge waste of money and other resources involved in U.N.—and even U.S.-sponsored peacemaking operations. Peacemaking today involves cocktail parties, negotiations at expensive resorts, private jets for Western representatives, and other elements of conspicuous leisure. The bottom line is that for all of the billions of dollars spent on promoting peace—and let us note that most of the money goes to pay salaries for staff and their comforts, in contrast to the relatively paltry sums spent on the comfort of well-being of the natives—the world does not seem very peaceful. As I write these lines, genocide continues unabated in the former Yugoslavia and Rwanda despite the presence of United Nations "peacekeepers," and ethnic conflict is occurring in about thirty other places in the world. Riesman writes of Veblen's criticisms of "organized futility," and of pretending to be helpful and industrious all the while one is being predatory (p. 66). One ought to extend these criticisms to the transformation of peacemaking into a business for the new leisure class. It would be a very Veblenesque approach.

The other component of contemporary peacemaking that Veblenism exposes is its implied contempt for the people to whom the West claim to bring peace and humanitarianism. One is reminded of the biblical story of Jonah, the reluctant peacemaker who hated the people of Nineveh, whom God commanded him to save, and refused to go there initially. Similarly, the much touted humanitarian and peace efforts by the United Nations in Somalia and Bosnia, to pick just two recent examples, resulted in failure and widespread feeling among the natives that the U.N. peacekeepers were their enemies. The citizens of Sarajevo spat upon and jeered Boutros Boutros-Ghali, the U.N. secretary-general, to demonstrate their outrage at the fact that the West feeds the Bosnian Muslims so that they can be killed later by Belgrade-sponsored aggressors. More than any other social critic, Veblen exposes the hypocrisy of pity organized along the lines of business and bureaucracy: Pity benefits the self-image of the leisure class but implies contempt for the objects of one's pity.

Thus, one should balance Riesman's exposition of Veblen's ethnocentrism, hatred of Wilson, and other contradictions in his two books on war and peace with Veblen's largely implicit though sometimes explicit call for a fundamental change in humanity to peaceable habits of goodwill based on his vision of matriarchal society.[45]

CONCLUSIONS

In the pages that follow, David Riesman offers the reader a treasure trove of insights based on his dual strategy of criticizing Veblen as well as offering an independent social criticism of the America, and world, that Veblen criticized. To repeat, this is a book by a social critic on a social critic. I contend that the insights of both of these towering figures in American social criticism, Riesman and Veblen, still seem fresh and ring true when one looks around at the contemporary world. The waste, fraud, corruption, and perfumed, prestigious decadence that the pessimistic Veblen uncovered is with us still, perhaps worse than in the previous *fin de siècle*. But the more optimistic and generous David Riesman is also right to point out the areas of social life that Veblen neglected, the genuine productivity, goodwill, even innocence[46] that co-exists with barbarism in America, and the world.

Stjepan G. Meštrović

College Station, Texas
July, 1994

NOTES

1. Technically, Veblen was not a *fin de siècle* writer. Except for his *Theory of the Leisure Class,* published in 1899, the rest of his books were published in the twentieth century. Yet one could argue that he wrote in the *fin de siècle* spirit that was characterized by pessimism, disenchantment, and a critical stance toward modernity's worship of *rationality* with a capital "R". See Stjepan G. Meštrović, *The Coming Fin de Siècle* (London and New York: Routledge, 1991).

2. Joseph Dorfman, *Thorstein Veblen and His America* (New York: Viking, 1934); John P. Diggins, *The Bard of Savagery: Thorstein Veblen and Modern Social Theory* (New York: Seabury Press, 1978); Rick Tilman, *Thorstein Veblen and His Critics, 1891–1963* (Princeton: Princeton University Press, 1992).

3. See David Riesman, "On Discovering and Teaching Sociology: A Memoir," *Annual Review of Sociology* 14 (1988): 1–24; Steven Weiland, "An Interview with David Riesman," *Michigan Quarterly Review* 27 (1988): 373–887; David Riesman, "Quixotic Ideas for Educational Reform," *Society* 30 (March/April 1993): 17–24; David Riesman, "Reforming Education: Untimely Observations," *Current* 356 (October 1993): 15–21; David Riesman, *Constraint and Variety in American Education* (Lincoln: University of Nebraska Press, 1956); David Riesman, *On Higher Education: The Academic Enterprise in an Era of Rising Student Consumerism* (San Francisco: Jossey-Bass, 1980); Gerald Grant and David Riesman, *The Perpetual Dream: Reform and Experiment in the American College* (Chicago: University of Chicago Press, 1978); Christopher Jencks, and David Riesman, *The Academic Revolution* (Garden City, N.J.: Doubleday, 1968), among many other works.

4. Along these lines, see also Jeff Biddle, "Veblen, Twain, and the Connecticut Yankee," *History of Political Economy* 17 (1985): 97–107.

5. See also Jonathan Schwartz, "Tracking-down the Nordic Spirit in Thorstein Veblen's Sociology," *Acta Sociologica* 33, no. 2 (1990): 115–24.

6. Still another provocative reference by Riesman to Veblen is that of a "wandering Jew who lacks an identity" and an analogy between Zionism and "Little Norway" (p. 26).

7. Zygmunt Bauman, *Modernity and Ambivalence* (Ithaca, N.Y.: Cornell University Press, 1991).

8. Thus, most of Durkheim's many commentators refer to him naively as a French sociologist without mentioning the fact that he was Jewish or descended from eight generations of rabbis. Important exceptions to this generalization are Harry Alpert, *Emile Durkheim and His Sociology* (New York: Columbia University Press, 1961) and Stjepan G. Meštrović, *Emile Durkheim and the Reformation of Sociology* (Totowa, N.J.: Rowman & Littlefield, 1988).

Simmel has not been taken seriously until recently in the United States due to his "non-scholarly" writing style, with minimal sensitivity to Simmel's possible motives. For important exceptions to this rule, as well as sensitive explorations of how Simmel has been apprehended, see Michael Kaern, ed., *Georg Simmel and Contemporary Sociology* (Boston: Kluwer, 1990) and David Frisby, *Georg Simmel* (London: Tavistock, 1984).

Sigmund Freud is no exception to this mode of analysis, of course. See Marthe Robert, *From Oedipus to Moses: Freud's Jewish Identity* (London and New York: Routledge, 1974).

9. Robert Erwin, "The Man Who Discovered America," *The Yale Review* 78 (1988): 46–61.

10. Mike Gane, *Baudrillard: Critical and Fatal Theory* (London: Routledge, 1991).

11. Jean Baudrillard, *For a Critique of the Political Economy of the Sign* (St. Louis: Telos Press, 1981).

12. See Chris Rojek, "Baudrillard and Leisure," *Leisure Studies* 9, no. 1 (1990): 7–20.

13. Stjepan Meštrović, *The Coming Fin de Siècle* (London: Routledge, 1991).

14. Pauline Rosenau, *Postmodernism and the Social Sciences* (Princeton: Princeton University Press, 1992).

15. Jean Baudrillard, *America* (London: Verso, 1986).

16. For a most recent summary of these debates, see Chris Rojek and Bryan S. Turner, *Forget Baudrillard?* (London: Routledge, 1993).

17. Francis Fukuyama, *The End of History and the Last Man* (New York: Free Press, 1992).

18. George Ritzer, *The McDonaldization of Society* (Newbury Park, Calif.: Sage, 1992).

19. Letter from David Riesman to Stjepan Meštrović, 27 May 1994.

20. Allan Bloom, *The Closing of the American Mind* (New York: Simon & Schuster, 1987).

21. Peter Schneider, "Invasion and Evasions," *New York Times,* 7 June 1994, p. A15.

22. John Darnton, "Thatcher Tells of '89 Plan with Paris to Rein in Bonn," *New York Times,* 18 October 1993, p. A10.

23. Echoing the French and the British, U.S. Secretary of State Warren Christopher asserted:

"There were serious mistakes made in the whole process of recognition, quick recognition, and the Germans bear a particular responsibility in persuading their colleagues and the European community. We were not in office at that time, but many serious students of the matter think the beginning of the problems we face here today stem from the recognition of Croatia and thereafter of Bosnia." (*USA Today*, 17 June 1993, p. 11A)

24. See Anthony Lewis, "Lessons of Yugoslavia," *New York Times*, 26 February 1993, p. A15. Consider also Margaret Thatcher's statement that "the Serbs use the same methods as the Nazis, which I never expected in my lifetime to see in Europe again" (*Bryan/College Station Eagle*, 27 March 1993, p. A1).

25. Letter from David Riesman to Stjepan Meštrović, 27 April 1994.

26. Letter from David Riesman to Stjepan Meštrović, 15 April 1994.

27. See Leah Greenfeld, *Nationalism: Five Roads to Modernity* (Cambridge, Mass.: Harvard University Press, 1992) and Stjepan G. Meštrović, Slaven Letica, and Miroslav Goreta, *The Road from Paradise* (Lexington: University Press of Kentucky, 1993).

28. See also Charles G. Leathers, "Thorstein Veblen's Theories of Governmental Failure," *The American Journal of Economics and Sociology* 48 (1989): 293-306.

29. Robert N. Bellah, "Civil Religion in America," *Daedalus* 96 (1967): 1-21. For an extensive discussion of the connections between Veblen and Bellah's, Durkheim's, and Tocqueville's concept of civil religion, see Stjepan G. Meštrović, *Durkheim and Postmodern Culture* (Hawthorne, N.Y.: Aldine de Gruyter, 1992).

30. Dinko Tomašić, *The Impact of Russian Culture in Eastern European Politics* (Glencoe, Ill.: Free Press, 1953).

31. Letter from David Riesman to Stjepan Meštrović, 7 June 1994.

32. See Riane Eisler, *The Chalice and the Blade: Our History, Our Future* (New York: Harper & Row, 1987).

33. Stjepan Meštrović, Slaven Letica, and Miroslav Goreta, *Habits of the Balkan Heart* (College Station: Texas A&M University Press, 1993).

34. Perhaps Veblen has more in common with Edward Bellamy than Marx, however. See Rick Tilman, "The Utopian Vision of Edward Bellamy and Thorstein Veblen," *Journal of Economic Issues* 19 (1985): 879-98.

35. For more on the differences between Marx and Veblen, see Stephen Edgell and Jules Townshend, "Marx and Veblen on Human Nature, History, and Capitalism: Vive la difference!" *Journal of Economic Issues* 27 (1993): 721-39.

36. In a letter to Meštrović dated 27 May 1994, David Riesman wrote: "I think there are great differences among Americans in terms of optimism and pessimism. I have the sense that much dissatisfaction with politics today refracts a sense of mistrust that amounts to pessimism, and I think millions of Americans are pessimistic about their own future and the country's future. There is also a strong streak of despondency."

37. Thorstein Veblen, "Christian Morals and the Competitive System," *Essays in Our Changing Order* (New York: Viking, 1943), 200-28.

38. David Riesman, *Abundance for What?* (New Brunswick, N.J.: Transaction Publishers, 1993).

39. Note, in particular, two essays reprinted in David Riesman's 1993 edition of *Abundance for What?*: "The Nylon War" (pp. 67-79) and "Some Observations on the Limits of Totalitarian Power" (pp. 80-92). In the former essay, first published in 1954,

Riesman correctly prophesied that consumerism would bring down the Soviet Union. In the latter, also first published in 1954, Riesman displayed courage by pointing out the limits to the "brainwashing" powers of the Communists. One has to keep in mind that these essays were published during the height of the Cold War. Riesman deserves credit for being one of the few intellectuals to write about the end of the Cold War—and accurately, at that—at a time when the end of the Cold War was practically unthinkable.

40. Letter from David Riesman to Stjepan Meštrović, 7 June 1994.

41. David Riesman, "Attitudes toward President Nixon: A Case of American Exceptionalism in Relation to Watergate," *The Tocqueville Review* 4, no. 2 (1982): p. 293.

42. Letter from David Riesman to Stjepan Meštrović, 7 June 1994. In a letter to Stjepan Meštrović dated 17 June 1994, David Riesman adds:

> "Another charge that I make against lawyers...is that they absorb much too large a proportion of our intellectually most talented and ingenious, and even imaginative, young people, now almost as many women as men, who graduate from college. It is also public interest lawyers, including pro-bono, often younger, lawyers in the big firms who have been active in striking down single-sex institutions, whether it is the attempt to have three all-black boys' elementary schools in Detroit, struck down by lawyers from the ACLU and NOW, or the lawsuits against the Citadel and Virginia Military Institute. (But there is also the earlier lawsuit against the Mississippi University for Women, in which Hogan, a commuter who wanted to pursue a nursing degree at the University was persuaded to pursue the case by zealous public interest lawyers, men in this case, even after he had left the field of nursing and his wife and youngster, had gotten a divorce, moved out of Columbus, Mississippi, where the University is located, and where the dissenting quartet of justices in *Mississippi University for Women* v. *Hogan* declared that something valuable was being destroyed for the mere convenience of a commuter.) Apart from the great harm done to potentially useful and now rare experiments in education, what a waste of exceptional talent in the litigious process!"

43. Letter from David Riesman to Stjepan Meštrović, 27 May 1994.

44. Letter from David Riesman to Stjepan Meštrović, 7 June 1994.

45. Thorstein Veblen, *Imperial Germany and the Industrial Revolution* (New York: Sentry Press, 1964) and *An Inquiry into the Nature of Peace and the Terms of its Perpetuation* (New York: Macmillan, 1917).

46. See David Riesman, "Innocence of the *Lonely Crowd*," *Society* 27 (January/ February 1990): 76-79. I should add that I see the *Lonely Crowd* as an incontestably pessimistic work, and fail to see innocence in the America of the 1950s that Riesman portrays. David Riesman disagrees with me on this point.

In a letter to Stjepan Meštrović dated 17 June 1994, David Riesman writes: "But in reflecting on *The Lonely Crowd*, I am repeatedly reminded of one pessimistic segment which seems to me truer today than when it was written: namely, the portrait of the inside-dopesters and the curdled indignance in the political process. Both of these cadres are even more pronounced today."

PREFACE TO THE 1960 EDITION

THE interpretation of Veblen offered by this book emphasizes above all the ambiguity, even the internal contradictions, of his thought. Inconsistency, as Emerson said, need
not be altogether a defect: it may reflect a complex and honest
mind working on inherently difficult problems. Yet the authors of
this Preface remain more critical of Veblen than do a good many
of those who have written centennial interpretations of his work
and influence; this is in some measure because we attempt to view
his writings as a whole, where contradictions are most in evidence,
rather than taking them book by book or theme by theme. Moreover, we attempt to link the man and the work, not to diminish or
explain away the latter, but to try to make sense of its incompat-
ibilities. Thus, for example, it remains a problem for us why Veblen
invoked over and over again the virtues of small-scale neighborly
life among peasants and savages, while at the same time praising
the industrial technology which worked in his view towards ever-
increasing centralization. So, too, we must ask what he intended in
attacking the psychology of classical economics for assuming men
to be passive, while at the same time he mocked at reformers as
tinkering busy-bodies. And, since war and preparations for war
preoccupy us as these pages are being written, we also want to ask
what kind of radical was the Veblen who, though strongly against
war, supported American entry into the First World War, when
LaFollette, Debs, and Randolph Bourne, along with many other
brave and far-sighted men, opposed it?

Such confusions of thought, compounded by obscurity of
expression, make Veblen impenetrable for many. It may be helpful, therefore, to dwell briefly on the types of ambiguity which
Veblen's readers must expect to encounter.

Veblen was a reserved and idiosyncratic person, who expressed, in a language all his own, attitudes towards American society which were then novel and are today still unconventional (it follows that, as one's judgments of America shift, so will one's reaction to Veblen himself). Veblen's wordplay, his thought, and his personality were for him means of concealment as well as of expression, and each can become a barrier to the reader seeking rapport with the writer. Henry Adams, unlike Veblen in so many ways, was like him in the obsessive impersonality with which he referred to himself, as in the famous third-person manner of his *Autobiography*. Both men, seemingly, felt inwardly crushed and suffocated by the Gilded Age of late nineteenth-century America: a world, as Adams wrote, in which a sensitive man could not bear to live without a shudder. And this led both men to hesitate in expressing their feelings. Yet these feelings leaked in, and were among the many influences pressing toward a climate in which educated people today feel free—sometimes virtually compelled!—to open themselves up, to express themselves, to be sincere and direct. Many students who have grown up in this more permissive milieu find it hard to be sympathetic with Veblen's indirection and irony; though they might bear easily with myth and symbolism in poetry and tale, they are impatient with an economist who doesn't come right out with what he thinks.

More muscular men than Veblen reacted to him in his own time with a similar impatience. Thus, H. L. Mencken said that Veblen's language often merely clothed the obvious in sonorous prolixity. He was right up to a point: Veblen was at times trapped within his self-defensive apparatus, and he repeated himself interminably, burying an unforgettable phrase—and the trenchant idea behind it—in wordy exegesis. Viewed, however, with less impatience and with sympathy for a man who could not believe that anybody was listening, Veblen's style strikes us, after many readings, as brilliant and inventive—a genuine contribution to American polemical and scholarly prose.

But it is a mixture of strangeness and simplicity in Veblen's intellectual framework that probably inhibits and confuses his would-be readers even more than do the complexities of his personality or the style he used as a mask. Because key Veblenian terms like "instinct," "institution," or "barbarian" are in common use, we are over-ready to assume we understand the special sense in which Veblen used them. In fact, it would almost be better to consider his terminology as one does Plato's *hubris* and *nemesis*, or Machiavelli's *virtu* and *fortuna*: words which because of their strangeness are rightly suspected to clothe unfamiliar meanings. Veblen, for all his claim to derive only common-sense conclusions from merely everyday words, in fact relied on an anthropology, an economics, a psychology, and a philosophy which are superseded or out-of-fashion today. Posing as the king's jester or the village idiot, he was actually encyclopaedic in his learning, and original, not as a researcher in the modern sense, but as an "arm-chair theorist" who made an extraordinary synthesis from derived materials.

What were these materials? In economics, Veblen followed the German "historical school" of Schmoller and Sombart, which emphasized the development of economic systems and institutions, rather than the mathematical interplay of economic interests within a capitalist system assumed to be eternal. In philosophy, Veblen was a disciple of Kant, taking from him especially the notion that men look out on their experience with pre-conceived interpretative categories. Despite his admiration for Darwin and his insistence on evolutionary method in every field of knowledge, Veblen distrusted Hegel's developmental logic as non-empirical and goal-directed ("teleological"). In fact, in his distrust of any romantic, Hegelian-influenced view of man and history, any utopian image based on a (not merely biological) understanding of man's essential nature, Veblen was very much in the Anglo-American tradition of hard-headed empiricism, more narrowly pragmatic than John Dewey or William James.

Yet at the same time his psychology was largely shaped by these two men, one of whom (Dewey) was a contemporary of his at the University of Chicago. James and Dewey insisted that human nature was active, unfolding, and whole. Veblen, from this same point of view, never tired of accusing his fellow-economists of retaining a conception of the human mind as merely passive and receptive, propelled by discrete external events, at a time when psychology had left this view behind. However, Veblen relied also on the concept of "instinct," which hardly seems holistic or purposive to us; nor did he link it with "impulse" as Dewey was later to do in *Human Nature and Conduct:* there were elements of reductionism in Veblen's thought, partly as a way of reminding himself that he was "scientific" and not nonsensically metaphysical, partly perhaps also reflecting his deep personal passivity and despair. (Freud, who handled the biological concepts of the instincts more inventively, also selected among current concepts of science those compatible with his more active pessimism.)

Anthropology was the one major field on which Veblen drew without at the same time feeling called on to reform it. It was a new discipline and, as he saw it, wholly and beneficially under the influence of Darwinian method. This anthropology which he knew and trusted conceived that all mankind had evolved through a definite sequence of social systems; and that the primitive mind, characterized by an "animism" which considered all things to be living and goal-directed, likewise evolved by regular stages toward science and secularism. Veblen's own schema of social evolution involved two essential stages. The first, "savagery," was for him peaceful, cooperative, and good. The second, "barbarism," was competitive, warlike, and spiritually oriented to personal rather than communal achievement, hence (as Veblen saw it) to a falsely teleological rendering of external reality. All this Veblen elaborated in great detail and correlated with definite stages in the development of technology, in his conception the dynamic, causal factor. The daring and satirical twist which Veblen gave to the then-common anthropological assumptions lay in his bland assertion that modern society was, in its essential tone, only a latter-day barbarism.

In this distinction between a peaceful, industrious, cooperative "savagery," and an aggressive, parasitical, competitive "barbarism," Veblen knitted together the intellectual strands which he inherited. The contrast between "savagery" and "barbarism" was for him a contrast of cultural atmospheres, of ways of getting a living, of personality types, of outlooks on the world. And this perception of bellicosity and peaceableness as fundamental themes of history and social psychology should not be confused with the conceptual machinery Veblen employed to express it. It is not particularly important whether a peaceful, harmonious society really existed at the dawn of history, or is only a hope cast in the form of a fictive past, like the "state of nature" of Locke and Rousseau. What matters is that Veblen's sense of the central problems of American society, when stripped down to this quintessential contrast of two ways of life, has enduring truth. To view modern civilization as still barbaric at its core seems less funny today than to those who laughed, in 1899 (at the end of the "splendid little war" with Spain), at *The Theory of the Leisure Class*.

Veblen's black-and-white juxtaposition of "savagery" and "barbarism" was in good part derived from the Populist atmosphere of the Middle West in the post-Civil War decades (Veblen was twenty in 1877). The historian Richard Hofstadter has brilliantly characterized the "folklore of Populism": the mélange of inarticulate major premises which held together this, the strongest popular movement in American history. Populists believed in a golden age of peace and happiness in the past; the natural harmony of society if uncorrupted by power and money; a "dualistic version of social struggles"; and a "conspiracy theory of history."* One does not have to read many pages of Veblen to find each of these themes, not merely present, but central to his thought.

In dealing with Populism, Hofstadter and others emphasize that, while it raised for the first time as public issues the great themes of modern American reform—such as the graduated income tax, government regulation of monopolies, direct election of Senators, government subsidization of farm surpluses—it also fostered darker currents of popular social attitudes: racism and isolationism, and a quasi-paranoid and demagogic cast of thought. Much recent writing has tended to emphasize these darker currents as contrasted to the more hopeful ones, not only in American Populism, but also in

---

* *The Age of Reform: From Bryan to FDR* (New York, 1956), p. 62.

many popular revolutionary movements; modern totalitarianism has made many non-Communist intellectuals uneasy about any forms of political militancy, with its inevitable exaggerations, its dangers for intellectual and artistic cultivation, its potential threat to an orderly, sober, and constitutional democracy. This book itself is not entirely free of the excesses hidden in this seemingly moderate approach. For we can see (especially clearly, perhaps, after eight years of the Eisenhower regime) that political moderation is not a lasting or creative quiescence; that an age of reform looks better than an age of stagnation; that the end of ideology could betoken the end of ideas. While there are undoubted linkages of content and form between, let us say, the elder LaFollette and the late Senator McCarthy, there are also enormous differences of tone, buoyancy, and context. The gentle, yet shrewd, humanity of Senator George Norris is somehow missing from our contemporary picture of the demagogic and mean-spirited side of Populism. All this has been well stated by C. Vann Woodward, who argues that, while the Populists were occasionally anti-Semitic, this was seldom a salient theme, and quite negligible in comparison with frequent courageous advocacy in the South of solidarity between Whites and Negroes.*

Veblen's future impact on our thought will probably depend less on his specialized contributions than on the outcome of this debate about Populism and about political radicalism generally. For it is a measure of Veblen's strength as a social critic that no rounded judgment of his work can be made that is not also a judgment of American society, now as well as then. If, as the antagonists of Populism assert, the evils perceived by the Populists were more imaginary than real, and in any case irrelevant today, and if the fear to be naive becomes a stronger political motive than indignation at cruelty and injustice, then the inclina-

---

* See "The Populist Heritage and the Intellectual," *The American Scholar,* XXIX (Winter, 1959-1960), pp. 55-72. Woodward adds that, when the Populist program failed, winning support from neither poor Whites nor poor Negroes, many Populist leaders themselves turned sour and rancorous, only then using racism as a form of attack on the status quo.

tion will be to stress the psychological sources of both Populism and Veblenism at the expense of (rather than in clarification of) their substantive content. A quite different approach will follow if one agrees, as we are inclined to do now, with William Dean Howells' summary of the Populist impulse (in his introduction to Hamlin Garland's *Main-Travelled Roads*): "They feel that something is wrong, and they know the wrong is not theirs." Undoubtedly, the Populists, including Veblen, oversimplified the wrong, and regarded the wrongdoers with a Philistine and at times vindictive hatred. But in reading Veblen we must never forget that he lived and wrote at a time when Americans, both on the land and in the cities, could and did starve to death; when homeless men wandered the roads without hope of public succor; and when the newly rich and complacent lived a far more Philistine life than their humanitarian critics, condemning those who failed not only to terrible poverty but to guilt for not having "made it" when, according to doctrine, anyone could.

All these aspects of Veblen's thought—his inconsistency and ambiguity, his heavy dependence on a variety of intellectual schools now out-of-style, the essential identity of his approach with the Populist outlook—can be illustrated by his writing and actions during the First World War. As mentioned above, and further elaborated in the text (Chapter V), when Veblen left academic life to join Wilson's war government it marked a startling departure from his customary ironic skepticism towards efforts at reform. His book, *The Nature of Peace,* wavers between an unusually exposed plea for intelligent peacemaking, and the more familiar claim to be attempting nothing more than "a systematic knowledge of things as they are."* In no other work does Veblen stray so often and so far from the naturalism he shared with novelists like Stephen Crane and Frank Norris: what Parrington calls "a pessimistic realism that sets man in a mechanical world."** Here is an inconsistency which calls not so much for analysis or satire, as for pondering by all

---

* *An Inquiry into the Nature of Peace and the Terms of its Perpetuation* (New York, 1919), vii.

** *Main Currents in American Thought,* III (New York, 1930), xii.

those who seek to combine social analysis and personal action for social change.

The dichotomy between peaceful "savagery" and predatory "barbarism" appears in Veblen's war writing as a contrast between the Allied and the Central powers. Like Woodrow Wilson's, Veblen's attitude toward peace and war embraced two powerful sentiments. One was a horror of war as such, a tendency to believe that no provocation could be sufficient excuse to unleash the holocaust. Wilson expressed this view most notably in his "peace without victory" speech of January, 1917, delivered just at the time Veblen was composing *The Nature of Peace*. In that book, however, Veblen was already straining forward to the new attitude adopted by Wilson in his war message of April: the conviction that autocratic governments could not be trusted to make a lasting negotiated peace, hence that war must be pressed on to victory "to make the world safe for democracy."

In hindsight, or even in the perspective of the many radicals who at the time refused to go along with Wilson, Veblen's identification of the Allies and the United States with democracy seems curious—as no doubt the phrase "free world," used indiscriminately to refer to the anti-Communist coalition of our day, will seem a generation hence, provided that the very antithesis allows a new generation to grow up. Before the war, Veblen plainly regarded American capitalists as latter-day barbarians; how is it that he suddenly sees the Germans as the real barbarians? How is it that the skeptical student of propaganda, who was later to dub advertising "creative psychiatry," fell so unguardedly for the anti-German war propaganda of the Allies and the Yankee Easterners whom Veblen had previously mistrusted?

Do we deal here with the frequent phenomenon that, the more suspicious a person is, the more gullible he can become? Suppressing and hence keeping unclarified his own radicalism, Veblen imagined that he could transpose into the conflict between the Allies and the Entente powers his dichotomy between peaceful habits and institutions ("savagery") and warlike and predatory ones ("barbarism"). And, concluding in terms now quite familiar to us (as we fight the Cold War with Maginot-Line slogans about Munich and appeasement) that Germany's dynastic state was not only evil and oppressive in itself but inherently expansionist and impossible to treat with, Veblen came to justify war itself, chafing as angrily as Theodore Roosevelt at Wilson's effort to mediate rather than fight.

And then, when Wilson did declare war, Veblen came for the duration to persuade himself that Wilson might go so far as basically to modify American capitalism in the interest of winning the war and making a lasting peace. Veblen did not realize that Wilson's anti-German moralism was not so sharp as his own, nor could he be aware of how tormented Wilson felt the very night before he asked Congress to declare war. So, too, Veblen's hopes for Wilson as a revolutionary blinded him to evidence to the contrary, such as Wilson's antagonistic attitude towards labor, towards Debs, and towards Mexican uprisings against American investments and dollar diplomacy there. (Such self-deception was to find devotees among Franklin Roosevelt's admirers in the Second World War and, *parri passu,* in the Cold War.)

Ironically, we know today that Wilson's pronouncement of the famous Fourteen Points in January, 1918, was in good part brought on by the Russian Bolsheviks, who published the secret Allied treaties and sent forth to the world the slogan of "no annexation and no indemnities."* Yet the Bolshevik slogans were themselves borrowed from the speeches of Wilson; and in this complicated interplay of appearance and reality, the sources of Veblen's later hatred of Wilson and angry pro-Bolshevism are to be found.

Thus, in the Veblen of 1914–1917, we meet a man whose mind was not the "hard clear prism" Dos Passos spoke of, whose stance was not the unwavering hostility to the status quo in all its aspects which is so often attributed to him. Rather this is a Veblen whose judgment was quickly questioned by scholarship,** as in other cases it was rendered obsolete by events.

* Cf. the authoritative and enlightening discussion by George F. Kennan, *Russia Leaves the War* (Princeton, 1956), Chapters VII, XII.

** Thus ten years after America's entrance into the war, Sidney B. Fay was writing in *The Origins of the World War* (New York, 1927), II, 522: "Germany did not plot a European War, did not want one, and made genuine, though too belated, efforts to avert one."

None of this, however, is said in a spirit of debunking Veblen. Few are the saints who utterly escape the temptation to join "their" nation in a moral crusade against an obvious international wrong-doer! And, to the extent that we have succeeded in overcoming the contamination of nationalism within ourselves, so that we can look with appropriate horror at the policy of deterrence and see through the fanatical rationalizations with which moral men justify it, we are in debt to that more fully human side of Veblen that saw war as the health of the dynastic (or, as we would say, garrison) state, and saw peace as the health of mankind. Beyond that, Veblen had a sense of the ways in which technology could be married to nationalism for war-making purposes, and of the contribution of the "underlying population" to a warlike animus, so that, while he is far from a complete guide to the present world conflict, he is a good preliminary one. Like other Midwesterners of a later generation— we think of George Kennan, Harold Stassen, Glenway Wescott, among many very unlike men—he found his way to an intellectually cosmopolitan outlook.

In Chapter 9 we compare Veblen with Henry Ford and Mark Twain, noting important similarities of outlook beneath obvious disparities. (More recent work on Mark Twain, emphasizing the tinkerer and entrepreneur in him, would not seem basically to alter our picture.) Now we would like also to compare Veblen with Thoreau in terms of the lasting significance both men have had in creating a style of dissent. No one now bothers with Thoreau's theories, such as the notion of "correspondence" between the biological and mental worlds; and in a hundred years, if the interpretation here advanced is correct, few will remember "the instinct of workmanship" or the contrast of "savagery" and "barbarism." No, the significance of these men lies not in theory, but in a total attitude towards their society. It is not a cheerful attitude: with Veblen it is still more bitter, withdrawn, and passive than with Thoreau. Nor is it a consistent one. Thoreau went to jail in opposition to the Mexican War but applauded the violence of John Brown; just so Veblen, as we saw, supported the Wilson administration in the First World War, while condemning war as barbaric.

Veblen, like Thoreau, turned back to the enduring qualities of nature and life itself, and arraigned American society as their betrayor. The cabins in the woods which both men frequented are a kind of symbol of this attitude. The fondness for nature and the natural, the rejection of all cant and hypocrisy, the "inner emigration," and in Veblen's case the unaggressive unkemptness and relaxed sexual attitudes—all these would seem to link the outlook of these men to those of our contemporary Beats, or to the J. D. Salinger characters for whom also a cabin in the woods becomes a symbol of incorruptibility. (Some of these analogies are touched upon in Chapter 8.) But the differences are as profound. Neither Veblen nor Thoreau sought escape from the political conflicts of their time, but instead took risks for what they believed in. Both men were disciplined workers who never dreamed that messy behavior would provide an alibi for messy work. And while both men shared a post-Enlightenment distrust of the ravages and ridiculousness of which the human, and perhaps especially the academic, intellect is capable, neither man praised mindlessness nor was fundamentally anti-intellectual—surely not the Veblen who remained a life-long scholar and devotee of "idle curiosity." If they rejected aspects of their world, it was with the hope of changing them.

And yet it is at this point that the tragic fate of both men becomes most evident. Being, like so many Americans, clearer about "freedom from" than "freedom to," they tended in their bitterness and isolation to become solitary rebels; both men hurt and spurned a companionship they might have had. Escaping from fierce constraint, they distrusted all given authority, all given institutions:* they sought (in Thoreau's words) "hard bottom and rocks in place, which we can call reality, and say, This is, and no mistake; and then begin."

We must indeed begin there—begin by seeing reality clear. But further steps, even towards the grasp of reality, require communal support, and this in turn depends on a human solidarity that neither Veblen nor Thoreau rejected, but that neither could

---

* Cf. the similar rejection of institutions by Allen Wheelis, a psychoanalyst influenced by Veblen, in *The Quest for Identity* (1958).

call forth in self or other. Veblen was driven by his epoch to asso-ciate solidarity with "savagery," that is, with a prehistoric peace-able tribe. However, quite rejecting folksiness and sentimentality, Veblen also insisted that man must make his peace with the ma-chine; much like C. P. Snow in his lectures on *The Two Cultures and the Scientific Revolution,* Veblen was sensitive to the snob-bery and subtle inhumanity hidden in literary hostility to tech-nology and to the modern world. Admiring both the matter-of-fact skepticism he believed industrial man to possess and the amiable unassertive humanity he attributed to pre-industrial man, Veblen was unable in his own life or in his work to bridge the two cul-tures, or to envisage a post-industrial world that might be both abundant and fraternal.

Much as Freud saw the advance of civilization as a trap, in which man's libidinal and aggressive instincts become turned against himself, so Veblen saw the increase of human productivity as the very source of exploitation and waste: he has few sugges-tions as to how economic abundance, the fruit of the workmanship of the race, can be used to join men in fraternal solidarity rather than to divide them in emulation and war. With a pessimism char-acteristic of him, but far rarer in his day than in ours, he wrote:

"History records more frequent and more spectacular instances of the triumph of imbecile institutions over life and culture than of peoples who have, by force of instinctive insight, saved themselves alive out of a desperately precarious institutional situation, such, for instance, as now faces the peoples of Christendom."

DAVID RIESMAN   STAUGHTON LYND
Cambridge, Mass.   New York City

May, 1960

PREFACE TO THE 1953 EDITION

B
Y and large, the books so far published in this series have been written by devotees. Zilboorg defends Freud against his critics, against misunderstandings; Paul Sears defends Darwin; Lloyd Morris, William James; Muzumdar, Gandhi. There is nothing the matter with that: love opens eyes as well as blinds them. The point is rather to have the reader of this book understand at the outset that I am not a devotee of Veblen. I find him more often interesting than attractive, more often pungent than wise. His admiring student, the late Wesley Mitchell, who has perhaps done more than anyone else to institutionalize "institutional economics" (in his writings and in the National Bureau of Economic Research), spoke of Veblen as a "disturbing genius," adding: "No other such emancipator of the mind from the subtle tyranny of circumstance has been known in social science, and no other such enlarger of the realm of inquiry." Other well-known admirers have made (perhaps would not today make) similar declarations, which strike me as extravagant. To be sure, we must not be too critical of the enthusiasm for Veblen of those for whom he did enlarge "the realm of inquiry"; America has not had many teachers who even pretended to do that but, just as women often think their first lovers invented the pleasures of the body, so students often think their first gifted teachers in person or in print invented the pleasures of the mind. Undoubtedly there are still a great many people for whom Veblen can be enlightening in the highest degree.

Veblen had an eye for much that was central in turn-of-the-century experience. A superlative artist and thinker outlives his timeliness or makes his time part of our time. But Veblen suffers from the extraordinarily rapid changes which have made his experience, not obsolete, but peripheral to our own. The Vested Interests of business which frightened him seem only marginal menaces to us, at least in the United States; indeed, Veblen helped make almost too great a dent on the myth of the business-man. He is credited by some with predicting modern totalitarian-ism in his *Imperial Germany and the Industrial Revolution,* where he foresaw the aggressive potentialities of dynastic ambi-tions married to a late and hence superior acquisition of the Anglo-American technology. But while this actually worked out pretty much as Veblen prophesied with respect to Japan, it is wholly insufficient for comprehending Nazism, from the under-standing of whose motives and methods Veblen is almost as far removed as the 19th-century utilitarians and "classical econ-omists" he ridiculed. Much of Veblen's system of analysis now appears oversimple, and not adequate for understanding con-temporary society.

But if change has made much of Veblen irrelevant, both where it followed his lead and incorporated his ideas into our vocabulary and where it left him (to use one of his own phrases) "sitting on a dry shoal upstream," change has also served to make salient certain themes in Veblen which were less important in his own day. The breadth of his social science interests, his concern for what was changing, his use of history as anthro-pology and anthropology as history—these help provide us with the image of a modern social scientist who is less specialized, less adrift in the merely contemporary, than most prevailing models. At a time when Veblen's kind of evolutionary anthropology is almost wholly discredited, it is important to see what vitality it may still have, at least as a counterpoint to comparative work in the Boas and Malinowski traditions. Veblen steadily recalls us to the study of fundamentals, even if they are not the same fundamentals that attracted him.

To some extent, these are specialist uses of the Veblenian past, particularly for specialists who want to become generalists as well. And to some extent, this re-interpretation of Veblen is written for them, in an effort to sift what is valuable in his legacy from what are, in one of his favorite phrases, "negative assets." As each generation needs to write its own history of "the" past, so each needs to re-evaluate the thinkers who comprise its intellectual heritage. But such general shifts of perspective as go on today among the specialists are, and should be, of interest to all educated persons. Moreover, I do not believe that the line between the academic specialists and the curious and observant reader is, or should be, too neatly drawn. Apart from his commentaries on Kant and a few passages of criticism of dead economists, obscure for those who do not know what Schmoller or Roscher, Boehm-Bawerk or Irving Fisher, stood for, there is not a line of Veblen which cannot be understood by a moderately well-read person—whether or not he can always penetrate his irony and "ultimate" meanings Veblen hid even from himself; in fact, the "difficulty" Veblen presented to his own age is like the "difficulty" of Van Gogh or T. S. Eliot or Stravinsky on their first appearance.

For such a reader, then, the call to read Veblen is a call to pleasure, to read him not so much because he has portentous things to say about the modern world but because of the recurrent charm of his intellect, the bite of his sarcasm, the period flavor of his hatreds and affections. And the call to read a book about Veblen is, I hope in this instance, also a call to pleasure, to the enjoyment of a relatively idle curiosity in the disentangling of Veblen's themes and motives, the effort to relate his work, in its uniqueness and typicality, to time and circumstance, and in the search for the personal flavor of a man who, more perhaps than most of us, aimed to be misunderstood, to elude friends and foes alike, and to pretend that the idiosyncratic style he has added to our life and literature was the mere matter-of-fact, ascetic form of a scientist's inescapable vocation.

D. R.

Brattleboro, Vermont
September, 1952

ACKNOWLEDGMENTS

SINCE I have been reading and reflecting and writing on Veblen for twenty years, it is impossible short of a long autobiography to mention or even recall all those who aided my understanding of him. (The selective bibliography with which this volume ends, as well as the very occasional footnotes, are intended more as a guide to the reader than as a statement of obligations.) I read Joseph Dorfman's *Thorstein Veblen and His America* on its appearance in 1934, and have returned to it many times; it is by all odds the most useful picture of Veblen and his background that we have and, without its conscientious fullness of detail, such interpretative work as mine would be badly handicapped. In my law school days, I encountered a number of admirers of Veblen and men whose attitudes towards law, monopoly, and life appeared to have been influenced by him: I think of Thurman Arnold, Felix Frankfurter, Walton Hamilton, Max Lerner, James A. McLaughlin. During this period, Carl J. Friedrich not only helped introduce me to Veblen but to much else that aided my perspective on him.

In the College of the University of Chicago it has been my good fortune to have had as colleagues a group more than casually interested in Veblen and in the significance of his work for contemporary social science; among them, I am indebted particularly to Daniel Bell, Mark Benney, Reuel Denney, Morton Grodzins, Abram L. Harris, Martin Meyerson, Helen Sullivan Mims, Milton Singer, Jay Williams, and Richard Wohl. I am also indebted to a grant from the Social Science Research Committee of the University of Chicago in aid of completion of the manuscript.

In the actual writing of this book, I owe most to Staughton

Lynd, a graduate student at the University of Chicago. After exchanging drafts and notes on Veblen for some months by mail, Mr. Lynd joined me in Vermont for several months of intensive work on the manuscript; chapters two and seven were first worked out by him, and the other chapters as well have benefited from his knowledge of Veblen and of the rural Norwegian background, his sensitivity to the intellectual climate of Veblen's time, and his interest in Schumpeter, Marx, Sombart, and other wide-angled economists. Mr. Lynd has somewhat more enthusiasm for Veblen than I, more belief that he had valid answers for some of the great economic and political questions; this view provided a useful counterpoise to my own less sympathetic opinion of Veblen's permanent intellectual achievement.

A number of friends have generously read the manuscript or chapters of it, and I have profited greatly from their criticisms. Especially to be thanked are Daniel Aaron, Carl J. Friedrich, Oscar Handlin, Richard Hofstadter, William and Virginia Miller, Helen Singer, and Lionel and Diana Trilling; several other friends are thanked specifically in text and footnotes. Sheila Spaulding prepared the index, and made a number of helpful suggestions. Although my main reliance was on written materials, I did consult a few individuals who had known Veblen, several of whom were good enough to read portions of the manuscript. I am indebted to recollections of Veblen given me by R. L. Duffus, Lawrence K. Frank, and D. R. Scott, as well as to some criticisms by Veblen's former publisher B. W. Huebsch. Dr. Isador Lubin, Veblen's student at the University of Missouri, his assistant in the Food Administration, and his friend thereafter, found time to read the manuscript in the midst of his duties for the UN. As the book was in galley proof when we could meet to discuss it, I have taken account of a number of Dr. Lubin's corrections and observations in footnotes. It goes without saying that neither he nor any other reader or informant is in any way responsible for the interpretations presented in this book—it also goes without saying that these interpretations, no matter how dogmatic their brevity may lead them to sound, are tentative and hypothetical: they are offered as contributions to the stream of discourse on Veblen.

My wife, Evelyn T. Riesman, brought to this book her substantial editorial gifts and her unfailing encouragement and interest.

I want to thank *The Journal of General Education* for permission to draw on my article, "A Lecture on Veblen," published by them.

CHAPTER ONE

GIANT OUT OF THE EARTH

When I was a freshman at the University of Chicago I ran smack into a small chapel of Veblenians who burned a frenetic candle of admiration in perpetual recognition of the master. I met the hero occasionally as he journeyed from one place of exile or retirement to the next. He was rarely of any sparkle when he spoke. But there was a very special aura of potentiality around his every mannerism. At first he struck you as a rumpled and crumpled Van Dyke; and there was always something worn and dispirited in the way he slumped around. His permissive irreverence chimed in with the mood of the twenties, and gave everyone with any claim to brightness the obligation to be smart. In the perspective of world ideological movements the man was an outlyer of Marxist disgruntlement, who avoided the political implications of a responsible Marxism, and contributed to the undertone of disapproval and alienation that characterized the posture of the well-turned-out intellectual in this country whenever our leading economic, political and social institutions were referred to. . . . In Veblen and Sandburg we have two of the Scandinavian imports who kept alive a highly personalized note in seeking for ways of feeling and seeing their way into the intricacies of a continent where the inner possibilities of modern civilization were blossoming in stupendous profusion. Sandburg was quiet and nostalgic and particularly personal: Veblen was quick and ironic and given to impersonalizing the particular observation.

From a letter to the author from Harold D. Lasswell

THIS book is not a biography of Veblen but an interpretation of his work. But because his work was in some good part original, we cannot understand it by merely tracing the "influences" of other thinkers and of the Zeitgeist upon him; rather, we are led to look to the idiosyncratic elements in him for what they will tell us about his ideas. Of course, it does not help

1

determine the truth of a doctrine to penetrate into its personal and psychological sources in its originator—any more than a psychoanalysis of Van Gogh explains the beauty of his paintings. However, such analysis can sometimes help us trace connections in a man's thought that might otherwise escape us. For instance, if we see Veblen as a man who felt himself deficient in the usual manly virtues of self-reliance, aggressive comeback, social effectiveness, and so on, we can suggest as a possible interpretation of much of his work that he is defending the "feminine" as against the "masculine" elements in civilization, and thus bring together otherwise unrelated strands. Likewise, we may be put on guard against some of Veblen's merely plausible generalizations if we look for evidence that he wished to build a closed system which would keep out critics by labeling them as "leisure class," or "barbarian," or "pecuniary-minded"—as other thinkers have used "bourgeois" or "defense-mechanism" as spring-guns against poachers.

Finally, it is sometimes possible through such "extrinsic" analysis to shed light on the intrinsic and intended meaning of Veblen, as of other authors. Thus, it is disputed among Veblen scholars whether his irony was a mask for radical thoughts he felt it unsafe to express openly, or whether it sprang mainly from deeper disenchantments, including a disenchantment with radicalism. If we then find that Veblen hid his emotions though not always his opinions even from his close friends, we may have, if not a clue to the meaning of his writings, at least a warning as to possible ambiguities lurking in passages that on first reading appear straightforward.

Obviously it does not follow from this that a man's writing may not transcend his competence and quality in other aspects of living. To reduce the work to the level of the man, or vice versa, is to misrepresent the man who, after all, produced both the work and his own character.

VEBLENIANA

Veblen left strict instructions in his will that no biography or other memorial of him be prepared—but fortunately these instructions were disregarded by his admirers. Never having met Veblen, my own picture of him is based on what these others have written and said; on Veblen's writings seen, in the process I have been describing, as partially symbolic of his deeper motivations; and on a painstaking effort to "reconstruct" Veblen in a way that would allow room for the interpretations of those who knew him. Joseph Dorfman's conscientious biography, *Thorstein Veblen and His America,* has been my principal source; others are cited in an appendix; readers are referred to them not only for more details but for contrasting views. And, above all, readers are referred to Veblen's own writings; they remain the court of last resort, and exegesis and interpretation, like program notes at a concert, should never be allowed to get in the way of direct access to the work itself. In fact, I feel this so strongly that, at least with men about whom whole libraries have been written—Shakespeare, Bach, Goethe, Marx, for instance—the task of allowing each new generation of students to approach them freshly seems almost to require some sort of willing suspension of critical traditions. Fortunately, with Veblen, just enough time has passed since his work was done to give some measure of detachment (especially if we measure time as we should, in terms of speed of social development), without the need for chopping down a forest of received interpretations (Dorfman's, for instance, are quite modest) in the hope of seeing him straight.

FATHER OF THE MAN

Veblen began his teaching career (save for an unhappy year spent at a pious Wisconsin academy after he graduated from Carleton College) at the newly-founded University of Chicago in 1892, when he was already thirty-five. He had no "vocation" for teaching, in the sense of wanting to get his hands on the young— in fact, he did his best, or not quite his best, to discourage students and stated that in his ideal university (described in *The Higher Learning in America*) there should be no students, only research apprentices. Rather, it was forced upon him, faute de mieux, because his family and his wife's family were tired of supporting him, because there was pressure on him to have an occupation, because he was interested in research (he tried at various times to get research jobs, once in the Library of Congress and once on an archaeological expedition), and perhaps because, in spite of his tendency to withdraw from people, he could not live entirely to himself.

He had done graduate work at Hopkins and then at Yale, studying philosophy and making a good impression on his teachers—this despite his gawkiness, his shy farm-boy air, and the fact that English had come to him as a second language late in his teens. For these were the days when few people went to college, and even fewer into graduate work, and the professors, not overwhelmed with ambitious students, could enjoy taking time to polish rough diamonds of farm or city-immigrant background, making gentlemen as well as scholars of them. (Veblen became a scholar who studied the gentleman.) Noah Porter, the President of Yale, greatly struck with Veblen's doctoral thesis on Kant, and fond of him—they took long walks together—tried to get him a post teaching philosophy, but such jobs were then mainly controlled denominationally and Veblen, though he used to argue theology with his neighbors and college-mates, was too much of an agnostic, too long emancipated from Lutheran fundamentalism to get a position.

Veblen went home again. That he was willing to do so, and could do so, tells us a good deal about his relation to his family and the other Norwegians of the midwest farming territories. For when they emigrated to America from the village communities of Scandinavia, they had not had a strong national identity; they acquired this as part of the process of "Americanization," when they encountered scorn from the Yankees who dominated the towns, where they were called "Norskies" and ridiculed (recall the expression "dumb Swede"). They were willing to shelter and put up with, if not to like, a *Landsmann,* a fellow-Norwegian even if, like Thorstein Veblen, he appeared conceited, pinned derisive nicknames on them, and refused to follow a plow and, even worse, would stand idly by and argue with those who were following a plow. Perhaps, like Veblen's father and his brother Andrew, who became a well-known mathematician, they took pride in his intellect and erudition, for this "lazy" youth was good at languages and read everything that came to hand. And, on his own side, while Veblen hated farm work and was wholly out of sympathy with the religious disputes that shook the "little Norways" of Minnesota and Wisconsin, he never sought to escape his Norwegian identity and affiliations. At Yale he greeted a Norwegian stranger as a fellow countryman. Some of his students regarded him as a Norwegian chauvinist, and Alvin Johnson noted that he laid on his Norwegian accent more heavily than usual when he had a distinguished visitor in class. He translated a long Icelandic saga after he left Yale (published late in his life as *The Laxdaela Saga,* with an introduction and notes by Veblen), tirelessly studied Norwegian antiquities, and travelled as a quizzical celebrity to Norway. There, given a first-class pass on the railroads, he played a characteristic trick on a conductor: he donned overalls and, being asked to leave the compartment, pulled out his pass and enjoyed seeing contempt replaced by obsequiousness. The incident may perhaps reveal how hard it was for him to feel at home in Norway or in little Norway, as a great man or as a scorned one.

Thomas Veblen, Thorstein's father, seems to have had no such problems of marginal identity. All his life he continued to speak only Norwegian, though he had come to America as a young man. Certainly, Thomas was a dominant influence in Thorstein's life. A hard man, more enterprising by far than his neighbors, he was the first man in the county to introduce farm machinery, going out of his way to import it from the East. To those not familiar with rural conservatism, the importance of this must be emphasized; even today, most farm innovations come about because of exhortations by county agents, who rely on demonstration farms and often on those who come to farming from other backgrounds where "grandfather's way" cannot hold them back. The elder Veblen lost his first farm, for which he had slaved and driven himself and his family, to a Yankee claimant who was aided not only by his command of the English vernacular but also by his tribe's command of legalism. Many commentators have, I think correctly, seen in his father's experience the germ of the dichotomy that Thorstein Veblen made between workmanlike machine industry and predatory and legalistic chicane. One might go farther and say that Thomas Veblen's willingness to learn new farming techniques but his unwillingness to learn new linguistic ones was the model for the son's admiration for production per se, accomplished without "waste," "naturally," without the frills of cultivation or nuances of style.

The father, as I have said, was a hard man who came back strong from his defeat, ending up as a substantial landowner and a power in the Norwegian community. In the year that R. L. Duffus, then a student, lived in Veblen's household, the latter mentioned his father only once, recalling him as follows (Duffus, *The Innocents at Cedro*, p. 59):

". . . when the elder Veblen went to town on a market day and happened to meet his son on the street he did not speak to him or give any sign of recognition. I gathered that the Professor thought this interesting but not extraordinary. If a man had nothing to say there was no use in talking, even to his own son."

In conformity with this maxim, which would not have seemed outlandish to some of the heroes of Rolvaag's novels, when Veblen *père* decided it was time for Veblen *fils* to learn something, he put him in a buggy destined for nearby Carleton Academy without consulting the boy, 17. Perhaps it is not surprising that he grew up into a man who never called his friends by their first names—and who claimed that his father had taught him more than any other man.

THE MOTHER

The mother was a softer person, whimsical and imaginative; she enjoyed folktales and the Bible. She tried, like many mothers in similar cases, to protect her son, who later termed such benevolent care for the young "the parental bent"—I think it would have been more correct, in terms of Veblen's own system, to call it the maternal bent. Much of Veblen's work may be read as an internalized colloquy between his parents: between one who calls for a hard, matter-of-fact, "Darwinian," appraisal of all phenomena and one who espouses the womanly qualities of peaceableness, uncompetitiveness, regard for the weak. I am inclined to think that Veblen is at his best when he takes the side of the one who is maternal, and is destructive when he tries to be "hard." Like many bright boys, he seems to have been impressed by the male who had the power and authority in his home to give commands, while at the same time developing unexpressed resentments against power and command of any sort. When, late in life, he saw in the hard-boiled, mechanically-adept engineers an elite who would take over the country and run it as a no-nonsense industrial republic, one may sense the return of the father in a Technocrat's uniform.*

It is plain that Veblen's parents, living vicariously in and for their children as so many hard-working immigrants have done, had high aspirations for him, which he must have felt as a tacit if not verbalized constraint. The psychiatrist George Saslow has suggested that parents of this sort—intense, not very loving, who have very high ideals for their children—tend to produce children who are abnormally sensitive to constraint, children who suffer from a sort of emotional claustrophobia when exposed to the expectations of others. I was greatly struck with the relevance of

* Commenting on these observations, Professor Richard Hofstadter has written me as follows: "I have always thought of Veblen as some sort of analogue of Dreiser (despite Dreiser's utter lack of humor)—perhaps because of that sense of massive and clumsy—almost bearish—effort one gets from both of them. But there's more to it, I think: Veblen seems very much like a number of the naturalist (so-called) writers of the turn of the century, in that a fundamental impulse of sympathy for and indignation over the condition of the underlying population is smothered by a sense of helplessness. The reaction is usually to swing back and forth from sympathy to a kind of apotheosis of strength, of the sort which you locate in Veblen. . . . What naturalism and Darwinism did for men of this sort was to give them a rationale and a cover for their 'hard' moments. So Veblen, Dreiser, Jack London [whose *The Iron Heel* is a most striking instance], Frank Norris, and perhaps many others. The difference with Veblen was that he was more often successful than most in keeping his fundamental regard for the virtues of Christian fellowship under wraps—only, as you say, in the war period and the very few years afterward did he try to humanize himself, to communicate, and to propound solutions for the social ills he had raged sardonic about so long."

this remark to Veblen, for I had already seen the theme of fear of constraint as a dominant one in Veblen's life, to be traced in his work, where it is connected with his distrust of pragmatism, his praise for "masterless men" throughout history, and his concept of "idle curiosity"; and to be traced in a variety of escape-maneuvers throughout his career.

One of these consisted in marrying a woman—his first wife, Ellen Rolfe—whom an autopsy showed to be sexually still a child, insufficiently developed to have children. Veblen used to say that he could not imagine himself as a father. (It is interesting how in his work he returns with relish to the theme of illegitimate births, as in the last paper he wrote, called "An Experiment in Eugenics"; likewise, the matriarchal societies he so much admired he tended to interpret in terms of male irresponsibility. In his recurrent references to "masterless men," who could be either insubordinate Icelanders or wandering Wobbly farmer-workers, he struck a note reminiscent of Whitman's quasi-homosexual concept of brotherly love in a world of men without women.) When, through his second marriage (entered into at 50 in part to escape further dependency on his friends, the Davenports, and perhaps also because his friends so strongly opposed it) Veblen acquired stepchildren, he felt himself helpless to protect them from his wife's strict regimen which she based on Veblen's own ascetic principles. Like many great scholars and economists who either did not marry or did not have children, Veblen appears never to have exorcised his own father.

Ellen Rolfe was, however, in one sense a sign of Veblen's emancipation, for she was neither Norwegian nor farm-bred; and, as a lover of fairy-tales and an imaginative person, she must have represented for Veblen his mother's rather than his father's principle. Daughter of a railroad magnate, and niece of the President of Carleton College, where she met and befriended the rather isolated and "queer" Veblen, she was of considerably higher status than Veblen, but like many bluestockings was willing to marry "down," despite family objections, if she could get a man of exotic personal style and intellectual promise. Although her life with Veblen, seldom if ever happy, became increasingly harried and strained, she was reluctant to give him up and felt, somewhat martyr-like, that she served in a good cause. Other than John Bates Clark, who taught Veblen at Carleton before going on to a distinguished career in economics at Columbia, Ellen Rolfe seems to have been the first person outside his immediate kin to recognize and admire Veblen's powers.

There are intimations that Veblen married her, long after their first meeting, with the resignation and lack of enthusiasm of his other "decisions." * Unable to get a teaching job, he was living off his family, claiming illness as he did later in similar situations; marriage offered solvency, financial and emotional. (Of what it offered or threatened in status terms we have no inkling, apart from the fact that his second wife was, in his friends' opinion, a lowbrow and "beneath" him). He moved to Ellen Rolfe's family place, continuing his seven years of reading and ruminating. The couple read Bellamy's *Looking Backward* together—it came out in 1888 and swept literate America. Ellen Veblen said it changed their lives, focussing their interests on social questions and apparently leading Veblen from philosophy to economics, of which he had got an initial taste from William Graham Sumner at Yale as well as from Clark at Carleton.**

* It is noteworthy that Ellen Veblen later became a Theosophist, member of a vegetarian, pacifist sect which plays down the differences between men and women and believes they will eventually disappear. On her death, she willed her body to science—showing a characteristic Theosophist attitude to bodies (unimportant) and science (important). A recent study by the psychologist, Hedda Bolgar, provides evidence that women Theosophists have usually been sexless, strong partners tied to weak men.

** There are many interesting parallels between Bellamy's work and Veblen's: the same willing acceptance of modern industrial routines; acceptance, too, of administrative centralization; the same hatred for competition and the same willingness to admit distinctions based on technical competence; the same rather ascetic kinds of preferred consumption, free of rivalry, gusto, and "waste"; a similar lack of feeling for most of life's ambiguities, potentialities, and risks—symbolized in Bellamy by his wish (in his *Equality*) to cut all cities down to a maximum size of 250,000. Yet there is more pleasantness and contentment in Bellamy than Veblen usually allows himself; Bellamy recognizes sex, if of a sugary Victorian sort, while Veblen gives no place to it in his writings; Bellamy was a preacher and leader of a reform movement (the short-lived Nationalist clubs), while Veblen was a self-abnegating scientist who looked with a jaundiced eye on reformers and their utopias.

THE GROVES OF ACADEME

If *Looking Backward* was one influence which led Veblen to go back to graduate work, in the hope of eventually landing an academic post, another was the fact that Ellen's father lost his fortune. In 1891, Veblen went off to Cornell to study economics under J. Laurence Laughlin, leaving Ellen behind him for the first of many separations that, on his side at least, appear to have been quite casual and without afterthought. In general, Veblen seems to have taken his friends where he found them and parted from them easily, as is the case with many men who are withdrawn from others and who fear constraint. Also typically, Veblen arrived at Cornell without advance preparation. Dorfman writes (pp. 79–80):

> "Laughlin often told the story of his first meeting with Veblen. He was sitting in his study in Ithaca when an anæmic-looking person, wearing a coonskin cap and corduroy trousers, entered and in the mildest possible tone announced: 'I am Thorstein Veblen.' He told Laughlin of his academic history, his enforced idleness, and his desire to go on with his studies. The fellowships had all been filled, but Laughlin was so impressed with the quality of the man that he went to the president and other powers of the university and secured a special grant."

One of the things that may have struck Laughlin as unusual was Veblen's characteristic, and often effective, strategy of appearing to have no strategy. (Of course, if Veblen himself had known what he was doing, this would not have worked: he "operated" only at the price of keeping his motives deeply hidden from himself.) He preferred to arrive unannounced (which meant that no expectations of him had been built up), and apparently helpless. Although the opinion has been widespread that Veblen was discriminated against by the orthodox because of his heretical and original views, Porter at Yale and Laughlin at Cornell were merely the first in a procession of eminent and eminently respectable men who intervened at decisive points to try to help him, to be sure not always successfully—the list including Taussig at Harvard, President Jordan at Stanford, President Hill at Missouri, Davenport at Missouri and Cornell, President Alvin Johnson at the New School, John Bates Clark (even after Veblen had written a devastating review of his work). Yet there is much objective evidence to support Veblen's feeling that he had been unfairly treated by the universities: he never attained a rank above associate professor, or salary above $3,000; his publicized affairs with women, never gaudy, led to his being eased out at Chicago, forced out at Stanford. Only at Missouri (of all places! Veblen must have felt) was he given any sense of security, of being wanted and defended. When, in the early 20s, Paul Douglas (now Senator) and other economist admirers after much effort lobbied Veblen's nomination for president of the American Economic Association, Veblen felt sufficiently bitter and vindictive to let his friends down by declining; as he later recalled: "It gave me great pleasure to refuse him [Douglas]. They didn't offer it to me when I needed it" (Dorfman, p. 492).

My point here is less to deflate somewhat the picture of Veblen as a victim of academic Babbittry—undoubtedly he failed to win the security and honor commensurate with his gifts—than to see the subtle and probably unconscious ways in which he conspired in his own exploitation. A careful study of the evidence in Dorfman's biography concerning Veblen's negotiations for academic jobs inclines me to think that he wanted, in some ways, to be underpaid and underranked in order to create an atmosphere in which not much would be expected of him—only $2,000 worth, so to speak. Just as a woman may never learn to read timetables and may miss trains and suffer much inconvenience in order to prove her femininity, so Veblen, whose wants were always simple, was willing to endure hardship and humiliation to prove his sometimes inconvenient lack of the usual conventionalities, capacities, and competences.

Consider, for instance, the now-legendary schemes he developed for dealing with students when Laughlin, willing victim of one of President Harper's famous raids on Eastern institutions, went in 1892 to the newly-opened University of Chicago and took

Veblen along with him as a lowly member of the Department of Economics. Veblen fended off students by talking in a monotone, by mumbling in his beard so that he was almost inaudible, by setting unnecessary prerequisites and warning students that the course would be difficult, and perhaps above all by making it standard practice never to give above a "C" grade (for advanced graduate students, a "B" is barely adequate).* One student described his practices as follows (Dorfman, pp. 248–9):

". . . an exceedingly queer fish. He never gave us an examination and at the end of the course, he would say that with our permission he would register 'C' grade for each of us to conform to the necessary ritual of university life. . . . Very commonly with his cheek in his hand, or in some such position, he talked in a low, placid monotone, in itself a most uninteresting delivery. . . . We never did really know him or much about him personally."

Veblen, who was interested in labor-saving machinery and was distressed when Dr. Lubin wasted motions in chopping wood, always seemed to have acted in an "economical" way himself and his grade of "C" appears to me to carry in one stroke many implications. It served to harass the administration and also the students who, as he knew, were often bucking for "As" and "Bs," for Phi Beta Kappa and scholarships. Instead of conducting a head-on fight against the injustices and absurdities of most examination systems, and against the student pressure for grades, Veblen operated by means of sly sabotage; indeed, Dorfman indicates Veblen's considerable delight in throwing sand in the gears of registrars and deans of students.** By giving a "C," moreover, Veblen

* Dr. Lubin has told me that when he corrected papers for Veblen at Missouri he was not limited to "C." He adds that one could hardly emphasize too much the ritualistic nature of the examination system in those days, indeed the whole university system, which Veblen ridiculed.

** Alvin Johnson has published his euphoric autobiography, *Pioneer's Progress*, since the above was written. In it (pp. 282–3) he tells of his effort at the New School to make it possible for a large audience to hear Veblen by installing a loudspeaker. On the first day eighty students showed up. When he became aware of the amplifier roaring back his whispers at him—"I was so ungenerous," Johnson writes, "as to regard this expiring voice as an affecta-

made an equivocal gesture on behalf of the common man, and against what he regarded as invidious distinction of persons— Veblen was so frightened of one human being taking precedence over another that at times he seemed willing to repress all equally. Most of his life, Veblen was incapable of fighting directly for the things he believed in; to do so would have meant having to take both himself and his beliefs, as well as the system against which he fought, much too seriously; it would have meant commitment. Like his seemingly detached writing, the "C" grade could be taken by others as an act of indifference and detachment, not aggression and revolt.

But there are still other implications of the "C." It saved Veblen from having to face individual students (he seems often to have "forgotten" their names), and from having to handle their sibling rivalries over grades. Indirectly, it informed his students that it was foolish and vain to try for a rational examination system, and no one seems to have dared protest Veblen's own system of distributive justice—perhaps an aggrieved student would have feared being thought predaceous. Not giving exams also meant not exposing oneself to student comment and questioning. And beyond all that, Veblen's entire mode of dealing with students put him in the protected position, not only of avoiding all competition with his fellow teachers for students, but also of having a perfect alibi when, as later at Stanford, he had only three students in a course; thus, he may have saved himself from being hurt—as teachers almost unavoidably are hurt—when students passed him by for others.

Whether in spite of or because of these masochistic tendencies, Veblen actually had during the course of his teaching career a number of devoted students; perhaps they enjoyed not only their teacher's gifts but their recondite discovery of them.

---

tion"—he put the microphone in the wastebasket and continued in a voice barely audible to the front row. The rest of the audience never returned. "A few days later, encountering Leo Wolman, Veblen said, 'Johnson thought he would make me popular. But I fooled him.' "

In most cases of sabotage, I suppose the saboteur does not escape unscathed, and here Veblen seems to have been the not unwilling but perhaps not wholly witting victim of his own sly tactics.

His students formed a loyal coterie to support Veblen in his recurrent financial and emotional crises; many followers (among them, Wesley Mitchell, Leon Ardzrooni, Joseph Dorfman, Walton Hamilton, C. E. Ayres, Horace Kallen, Lewis Mumford) sought to carry on his intellectual mission in their own teaching and writing. What students found in him is sensitively put by two observant ones whom Dorfman quotes. Elizabeth Narden declared:

> "His detached, free-ranging intellect attracted, and yet it seemed a mutilated personality . . . in the main one found the margin from economic shaping not too large. . . . The whole effect was towards criticism, skepticism of watchwords, fine sentiment, prides, prejudices, no passion of hope or preference, no scornful explosives or condemnations, just a remorseless massing of facts that drove home the plasticity of the human mind under economic facts, however free it fancied itself. I think we Middle Westerners recognized in him a real citizen of the world, and we liked the wit and urbanity we found in him personally."

And Mrs. Winifred Sabine (wife of Professor George Sabine) stated:

> "One needed to get close to Dr. Veblen to 'get' . . . the small and delicate shadings of meaning he was eloquently, but not forcibly conveying. . . . Finally, it seemed to me that the irony, the understatement, the objective unconcerned tone might almost be thought of as devices for concealing feelings too deep to desire easy expression."

In interpreting Veblen's academic life, of course, we must put ourselves back in the university world of a generation or two ago, when there were not so many serious students and professors as there are today—and when very few students or colleagues would have made much effort to understand a "queer fish," or to make allowances for a learned, original, but "difficult" man. To his dying day, Veblen remained bitter about Harper of Chicago and Jordan of Stanford who had let him go. Footloose of spirit, he failed to find the academic home he needed where he could feel secure and unharried, neither a charity case nor a pawn in an inter-university struggle for eminence.

THE RESISTANCE MOVEMENT

If we take these and other indications together, we renew our hypothesis of a man abnormally sensitive to constraint, including the constraint imposed even by one's own, let alone anyone else's, intellectual system—but a man all the more driven for that very reason to ferret out the sources of constraint in economic and social life generally, as if to insist, against any inner testimony, that freedom and spontaneity are illusions. Once, when a student in his course on "Economic Factors in Civilisation" asked him whether individual achievements did not contribute to civilisation, Veblen replied (quoted by Dorfman, p. 315):

"Well, you will find, Mr. ——, that all through history, when there was need for a sermon to be preached, there appeared a preacher to preach it."

Did Veblen also think that when there was a lecture to be given, there was always an anonymous lecturer—himself—to give it? Certainly, he took little pride in his courses—when a student asked him to repeat something, he said it wasn't worth repeating, and he hated to have students take notes. And likewise he took little pride in his books, greeting references to *The Theory of the Leisure Class* by speaking of it as "that chestnut." Thus, he disengaged himself from all his productions as if he did not want to be held accountable for them, or have more in the same vein expected of him.

But in a way he *was* detached from what he said and wrote by his inability to take an aggressive attitude towards his own knowledge and grasp of the social process. He was probably one of those men who, when asked a question, forget that they know anything. His usual failure to cite his sources in his writings would seem to have been due, to some extent, to a desire to seem original—a "natural"—and to a slightly greater extent to a desire to evade another academic ritual, another debt, but, in addition, to some inner fear that a citation would act as a constraining force, limiting what he could say. Thus, for instance, if he should rest a particular statement about the handicraft era on Sombart's treatment of it, he would either have to put himself under obligation to Sombart's interpretation or to show why he departed from it, whereas by a rare, vague, and general reference he maintains his superiority to his sources. This practice, and many other elements in his make-up, led him to seek the doubtful security of abstraction—including an endlessly abstract and earnest call to other economists to be concrete. For abstraction allows one to glide over difficulties presented by individual instances—while at the same time it may give even the most erudite thinker the feeling that he doesn't really know anything, as Veblen often said and must have half-believed that he didn't. His books proceed by repetition and restatement rather than by elaboration and expansion of a theme; as we would expect from a man who fears constraint, he never wrote from an outline—or allowed editors to tamper with his manuscripts (which good editing, not of his magnificent sentences, but of his needless repetition might have greatly improved). Thus, his inability to take command of his own work as a system of thought was not due to its intractability to systematisation (as I trust this book will help show) but to his own unwillingness to take the credit and risk of saying just what it was that was central for him—which would have meant, of course, saying who he was.

Dorfman recounts an incident from Veblen's later years which seems highly symbolic of these attitudes (p. 499):

> "An unscrupulous neighbour . . . was stealing from Veblen's property some drain pipes, lumber, and other materials purchased for a new garage. All the while Veblen sat smiling quietly, in the shadow of a tall bunch of cane growing in front of the house. The thief never knew that Veblen knew; neither did Veblen know that another neighbour was witnessing the entire spectacle."

Here it is Veblen's property, not his intangible knowledge, to which he cannot commit himself. Since when one's property is being taken in one's presence, one is expected to do something,

Veblen was here in his customary fashion evading a powerful demand, and suffering the consequences. He preferred to watch with a show of amusement the drama of the theft just as, in dealing in his books with the crimes of the Robber Barons, he preferred a stance of humor and detachment; or as, when asked once to state his views on the first World War, he replied that he greatly enjoyed watching the monkeys dancing in their cages—much as he was amused when a Phi Bete at Stanford could not harness a horse. There is in Veblen's outlook on human culture, even as in his observation of the theft, something of the voyeur who sees without, presumably, being seen—Veblen never doubted, so far as his writings and his published conversations show, that *he* was scientific, and objective, even if everyone else was not. And here, like many guileful men, he was naive: in the contempt he harbored for people, he thought he could fool them, just as he thought he was unobserved in observing the thief.

One is reminded here of the close unconscious connections between exhibitionism and voyeurism: Veblen enjoyed the thought of someone being observed, although he would have preferred that he be the someone. While consciously seeking to remain anonymous and avoid limelight, Veblen's classroom tricks, along with his love affairs, called attention to him while at the same time punishing him for this very guilt-laden performance. Very likely, he dreaded external constraint because he so deeply needed it to keep these forbidden impulses in check. His strategies of non-compliance are in this interpretation only the end product, codified by recognition, of a repressed inner urge to show off.

In this connection, the incident of the thief sheds further light on Veblen's feelings against authority. Much as he was ready to disown his books even before they were criticized—for how could *he* be an authority?—so I feel he sided with the thief against himself, against his own withdrawn and passive kind of person; so, too, he sided with the thief against the authority of the law. And perhaps he sided with the thief as the representative of the cosmic forces that were disrupting his plans for a garage.

However, what I have said should not be taken to indicate

that the fear of constraint or the feelings against authority I have sought to trace in Veblen are peculiar only to him. They are widespread in the academic culture, though some fields, I suspect, are more appealing than others to men of this type; sociology more than psychology, for example; and economics more in Veblen's day than economics now, when it has become immensely larger, more successful, more organized. More generally, Veblen seems to have anticipated a theme—the fear, not of failure, but of success—which has in recent years become much more dominant in American life than in his own day (when the major theme, of course, was the fear of failure); and, on the whole, it must be said that Veblen's society gave him what he appeared to ask for and left him to relative obscurity. To be sure, the theme of the fear of success is an old one in terms of the quasi-religious dichotomy between success and saving one's soul, or one's integrity. And Veblen's inability to rise in the academic and worldly hierarchy is often interpreted as the price he paid for his refusal to conform, his critical vision and outspokenness. But this is only part, and I think not the major part, of the story. More important was Veblen's fear of eminence, of the dark unnameable dangers attendant on putting oneself forward, out in the open, an object of critical notice, a target before spectators. Since I have sought, in *The Lonely Crowd,* to suggest some of the psychological and institutional sources of this modern fear of success, I shall not develop the matter further here; but I do believe that one of the reasons that Veblen is so attractive to many American intellectuals today, beyond the actual contribution of his work, is that they sense in him motivations that prefigure theirs; that is, it is his realms of failure and despondency that attract them, and not his realms of success.

FAREWELL TO REFORM

It was at Chicago that Veblen had the most sympathetic and stimulating colleagues and where most of his best work was done. His principal ideas (other than the theory of late-coming industrialism that animates his *Imperial Germany and the Industrial Revolution*) can largely be found pretty well developed in the series of essays and reviews he wrote between 1892 and 1906 for the *Journal of Political Economy* (which he edited) and the *American Journal of Sociology,* both published at Chicago as manifestations of the academic entrepreneurship that resulted from combining Rockefeller's money with Harper's dynamism. Other manifestations were John Dewey, Jacques Loeb (a biologist, discoverer of "tropisms," who greatly influenced Veblen), the sociologist W. I. Thomas (like Veblen, a gifted maverick who was forced to leave the University because of "woman trouble"), the social psychologist George Herbert Mead; there were others, too, including the anthropologist Boas at the Museum, but these indicate the nature of the galaxy. Many of these men were reformers as well as researchers; the city of Chicago in their day buzzed with the progressivism of such men as Henry Demarest Lloyd; and after the turn of the century the city began to develop a literary movement premised on realism and reform. (Floyd Dell, one of the leaders of the latter, has told me that he and his group greatly admired Veblen; *The Theory of the Leisure Class* was almost a Bible among them.)

Veblen responded to the ideas of his colleagues, but not to their reform activities. From Dewey, as well as earlier from William James, he gained a renewed sense of man as an active being, one who selects his environment as well as is shaped by it. From Loeb he got a sense of the biological substratum of human activity; Loeb in turn acknowledged his indebtedness to Veblen's "instinct of workmanship"—these being the days when psychologists collected and classified instincts as a limited set of determinants of human action and social cohesion. Loeb, too, as a brilliant natural scientist, appears to have helped give Veblen his life-long credo that only a social science shaped in the image of post-Darwinian biology could lay claim to being "scientific"— this, for Veblen, meant free of value judgments, cold, impersonal, tough-minded. But Veblen admired none of the Chicago group as much as he admired his former Yale teacher, William Graham Sumner.

Sumner, minister-turned-professor, was one of the most impressive and important of the American Social Darwinists; he liked to insist on the very narrow limits within which men's reason could control their destiny and denounced reformers and do-gooders, though one himself (he campaigned aggressively for free trade, and against the War with Spain and Imperialism). Sumner's role as a big, blustering, outspoken man of the world (in class, he urged his students to "get capital") may have appealed to Veblen where shyer, more diffident men such as Dewey, more akin to his own temperament, did not. But the ideological affinity between Sumner and Veblen is more complex, and a famous passage from Sumner may help indicate its nature:

> "The great stream of time and earthly things will sweep on just the same in spite of us. It bears with it now all the errors and follies of the past, the wreckage of all the philosophies, the fragments of all the civilisations. . . . It is only in imagination that we stand by and look at and criticize it and plan to change it. Every one of us is a child of his age and cannot get out of it. He is in the stream and is swept along with it. All his sciences and philosophy come to him out of it. Therefore the tide will not be changed by us. It will swallow up both us and our experiments. It will absorb the efforts at change and take them into itself as new but trivial components, and the great movement of tradition and work will go on unchanged by our fads and schemes. The things which will change it are the great discoveries and inventions, the new reactions inside the social organism, and the changes in the earth itself on account of changes in the cosmical forces. These changes will make of it just what, in fidelity to them, it ought to be. . . . That is why it is the greatest folly of which a man can be capable, to sit down with a slate and pencil to plan out a new social world."

Sumner was an enthusiast campaigning against enthusiasm (as today men like Karl Popper and Michael Polanyi and Von Hayek are fanatics campaigning against fanaticism). While Veblen was no enthusiast, he nevertheless shared Sumner's zest for discovering the futility of human action and, in a wider ambit, for ridding social science of what he regarded as theological, Hegelian, and reformist preconceptions. It was this attitude, I believe, rather than caution which kept Veblen remote from the Progressive and Populist stirrings in and around Chicago, and from the reformist efforts of his colleagues.

Why should a discovery of the limits of human action, and of the insignificance of the individual, arouse enthusiasm and zest for further work? We come here on the age-old paradox that fatalistic creeds (e.g., Calvin's, Marx's, Mohammed's) seem capable of arousing men to frenzied action. In his brilliant chapter on "Desperate Naturalism," as he terms Sumner's position, Herbert Schneider writes as follows (*A History of American Philosophy,* pp. 396–7):

> "To most men this submission to existence comes naturally as an adaptation to environment, but in every generation there are sensitive spirits to whom the discovery that man shares an animal existence and an animal faith with other species comes as the revelation of poetic truth. In their unreflective thinking they go along with their fellows, 'conquering' nature and managing their efforts, but in the privacy of philosophical reflection they awake from their pragmatic nightmares to observe calmly how even they are caught in the grip of natural forces. This knowledge of their bondage then appears to them as a precious liberty, not granted to other animals, of living in disillusionment; they 'bear their fetters with an air.' They now play the role of seers. . . ."

"WHAT IS ONE TO DO . . . ?"

For Veblen, there was not even this contradiction between his philosophy and his management of life, for the latter was a continuous surrender, helpless rather than pragmatic. R. L. Duffus, who lived for a year under Veblen's roof while working his way as a student at Stanford, pictures his employer as living in a kind of careless disorder, more a consequence of inattention than of pose, surrounded by animals, stray students, and occasional motherly women—"what is one to do," Veblen, again helpless, complained to his Stanford friends who chided him for making things difficult by amatory scandal, "if the woman moves in on you?" In his Cedro cottage near Stanford, he let nature move in on him, so to speak, not so much because he was a nature-fan (his botanizing was more scientific than fond) as because he was not a human-nature-fan, and because he preferred to put up with whatever came handiest; he did not struggle against the cosmic forces.

Dorfman describes his attitude very well, as it manifested itself in his last years, which were spent in his mountain cabin (p. 498):

"For the cabin he built himself an outdoor chair. . . . Not a leaf or a weed or an insect was disturbed. Wood rats had free access even to the larder, and a skunk would brush itself against his leg, as a cat would. Veblen would stand or sit very quietly for long periods. He was never sentimental concerning 'Nature,' never even articulate. He seemed to consider the human relatively unimportant among living things."

Likewise, according to Dorfman, there was no conscious asceticism in Veblen's mode of life. He was actually neat in dress, enjoyed wearing rugged clothes "so coarse they would almost stand alone" (Dorfman, p. 498) which he preferred to buy at mail order, and liked the utility more than the effrontery of fastening his watch to his vest with a big safety pin. Perhaps what he himself referred to as his "tough skin" gave him pleasure in contrast to the sensitivity of his easily-wounded spirit. His photographs, showing his long hair, his bushy eyebrows, intelligent eyes, give me the impression of a handsome man, and it is perplexing why his contemporaries found him unprepossessing.* It may be that what was felt to be lacking was vitality: someone who has handed in his resignation to life, in 19th-century Ameri-

---

* In privately-printed "Recollections of Thorstein Veblen," his University of Missouri colleague, Jacob Warshaw, noted that at home, in his loose dressing-gown, he looked "not nearly as anemic and fragile as in his street clothes"; and that, indeed, in private with one or two cronies he could be gay, unaloof, even smart-alecky—altogether different from his public reserve.

can culture at least, may be appealing but will hardly strike others as an impressive fellow.

It is interesting that Veblen's two wives, although very different from each other, were, each in her own way, enthusiasts, with a penchant for action. His second one was given to radical statements and explosions, and Mrs. Sabine suggested that he probably enjoyed these, as a kind of vicarious release. But he was annoyed when his first, and more brilliant, wife got attention at a party; and I surmise this was due less to jealousy than to hatred for the childishness of her enthusiasm: there was something in him which made him wish to crush an innocence he himself could never recapture. For Ellen Rolfe Veblen was by no means attuned to the machine process, or matter-of-fact; she was, on the contrary, a very romantic, high-flown person; and Thorstein Veblen could not leave her to her fancies, but felt compelled to deflate them, much as he deflated doctrinaire and wishful students. But even here he often proceeded by indirection, leaving love-letters from admiring women where his wife would be apt to come upon them. Indeed, there is testimony in both Dorfman and Duffus of a kind of practical-joking temper in Veblen, a buried sadism. Leon Ardzrooni tells the story of how Veblen found a hornet's nest while on a walk and, meeting a farmer with an empty sack, asked him if he could borrow it for a while; he returned to the nest, put the hornets into the sack, then returned it to the farmer with a "thank you"—the farmer, says Ardzrooni, is still looking for Veblen (Dorfman, p. 499). Then there is Alvin Johnson's (unpublished) story of an elderly man going to visit Veblen and asking a man on the way for directions to Veblen's cottage. The man gave him directions; the visitor walked wearily on to an empty cottage, only to discover that it was Veblen who had directed him.

In milder form, this same streak appeared in Veblen's dealings with students; there, too, he liked to slip a hornet's nest into the sack. One former student, the Reverend Howard Woolston, is quoted by Dorfman as follows (p. 250):

"Veblen was an impressive teacher and an irritating leader. He encouraged the novice to jump into a bramble bush and scratch out both his eyes. When the smarting youngster came back with tales of grief, the shrewd mentor slyly indicated ways to toughen a tender mind."

Another student speaks of Veblen's custom at Chicago (he also did this later) of having a student take charge of the class, with Veblen himself in the role of student asking questions of the temporary teacher—a way, whatever its objective merits, of avoiding the teacher role as an authority. The student reported (Dorfman, p. 209):

"I recall three very strenuous days during which I took over the outlining of the building up of the capital structure and foundation of the Steel Trust by Carnegie, Frick, and Morgan. He was a merciless questioner when he became a student and caused me no end of discomfiture and created much merriment, mostly at my expense."

We might note in passing that, while in his books Veblen studiously avoided personalities, preferring such abstract personifications of historical trends as "Captain of Industry," "Captain of Erudition," "A Soviet of Technicians," and so on, in this course he much enjoyed the details of skullduggery on the part of the leading financiers and also, according to student report, was not averse to mentioning the private foibles of the great. No one, in fact, seems to have escaped his barbs. Thus, at Missouri where he was brought by Davenport and while living in the Davenports' cellar (which he entered through a window), he used Davenport's text in one of his courses to poke holes in it relentlessly. Similarly, I have already referred to his long review of the works of John Bates Clark, where the mask of impersonality served as a rationalization for cruel, almost nihilistic dealing with a teacher and benefactor—explicable but certainly not justified by Clark's dominant position in American economic thought at the time—even Veblen felt a bit troubled afterwards.

Men of Veblen's sort, who underestimate themselves, often are unaware of their power to hurt others—"who, little me, how can anyone take me seriously?," they seem to be saying. This pattern doubtless played its part in convincing Veblen and his friends that Veblen had been shabbily treated by the university world, for they were not aware of how aggressively he behaved towards authority and how, in many cases, the authority responded with more patience and less vindictiveness than might have been anticipated. In Veblen's whole posture here, there was something of the child, who is unable to realize that he can hurt his parents' or other adults' feelings—or, in any case, feels he should readily be forgiven, since he is not fully responsible.

In much the same way, Veblen's inability to commit himself (up to the First World War) to any person or cause is partly attributable to the converse feeling of the child—how can he help anyone? how can his support or intervention matter? When in his writings he made sarcastic remarks about Dewey, James, Peirce and the pragmatist movement,* he could hardly have believed he was being extra rough on thinkers who were, in many respects, his intellectual allies—the notion of an alliance would have meant taking seriously the weight he himself could throw.

Likewise, though he leaned on and learned from Marx, he continuously sought to detach himself from Marx as well as from the Marxists, and made more of his differences from them than of his large areas of agreement. Some commentators have laid this to his cautious and not unjustified fear of the academic Vested Interests; he knew that President Harper felt that Veblen didn't advertise the University of Chicago; and he observed the fate that often befell campus radicals (so well memorialized by Upton Sinclair). Yet his refusal to identify himself with Marx persisted even when in the years immediately after the First World War he was writing patently Marxist pieces for *The Dial*. In my judg-

---

* I do not speak here of the genuine differences between Veblen's and other varieties of pragmatism, such as his emphasis on unpragmatic scholarly curiosity and his Social Darwinist negativism towards reform. Rather, I refer to those passages in which Veblen uses "pragmatism" as an epithet (once he explains lamely in a footnote that he is giving the term a special twist), or where with typical ironic undertow he speaks of the "latter-day psychologists, whose catchword is that The Idea is essentially active." Since Veblen shared a great deal with the writers he thus deprecates, he was himself the recipient of many of his own shafts.

ment this was not political caution on Veblen's part—Veblen never sought to hide his caustic view of business and political leaders. Rather, Veblen felt himself put off by Marx's dual role as scholar and propagandist; he cared too much for an objective science to be comfortable with Marx's mixture of strategy and prophecy. Ernest Manheim has pointed out to me how "American" Veblen is in his uncommitted griping, his un-Marxist refusal to relate his strictures to a party program. Yet my whole impression of Veblen is that, underneath all specific good reasons for acting as he did, his was the behavior of a somewhat schizoid person who fears entangling alliances, fears the claustrophobia that may come of having colleagues, and prefers the relative anonymity of the homeless wanderer. Veblen identified himself, half-ironically and half-sympathetically, with the emancipated, wandering Jew who lacks an identity, who has left his tribal gods behind him and not found new ones—and whose contributions to culture come at the price of his marginality and alienation; for whom, also, capture by nationalistic Zionism means return to a stifling, parochial complacency akin to that of "Little Norway."

THE SIMPLE LIFE

Some men who are not attached to people are attached to things; Veblen seems to me to have been attached to neither. His "homes" were of the barest (at times he made his own furniture, or used packing crates). When he moved, he would leave his books—those precious "children" of many intellectuals—behind; like his friends of the moment, they had served their purpose. Duffus writes (*The Innocents at Cedro*, p. 88) that Veblen

> "did not wish the emotional nexus any more than he did the cash nexus. He would win disciples for his ideas, never for his whole hidden and involved personality."

Perhaps it was just this challenge of the "hard to get," these defenses in depth—especially in a country whose masculine ideal was in Veblen's day one of aggression and lack of depth—that drew women to him. Duffus writes (pp. 92–3):

"It is easier to believe him capable of affection than of passion. I think he did regard his first wife, Ellen Veblen, with affection, and that during his marriage to her he was kind to her, except in the one essential of being faithful. That he could inspire an abiding devotion in a woman, in spite of everything, I know from what Ellen Veblen told me. . . . One lady, whose opinion I respect and who did not like him at all, said to me once that Veblen was a case of a man who did not discover until well on in life that he *was* attractive to women. . . . I do suspect, and what I saw at Cedro Cottage confirms me, that he was as often pursued as pursuing."

He had a plain shack up in the hills, overlooking the Pacific; he liked to ride up there for rendezvous, or drive his cart. However, as Duffus described matters Veblen was anything but romantic about women, or visibly stirred by them. They were convenient, and could be helpful.* His second wife seems to have mothered him, sending her own children by an earlier marriage out to get him fresh cream, and allowing them to sleep late (and miss school) lest they disturb their step-father. Like the four women who called themselves "the Virolas" and who took care of Veblen during part of his New York stay, she may well have viewed herself as having charge of a national resource!

Beyond that, it is my impression that Veblen enjoyed being in a situation where he was not expected to shine intellectually and therefore preferred the less demanding company of women —not that women don't have expectations, too, but they are often more willing to cooperate in having them met, or more patient when they are not met. Some of the most poignant stories in Dorfman's biography concern meetings or parties arranged for Veblen when he became better known, where he would sit miser-

---

* Since the foregoing was written, Professor D. R. Scott, who knew Veblen well at Missouri, has suggested that only with women was Veblen able to overcome his loneliness; they provided "a kind of psychological relief: as a form of contact with the world of human relations from which he had effectively banished himself." "A Recollection of Veblen at Missouri," *The Missouri Alumus*, vol. 41, p. 12 (Feb. 1953).

ably silent, stubbornly unable or unwilling to "give." And Duffus details the silent meals at Cedro, where Veblen would only on rare occasions open up to the young, admiring students who lived with him and took care of his modest wants. At a faculty meeting, too, he was almost always silent, even if questions that concerned him were being discussed, and even if friends of his, under fire, looked to him for succor (in *The Higher Learning* he referred to academic committees as committees for "sifting sawdust"). Duffus writes (p. 59):

> "Apparently he could talk to farmers and working people more easily than he could to so-called intellectuals. He told us once of conversing with an Icelandic fisherman in Icelandic . . . and how when the man wanted to swear he had to break over into English to do it."

In the 20s Veblen began to go in the summers to a Wisconsin island where he lived among Icelanders; he appeared to enjoy leading them in games, footraces (he could, though over 60, outrun them), and other folkish pastimes.

But this un- and anti-intellectual side of Veblen is of course not the only side. At Chicago he liked to take long walks with select students. At Stanford he formed a fast friendship with Guido Marx, Professor of Machine Design, and with Rolfe, a classicist, and with the latter and a favorite graduate student studied Homer and Minoan antiquities. Though he gave Duffus the impression that "the ideal situation for a professor . . . was not to have any students at all" (p. 60), Dorfman reports him as missing students in his last years. He was more dependent on people—and for more than comfort or silent company—than he probably wanted to be.

VEBLEN IN WASHINGTON

All this comes out most clearly in the War years, when the withdrawn professor entered a new phase as amateur politician and publicist. He was taken up by some Wilson administration officials and, glad to get away from Missouri and teaching, was given a job in the Food Administration. To be sure, he had had some notoriety before this, when *The Theory of the Leisure Class* attracted the attention of William Dean Howells, but this had in the meantime died down—so much so that Veblen had had to subsidize publication of some intervening books. And he was, as former editor of a leading journal and as a frequent contributor of articles and reviews, prominent among economists, at least in America; he was always someone to be taken account of, whether for praise or dispraise. Though not widely known in Europe, he was sought out by visiting dignitaries at Missouri, and it was said on the campus that he was a famous man, if caviar to the general. But the War, which stirred up so many people and passions, helped find Veblen a wider public and gave him the feeling that perhaps after all it was possible to change the world. At 60, he became a reformer.

Of his work and his mood in this period, more will be said in chapter 5. Now we should note that Veblen greeted his departure from academic life by publishing *The Higher Learning in America* which, only half-jokingly, he referred to as "a study in total depravity"; the first draft was so vitriolic—the published one is hardly mild!—that Ardzrooni persuaded him to rewrite it. It is characteristic of Veblen's dependency that he did so; even more striking is the fact that he long withheld the book from the press at the instance of President Hill of Missouri—one of the very Captains of Erudition the book excoriates.*

Veblen had made various efforts before then to leave Missouri, but the negotiations always seemed to break down, despite many glowing letters of recommendation he could muster from the country's leading economists. He seems not to have had very good judgment about the jobs he applied for, as when for instance he was turned down by the Librarian of Congress as too bright for a routine bibliographic post; or to have had good judgment about his sponsors, as when one man he got to write for him called

---

* In private conversation, as Isador Lubin states, Veblen admitted that President Hill was, as presidents went, a very decent fellow, just as he would admit that individual businessmen (Lubin's father, for instance) were not wholly nefarious. I report this not to criticize Veblen for inconsistency; on the contrary, I think that like any artist he is entitled to select and emphasize and even exaggerate—indeed, cannot help doing so.

him "a big bluff": like many suspicious men he probably had difficulty distinguishing friend from foe. Paradoxically, what he really
needed was a patronage sinecure, without expectations—the very
sort of sinecure his insistence on workmanship and his similarly
puritanical intolerance of "waste" helped make seem suspect and
immoral to Americans.

Veblen had found the city of Chicago ugly, but he found
Columbia, Missouri, where the University is located, much less
bearable. And he resented the kind of pressure his benevolent
colleagues sometimes put on him; thus, Dorfman tells the story of
one professor who had persuaded Veblen to vote in a close town
election and came to take him to the polls, only to find that he
had lit out for the woods; likewise, when his friend and colleague
Stewart solicited him for the YMCA, he was passionate in refusal,
saying he thought it "a bourgeois and capitalist agency to defend
the existing order."

He went to Washington, as other men have done, in the hope
the existing order could be overturned. First, he thought the
defeat of the Kaiser's Germany, a nation which he viewed (as
we shall see) through the glasses of Allied propaganda, would
accomplish this. The literati, however, assumed that as a socialist
he must be against the war; he was invited to a pacifist dinner
along with Max Eastman, who reported to Dorfman that Veblen
refused to discuss politics but enjoyed "a frivolous, or at least
lowbrow conversation with a very beautiful girl we had the sense
to put beside him"; the incident shows that Veblen did not alter
his personal style of evading such "male" topics as politics to suit
his new reformist views. But he was nevertheless pleased when his
tract, *The Nature of Peace*, won favorable notice from Francis
Hackett and other radical intellectuals. Veblen said: "Now they
are beginning to pay some attention to me." (Dorfman, p. 371.)

In Washington, however, people had other fish to fry and did
not pay much attention. Veblen secured interviews with Brandeis
and Newton Baker, but was chagrined not to be taken up by
them, and to find that many officials considered the war already
won—and hence radical reforms in mobilizing the American
economy unnecessary. Later, he was given a chance to submit

plans, through Walter Lippmann, to the House Inquiry on the Peace, and again was disappointed when these were not accepted. In all this, Veblen appears to have been somewhat naive to assume that an elderly professor, inexperienced in practical affairs, would be eagerly welcomed even by his sympathizers in office. He expected miracles from the War itself—and possibly also as a result of his own willingness to come out, at long last, from behind his shell.

VEBLEN THE JOURNALIST

He became anxious to leave Washington, and turned down a $4800 job with the War Labor Board offered him by one of his former students; this was far more than he had ever earned, and perhaps too much for the man who told Leon Ardzrooni after the latter had arranged for him to become a contributing editor of *The Dial* at $2500 that he didn't think he was really worth 25¢.* (Veblen was present at one meeting where the terms of his service for *The Dial* were set—he was to write only when and how much he chose—but characteristically he did not say a word.)

Veblen poured into his *Dial* writings the full fury (of which we have come to see so much in the second Roosevelt era) of the public official scorned. He drew much the same picture of Wilson which was to turn up later in the Communist press: a silk-hatted hypocritical thin front for pudgy bankers. But he had trouble fitting his style to the demands of a weekly journal; when asked to write 1000-word pieces, he said it took him that long to get started. And then, as I have indicated above, he refused to allow any editorial tampering with his work; the famous incident of the

---

* Ardzrooni had by this time replaced Davenport as Veblen's Man-Friday; it was he who arranged, when about this time Veblen's second wife began having delusions of being persecuted, that she be placed in a sanitarium, and her children sent to Stewart, another student and former colleague, at Amherst. When at one point Ardzrooni had to leave New York, Mitchell arranged for Isador Lubin to come there from Washington to look after Veblen in his place. Lubin believes Veblen turned down the Labor Board job not because of the salary, which he would have liked, but because of doubts whether he could accomplish anything in a conservative bureaucratic setting.

"sexton beadle" dates from this period. As Lewis Mumford, then also a *Dial* editor, tells the story ("Thorstein Veblen," *New Republic,* Aug. 5, 1931, p. 315):

". . . Veblen had characterized Samuel Gompers as the sexton beetle of the American labor movement. In preparing the ms. for the printer, one of the editors had automatically changed this over to sexton beadle, in order to make sense. Veblen was furious: his white ashen face was more ashen than ever with anger—such anger as seemed especially terrible in the mild and reticent person that Veblen always was. He wanted to know if the unknown dunderhead who had mutilated his copy did not realize that a sexton beetle was an insect that spent its life in storing up and covering over dead things? Besides, there was an overtone in the illusion: Gompers looked more like a beetle."

We note here, to return to the matter later, the "insane" rage of the claustrophobe when faced with unmanageable constraint—Veblen clearly felt *he* was being mutilated. Nevertheless, Veblen, in spite of his own and his fellow-editors' misgivings, was actually a highly effective radical journalist, helping to create a style which was imitated by left-wing writers—and also a set of attitudes such as the facile contempt for the "safe and sane" Gompers and other leaders of the A.F. of L. which has since been standard operating practice for the Bohemian intellectual. In similar mood we find him writing (in *The Freeman*, in 1921) that the Soviet

"displaces democracy and representative government, and necessarily so, because democracy and representative government have proved to be incompetent and irrelevant for any other purpose than the security and profitable regulation of absentee ownership"—

and then adding (speciously, despite possible derivations of the Soviet from the old Russian commune or *mir*) that "the Soviet appears to be very closely analogous to the town-meeting as known in New England history." In the same vein he goes on to say that "Socialism [as distinguished from Bolshevism] is a dead horse," and its hope to take over rather than scrap current political organization, an idle fancy. While the old, cautious, self-protective Veblen appears in the comment that, while the Old Order is dead, the New gives no considerable grounds for optimism, this and other articles of the post-war period show how readily Veblen's skepticism and cynicism led him to become (like Sorel in a similar case) an effective spokesman for the "wave of the future" muscularity of Bolshevism, his sarcasm now used solely as an offensive weapon.

This development, which put behind the American Communist movement the apparent sanction of science as well as an indubitably "native" name and tone, made Veblen something of a model for young American radicals. His enemy, Mencken, wrote in 1919 that Dewey had been overthrown by Veblen among the "intellectual soviets," that "the newspapers reported his every wink and whisper," that there "were Veblenists, Veblen clubs, Veblen remedies for all the sorrows of the world . . . even, in Chicago, Veblen girls." Randolph Bourne, Maxwell Anderson, Mumford, Laski and many others joined the claque. However, for reasons already partly apparent, Veblen placed his own faith for revolution not in propagandists but in engineers and technicians, and in 1920 he persuaded his former Stanford colleague, Guido Marx, to give a course at the New School, where he was now himself teaching, on "The Social Function of the Engineer." At that time Howard Scott, who later became the leader of the Technocrats, appeared on the scene; there were not many others. Still, Veblen seemed to harbor the hope, at once grandiose and menacing, that the younger technicians (like the younger economists and, in some unspecified way, the young generally) were only awaiting a lead before organizing their restlessness and insubordination to replace the Vested Interests and the National State with what Veblen, in a memorandum he then wrote, called "A Practicable Soviet of Technicians"—Bellamy's industrial army with a vengeance.

Again in his last published article, "Economic Science in the Calculable Future," Veblen distinguished between the elder statesmen of economics, corrupted by the pecuniary culture and its hedonistic calculus, and the putative younger generation who would be oriented to technology, not accountancy, to the productive process, not "classical" theory. But now, in 1925, he could promise the young scant hope of power, instead only mistreatment at the hands of the academic Vested Interests. The fact is that the younger economists, including Veblen's students and disciples, were on the whole not in sympathy with his pro-Soviet stance. Thus, he had little experience on which to base his faith in the young. Rather, we must look at Veblen himself when young in an effort to grasp some of the sources of this faith in youth—a faith tenaciously embraced by a man who consciously rejected what he would have termed "metaphysical" beliefs in untutored or "natural" human goodness.

Veblen never broke with his own father. As a boy he adopted his father's stern reticence, his preference of machines to men, his willing submission to "reality." Unconsciously, underneath outward compliance, he sabotaged the father—by "illness," by not becoming a success (as his brother Andrew and his nephew, Oswald, a mathematician, did), by ironical evasion of the hopes and loyalties that Thomas Veblen, spokesman for "Little Norway," stood for. The violence with which Thorstein Veblen in his declining years attacked all authorities would thus seem, *inter alia*, to represent the return of the repressed hostility against his own domineering father. But such ambivalent hostility, by necessary compromise, partakes of what it fights. In locating the revolutionary cadres of the New Order in the engineers and technicians, and in those economists who were least "scholarly" and most like engineers, that is, in Veblen's view, most hard-boiled and unsentimental, the son projected upon the young the very qualities he had himself admired in his own father. It was not innocence, then, save of pecuniary guile, that he sought in the young, but the marks of cold-eyed, self-repressed, unenthusiastic, ruthless, "scientific" upbringing.

Veblen's later writings are studded with paeans to this new Common Man, made in his father's image. He is someone given to "submergence of the personal equation" (*The Vested Interests and the Common Man*, p. 40), who is (p. 46) "not so familiar with the recondite wisdom of the past, or with subtle definitions, other than the latter-day subtleties of the market, the crop season, the blast-furnace and re-finery, the internal-combustion engine, and such like hard and fast matters with which he is required to get along from day to day."

By the same token, the common man eschews too much intellec-tion, too many value judgments; as Veblen continues (p. 47):

"By consequence of much untempered experience the common man is beginning to see these things [i.e., the "cer-tified make-believe" of private property] in the glaring though fitful light of the mechanistic conception that rates men and things on grounds of tangible performance—with-out much afterthought."

This worship on Veblen's part for the "simpler and cruder" men and ways of life did not of course mark a radical break from his earlier thought, most of which is merely repeated in the later writings. Rather, the latter replace subtlety with stridency, gentle irony with sarcasm, shadings of respect for the past achievements of mankind with impatience. And Veblen appeared to be re-warded for thus becoming a caricature of himself by the new audience he was attracting—and, in some who admire intransi-gence and "toughness" above all other human responses, still attracts.

However, as may be imagined, Veblen's former students and economic colleagues were not pleased at the new company he was keeping. Walton Hamilton, reviewing a collection of Veblen's more technical essays in 1921, sought to defend him against his growing reputation, noting with dismay that "In this season's most 'significant' novel the heroine who fights the smugness of the small town with affectation reads Veblen," and pointing out that Veblen's thought was beginning to be inflated to cosmic propor-tions. Another former student, H. Parker Willis, felt that Veblen had completely changed, and had become estranged from his former close intellectual associates.

It can always be argued in this way that the laity "spoil" a thinker—and to be sure they, like everyone else, read his work selectively—but in my opinion this frequently occurs with the thinker's conscious or unconscious cooperation. What the War and its aftermath had done for Veblen was to destroy, pretty much for good, the amalgam of hope and despair he called "science," or "the evolutionary point of view," and to leave him prey to the general intellectual currents of the age, first of quasi-racialist anti-German feeling, and then of no less bellicose anti-Wilsonian and anti-American feeling—with all hopes transferred to the Bolsheviks. Veblen was at this time physically and psychologically too old to recover from despair, to build a new theory or a new skepticism; always inclined to be passive, he was ready to accept the Bolsheviks as earlier, in his Darwinian phase, to "accept the universe." (Of course, to many Americans of this period the Bolsheviks were underdogs, their tough talk no match for the Allied concert of powers: we must be careful not to read back to 1919 our contemporary image of Bolshevism.)

But Veblen's pro-Soviet and Technocratic hopes were short-lived—indeed, he later admitted, the Palmer raids and other signs of anti-"Red" hysteria fooled him by allowing him to think the Americans more disaffected and ready for violent change than the era of normalcy showed them to be. He was not the first revolutionary to take the wild fears he and his allies aroused in conservative quarters as a sign of his movement's strength. Yet he had enough energy left to make one last major assault on the Vested Interests in *Absentee Ownership*, published in 1923, in which he combined the analysis of credit and "intangible assets" developed in *The Theory of Business Enterprise* (1904) with a scathing critique of advertising and other modes of vending such assets that had luxuriated in the interim. It is in many passages brilliant, but overlong and highly repetitious, both in its own terms and in terms of Veblen's earlier work; it is interesting that Veblen asked a friend to point out the repetitions in the manuscript, but, as Dorfman says, "most of Veblen's friends felt that he could never be repetitious" (p. 467)—perhaps it "cost" so much to be a friend of Veblen that only devoted and uncritical disciples would stay in his circle, or perhaps he was too easily offended, on the basis of his own self-doubts and withdrawal, to be able to take criticism even when he asked for it. When he took the manuscript to B. W. Huebsch, the publisher (now of the Viking Press) who for many years had admired and befriended him, Veblen acted like a little boy bringing in something objectionable; a Huebsch associate told Dorfman (p. 485):

> "Huebsch told me that Veblen had stolen into his office like an interloper who wished to ask for a dime, but sat fidgeting in a chair for about an hour while Huebsch made conversation, and had finally with a great effort of will dumped an untidy parcel of manuscript on the desk, stating that it was something he had written but probably not of the least interest to the publisher or anyone else."

If Veblen had so little love for his own productions, and perhaps for himself, it is not surprising that he did not anticipate love from others. Beyond that, to deliver a manuscript seems in a way to deliver oneself, and by this time as Dorfman writes, "His protective mechanism of silence had become his master" (p. 424). Even when R. H. Tawney came to see him, or when, at his own invitation, industrial experts called, Veblen could find nothing to say—unless he asked questions himself, as he had done as a teacher, to avoid being questioned. It is remarkable, as with so many other creative and neurotic men, that the work got done at all, that there *is* a Veblen shelf to outlive its author's agonies.

THE STYLE AND THE MAN

The agonies, to be sure, reveal themselves in the formlessness of Veblen's books. What is striking about Veblen's style, both early and late, is that sentences and even paragraphs and pages flow, while chapters and the books themselves not only lack organization (Veblen's first book is the only one to have an index) but take two steps back for every one forward. It is as if Veblen hit and ran, and then, finding himself unhurt—perhaps thinking it was because no one heard him—hit again, only harder, then ran again, only further. In print as in person, he appears not to have felt that he had an audience, that he could communicate: his books and even his long articles, taken as a whole, convey an obsessive quality, as of a man who fears he will not be heard—but also that he will be heard, and therefore committed.

It goes without saying that communication is a two-way affair, and the other side of Veblen's inability to make himself heard was his inability to listen to the meaning of many intellectual attitudes which might have proved provocative to him. Thus, the narrow circle of his friends is matched by the narrow circle of his citations: he read the economists he despised and a few of the more or less socialist writers he admired, but never seems to have confronted Max Weber, Michels, Pareto, Mosca, and others who took a much more pessimistic view of society than even he did, a view which regarded, not technology, but large-scale organization as the keynote of modern times and hence saw little difference between socialism and capitalism. Increasingly, this man whose erudition has been so much praised—and who did, of course, roam widely in the natural and social sciences, in history, philology, and philosophy—seems to have read books on modern society he could dismiss as written by idiots, save for Spencer and socialists like the early Sombart, from whom he borrowed many concepts. Thus, he avoided certain crucial criticisms that writers such as Durkheim or Simmel would have presented for his own line of thought.

In his personal contacts, he must have been equally unlucky. He had no Engels, not even the gifted, irascible disciples such as Freud had (nor did he, like Freud in his first lonely days, "invent" a colleague in a Dr. Fliess, whose limitations Freud avoided seeing). His Chicago colleagues must have seemed to him too heavy-minded, too "serious," too hot-eyed to reform the world, and too eager in their expectations of him. And if one thinks of his well-known students, they too, were serious people, not given to ambiguity; of those whose work I know, only Walton Hamilton seems to possess something of Veblen's ironical quality rather than dutifully responding to his pronouncements. Perhaps Veblen would have been "saved" had he in his first academic years found even one good friend who understood him, who was not put off by him or on the other hand taken in by his cries of helplessness—a friend with whom he might have established give-and-take relations, both intellectual and social, a friend as playful with ideas, and as unbelligerent, as Veblen in his own best mood could be. With such a friend, I sometimes think, Veblen might have developed as his life went on, rather than retiring to the relative isolation of his cottage at Cedro, and clinging ever more tightly to what were his grand heresies of the nineties.

Yet on second thought I realize that had Veblen had an easier and more direct access to people, he would in all probability not have continued his magnificent mode of indirect access through abstraction. In a country as inhospitable to theory, to idle curiosity, as America mainly was in Veblen's day, only a character-conditioned refusal to become tempted by practical life tasks could sustain the sort of detachment from the culture, Veblen's achievement, which we his heirs can take much more for granted. The pioneers on any frontier pay the price, and win the rewards, of a hardihood they cannot help—and one of the reasons why Veblen's hopes for the young economists were illusory is that, to the very extent they could learn from him, they could avoid his destiny.

That destiny, by the post-war period, was beyond revision even by change of luck. At the New School, teaching appeared evermore to be beyond his powers, and he used every pretext to avoid his classes, much as he left his stepchildren to the care of his friends. He declined lectureships, and let fall various negotiations for jobs. While a generous student subsidised his New School salary, he lived near the School at the "Virolas" and took lunch with whatever colleagues were around. One of these, Lawrence K. Frank, describes him as usually uncommunicative, but occasionally doubling over to laugh silently and inwardly at some joke. Another, Harold Laski, recalls him as a man who "delivered himself in a half-oracular, half-ironical way of extraordinarily pungent judgments upon men and things" (Dorfman, p. 451). On the whole, however, he seemed unable in these closing years to liberate himself—save for brief summer periods with his Icelandic friends—from his mood of despondency and helplessness. He had

had such spells before, as a youngster, again after his graduate work at Yale, and yet again at Missouri. But now, with his hopes for the coming revolution dwindling, even the efforts of the friends who closed about him could not lift his spirits, and if one can let oneself die of a broken heart, I guess Veblen did so. Had the Depression come a little earlier, he might have felt somewhat less gloomy—the British General Strike of 1926 had given him a short-lived hope—but his end in 1929 preceded by two months the crash of the credit structure he had always, with a country boy's suspicion rather than a country boy's wonder, hated and feared.

This last, sad period of Veblen's life is perhaps best symbolised, not by what he wrote, but by an incident reported in Dorfman's book. Reference has already been made to the mountain shack Veblen had built in his Stanford days—he had built it out of lumber from a wealthy estate and had been very pleased with his shrewd bargaining. By a realtor's error, the cabin during Veblen's long absence had been included in a sale of the surrounding property; however, a friend of Veblen, without telling him, had rectified the mistake and secured a recognition of Veblen's title. Veblen went with this friend and others to visit the site in 1920. When he got to the cabin he thought, before anyone could dissuade him, that the neighboring landowner had seized his property; Dorfman writes (p. 456):

"He took a hatchet and methodically broke the windows, going at the matter with a dull intensity that was like madness, the intensity of a physically lazy person roused into sudden activity by anger. If there were to be any disputes about the ownership, he intended to make the place thoroughly uninhabitable for all concerned."

The incident reveals not only the intensity of a usually slow-moving person, but the destructiveness of a usually inhibited one. And it reveals with an irony almost too true to be good the enemy of absentee ownership and of sabotage caught in the toils of both. It is as if he felt doubts about his ownership *of himself* and hence had to resist with desperation any trespass on what William James described, in his *Psychology*, as the physical trappings of the Self; as if he were preternaturally conscious of sabotage because he was always laying waste in frustrated helplessness his own not fully utilized powers.

We may read the incident also in another way. As a farm-boy turned intellectual, Veblen must even as a boy have differed in his tastes and interests—hence in his form of masculinity—from the other Norskie boys around him; perhaps his mother helped cue him this way, much as Irish mothers often cue their softer and brighter boys to be priests. But in a family with such a father as Veblen had, keen on "modern improvements," the son could not find his vocation in the ministry, which would have been a role the community understood. Instead, without models in "Little Norway" to guide him, he was sent to make his way in the academic community, but there, too, though he became cosmopolitan in his intellectual reach, he never became "one of the boys." He lacked the kind of energy and social compliance necessary to compete in the approved manly and sportsmanlike ways that enabled other farm boys to feel at home, within a short span of years, as Captains of Erudition.

Instead he fought back against the cultural definitions of masculinity and femininity passed on him and such as he by Americans. He turned his lack of conventional masculine prowess (a lack which, as in so many similar cases, must have made his success with women all the more irritating to his academic colleagues) into an attack on the institutions and human types of a predatory capitalism, and into a defense of the peaceable types who throughout history had been overcome by masculine force and fraud. Much of his work may be seen as a passionate defense of women; Veblen regarded women as the great oppressed cadre, whether they were the slaves of marauding tribes and thus the first "private property" or the 19th-century slaves of fashion who bore the brunt of male emulation; intrinsically freer than men of such superstitions as nationalism, the women were the core carriers of social decency and simplicity underneath the perversions and rituals created and dominated by men.

Unable to asseverate these views directly, he hid like a court jester behind a "masculine" facade of science and objectivity. But out of this conflict of genders he produced (for social science) a new genre: irony.* The boy whom his neighbours could not understand reacted by creating a style of intentional ambiguity (though to be sure one in which Veblen himself was occasionally caught not knowing what he originally thought). Too "passive" to force his data into a watertight theoretical scheme, he nevertheless wrote with sly aggression against the data, against the reader —and against himself. And he meshed into his stylistic compromise his "feminine" awareness that he could not change the unreasonable world and his "masculine" protest against human helplessness and resignation, including his own.

In our culture, achievement means entering a vocational ladder at a relatively early age, but Veblen got his first real job only when, at the age of 35, he went in Laughlin's baggage to the University of Chicago. Thus, he was a "boy when he should have been a man." But here, too, he turned his discrepancy to account: his irony may be seen as the reaction of a mischievous boy in the schoolroom—Till Eulenspiegel's *Lustige Streiche* or Tom Sawyer. I might go further and suggest that one of Veblen's greatest concepts, that of "idle curiosity"—the spirit of playful inquiry, unrelated to any immediate pragmatic need or gain— might be thought of as a defense against the all-too-practical, all-too-grown-up people who wondered, both on the farm and later, where Veblen's "lazy" and speculative mind would lead him. In this, he reminds us of Thoreau.

* This statement needs to be qualified by recalling that some precursors of social anthropology have been heavily satiric—Swift, Goldsmith, Lowes Dickinson come to mind. And of course Marx was frequently caustic and sarcastic in the highest degree, though too heavy-handed much of the time to be called truly ironic. Veblen's contemporary, Georges Sorel, was a gifted user of irony; like Veblen, he had less hope for the revolution than Marx, less confidence in the working class, and more awareness of the ambiguities of the dialectic. Perhaps it would be more accurate to say that Veblen elaborated a new variant of an old genre. A good analogy to his style, suggested to me by Mark Benney, is the uniform of the cowboy, which takes the most masculine elements of a work dress and combines and embroiders them in somewhat feminine modes; similarly, Veblen pretends to be workmanlike and matter-of-fact but involutes what he has to say in ceremonial linguistic panoply.

I need hardly point out that people could have understood Veblen had he been a reformer; that was in the 19th-century a familiar nonconformist role, a kind of orthodox and sanctioned "impracticality"—the term "boy scout" for the reformer, which relegates him, too, to childhood, is a later invention. (Indeed, it was in the post-war years when Veblen acted as a reformer or was regarded as one that numbers of people began to "understand" him.) But a curiosity that aimed at neither adjusting to the world nor at changing it—that was "idle," that was childish. It was typical of Veblen's soft way with wrath that, rather than resist the label, rather than argue that he, too, was practical and effective, he accepted the accusation and turned it into praise, by relating idle curiosity to the distinctively *Ur*-human traits which led men out of savagery and into the scientific age. That is, his mode of defense was irony coupled with research, not apologetics and not counter-attack.

Defense, however, is not enough to prevent the infiltration of the enemy. While on the one hand Veblen saw in idle curiosity the human quality of disinterested and playful response to the world, a kind of surplus, on the other hand he conducted the most relentless battle against all "idle" production and consumption, which he termed "waste." The same man who defended women and the peaceful pre-predatory stage with which he imagined human life to have begun, before patriarchial control brought in its train property, slavery, war, and emulation, could later welcome the ruthlessness of the Bolsheviks and delight in their disregard and contempt for political and cultural freedom. Some of Veblen's friends have told me that I take too seriously his verbal fireworks in favor of the Soviets—that these were intended more as an attack on American crassness, patrioteering, and economic exploitation than as a defense of dictatorship and terror, especially so as the Soviet Union was then relatively weak and powerless. Perhaps so, but it is nonetheless striking that a man as sensitive to constraint as Veblen, should have let the Bolsheviks play for him in the later years the role played in his earlier writings by the peaceable and inefficient Savages, the role of implicit critic of America.

Still, we cannot help but feel that Veblen managed to turn his contradictions, even his limitations, into assets, especially if we look at his work with the perspective of today. For what strikes us then is less the intellectual contribution Veblen makes to our own understanding—other contemporaries of his, more truly original, are of greater importance to us—than the brilliant reinvention of irony as a mode of approach to theoretical questions. His writings have a drama and dash his life lacked; his created Captains of Industry (the phrase is Carlyle's) and of Erudition, his predatory Vikings, his amiably ineffective Savages have become part of the folklore of our capitalism. Veblen managed in his best moments to use a verbal complexity almost as remarkable as Conrad's to create living abstractions out of the very perils and frustrations of his own concrete existence. Whereas the skeptical and rebellious Vilhjalmur Stefansson, born of Icelandic parents on the Dakota prairies, went and lived among the peaceable Eskimos whom Veblen so much admired, the latter went and lived among the Yankees. Much of his literary energy comes from his use of the adaptive art of mimicry—he captivates us by weaving the pedantry, pomposity, legalism, and pretense of provincial America into a style at once witty and revealing. Almost any passage of Veblen (other than his doctoral thesis on Kant) is instantly recognizable—a final ironical tribute to a man who believed, not in distinction of persons, but in a "commonwealth of ungraded men."

CHAPTER TWO

VEBLEN'S SYSTEM OF
SOCIAL SCIENCE:
Workmanship Versus Wastemanship

Analyze the most talked-of men of the [gilded] age and one is
likely to find a splendid audacity coupled with an immense
wastefulness.
            Vernon Louis Parrington, *The Beginnings of Critical
                        Realism in America*

JOHN GAMBS, in his study of institutional economics, *Beyond
      Supply and Demand*, remarks that Veblen (unlike Bentham),
      has never had a John Stuart Mill, a disciple who would organ-
ize his thought into a single, logical system. The difficulty in doing
so does not lie in any lack of logic in Veblen's thought. On the
contrary, Veblen's was both a logical and an abstract mind. Like
Marx, he came to social science from philosophy, and he was at
his best in uncovering the assumptions of another person, another
epoch, or another social class.

This pursuit of coherence extends to such seeming inanities
as the fashions of women's dress. In one of his earlier essays, "The
Economic Theory of Woman's Dress" (1894), he concludes that
the seeming whimsy and silliness of dress itself garbs a stern logic
which commands that every stitch combine expensiveness, novelty
(testifying to the dress' unfitness for repeated use), and restric-
tions which prevent the wearer from doing useful work when so
clothed. As Freud sought to show the rationale behind the seeming madness of his patients, so Veblen all his life delved for the
logic underlying seeming economic and political absurdities. Thus
in writing an essay on "Dementia Praecox," as Veblen termed the

45

Red-scare of the early twenties, he tried to expose its inner rationality: who got what out of it, when and where.

SYSTEM OR SYMPTOM?

It would seem that if we want to know whether what Veblen said about the world is true, it would not matter that he arrived at this truth by projecting onto the world his unsuccessful struggle to discover consistency within himself. But the fact is that we cannot avoid the preliminary problem of deciding whether Veblen meant what he said. At first sight he appears to present a very tightly-woven picture of modern capitalism as the demonic disguise of earlier more open brutalities. But he does so from the base-line of a lax and meandering presentation of his own assumptions; we do not know where he stands and hence how literally to take him. Could he be writing a fairy tale, as grim as such tales usually are, as a form of reporting his personal terrors and doubts?

Take, for instance, his frequent defense of himself against the charge of using loaded language. What he does is to declare emphatically that he is merely using the language of the common man because the latter's habits of thought constitute the very institutions under scrutiny. Did he at bottom believe this? Or is he like many people who say, in only seeming innocence: "I didn't know it was loaded?" His repeated insistence that he is a value-free, "opaque" scientist, his contempt for his colleagues who allowed reformism to show, leave the answer in doubt. Likewise, when in *The Theory of the Leisure Class* and elsewhere he seems to be strenuously excoriating unfunctional consumption as waste and artifice, he will as often stop to observe that this judgment is passed only from an economic point of view, while an aesthetic or religious premise would allow a different conclusion. Does he really mean his relativism here, which permits contradictory standpoints to remain unresolved? Or does he, as I believe likely, mean to subsume virtually all worthwhile human activity under the rubric of "economic"? At times, Veblen himself, caught in the paradoxes of his irony, appears to be unsure what he is mocking and what he is glorifying. And here his cherished self-image as a scientist wholly free of value-judgments prevents his arriving at a truer awareness of what he is up to.

Still another source of interpretative difficulty in Veblen springs from his unwillingness to commit himself by presenting his own principles: he prefers to tear down the models of others and to proffer his own subtle insights as everyday notions, pretending that the common man had known these things all along, and that only the academician, with the trained incapacity of his craft, could possibly fail to see them. By the same token, he cannot decide when he writes a book what is central, what peripheral; a footnote is as likely as the text to contain crucial matter, inserted as a seeming afterthought. And, in his endless repetitions, it is as apt to be a favorite phrase as a favorite thought or principle to which he obsessively recurs. Only in a short article or review, and to some extent in *The Instinct of Workmanship* and the journalistic collection, *The Vested Interests*, can he sustain a position. Typically, he will introduce some reforming plan of his own with the words "it has been suggested," as if it were somebody else's idea; of his projected Soviet of Technicians he states that it "will apparently" take such and such a form, as if he were describing some highly probable event; or he will refer to some hope of his as the direction in which the brute trend and drift of things are tending.

This pretense of impersonality, together with the fear of constraint we have already discussed, meant that Veblen—for all his praise of matter-of-factness—was most uncomfortable with detail. He prefers to allude and elude even when dealing with a subject like the life of the farmer which he had known at first hand. In the chapter on "The Higher Learning" in *The Theory of the Leisure Class* there is the revealing comment that it would not be difficult but would be mechanically tedious to trace the correlation between growth of collegiate wealth in midwest colleges and "the date of acceptance—first into tolerance and then into imperative vogue—of evening dress for men and of the décolleté for women, as the scholarly vestments proper to occasions of learned solemnity or to the seasons of social amenity within the college circle." Generalization here appears as a form

of labor-saving machinery. There is no necessary harm in that—
Veblen is the opposite extreme from the stereotype of sociologist
who, with no philosophical training, consumes his time affixing
exact degrees of significance to insignificant correlations and
never gets around to discovering anything new about society. But
the danger lies in the possibility that Veblen shut himself off
from much that was new by his very propensity for abstraction
and generalisation. Had he in this case, for instance, made an
actual investigation, he might have discovered that, if wealth
were great enough, it might induce indifference to dress, or that
there were denominational differences irrespective of wealth, or
rural-urban ones, and so on—all the buzzing, booming confusion
of American life which Veblen somehow, thinking he understood
it, did not continue to grapple with.

THE QUEST FOR CERTAINTY

To be sure, the nineteenth century is full of thinkers of
parentage and emotional constellation very different from Veblen's who were similarly sure they had the key to history.* Darwin
was one of the sources of confidence all these men had in common; the generally peaceable international scene from 1870 to
1914 was another. In each thinker the search for theoretical consistency seems to us today to be truncated, to stop too soon, to
have too great a fear of ambiguity and bewilderment in the face
of the universe. It is not so much that these men jump to conclusions: they start with the conviction that conclusions there must
be. Thus, whereas Veblen greatly admired Hume's skepticism,
on the whole he applied it as a debunker of capitalism rather than
as a radical self-critique. And as his life wore on, he seems to have
become steadily less open to new evidence, or even interested in
any that did not sustain previously cherished views. The result is
that, though his output spans a period of nearly forty years, one
finds little unfolding, little development in it—only a change

* Yet this similarity should lead us to look for at least moderate similarities
in their upbringing. Cf. the work Else Frenkel-Brunswik and her co-workers
have done on the psychological roots of intolerance for ambiguity coupled with
the fear of introspection. See, e.g., her article in Robert R. Blake and Glenn V.
Ramsey, *Perception: An Approach to Personality* (1951), pp. 356–419.

towards greater rigidity. When he first comes on the scene he is already a mature thinker: as an undergraduate at Carleton, he was debunking theology, satirically commenting on his fellow-students (as he had earlier fastened nicknames on the Veblens' neighbors), and following with interest the literary and political iconoclasts of the day, such as Ibsen and Henry George. To this kind of literary iconoclasm, Veblen later added the iconoclastic tendencies in post-Darwinian science; thus armored, he sought to direct economics away from its abstractions towards "the practical exigencies of modern industrial life" (*Place of Science*, p. 81). Yet, since men cannot live and work without abstractions, Veblen's picture of "modern industrial life" (the phrase is itself an abstraction) is strewn with undigested lumps of the now largely discredited psychologies and anthropologies of the late nineteenth century. And since, as I have suggested, Veblen could not long tolerate uncertainty he sought escape from the ambiguities of his cross-disciplinary efforts by building new webs of abstraction, such as his instinct theory or his theory of evolutionary stages through which men had passed from Savagery to Barbarism (of several sorts) to Capitalism—with Socialism at the far end. Indeed, Veblen's partial failure helps us to see how much more difficult it is than he had supposed to harmonize the abstractions of economics with those of anthropology and psychology; this is an intellectual task still far from accomplished, but one which we can now see is not facilitated by substituting one set of fashionable abstractions called "reality" for another. A greater willingness to accept confusion and temporary inconsistencies in theoretical framework might have enabled Veblen to develop rather than restate his views, and to perceive a few more of the then-unadvertised events that were to transform the everyday life of man in his own lifetime, such as the beginnings of assembly-line production, and the first stirrings of colonial revolt.

To be sure, there are times when Veblen appears to recognize the limits beyond which his thought could not go. He now and again declares that the impersonal Darwinian forces that move mankind are obscure and, in their cumulative working out, unpredictable; occasionally, he will speak of the evidence he has marshalled as "not unquestionably convincing" (see, e.g., *Theory of the Leisure Class*, p. 361). But usually this kind of disclaimer turns out to be a preface to a prophecy—and prophecy based always on the assumption that there is such a thing as a social *system*, that society is systematic and not chaotic, that men are not, like kings with their court jesters, able to make fools of their scientists' accounts of them.

Most social science of the last century has proceeded, to its glory and at its peril, with this assumption of the uniformity and malleability of its human "objects"; and it is not surprising that the world today, despite all Veblen's effort to catch "the main drift," is not the one he foretold. And yet he did produce a number of startling predictions. Not so much his forcible systematizations as the detachment he achieved, or, more likely, possessed from the beginning and accepted, seems to have been one essential element in his anticipation of the aggressive potentialities of an industrialized Japanese feudalism; of the change in the Second International toward patriotism in World War I; of the Great Depression; and, if he did not predict World War II in so many words, at least he had a belief at the time of Versailles that another war was coming, and had an awareness of the military power that revived German feudal attitudes would have.

Explaining to the British in the summer of 1952 what she regards as the increasing conservatism of American academic life, Mary McCarthy stated that professors who take consultant jobs in business and government get to understand too much to be able to criticise—but in a curious way this close connection also limits understanding, for it is hard not to share the hopes and fears of those who treat us well. Veblen did not suffer the loss such luck can bring—at least until it was too late for him to change. The pessimism induced by his personal tragedy prepared him to foresee the disappointments of the hopes of liberals and socialists alike. The skepticism he looked for in the industrial worker * was

---

* So far as I know, Veblen never personally discovered any workers in large urban industry who fitted the picture he held of them. But he did discover the Wobblies, the I.W.W., who were mainly the least urbanized and industrialized workers—they were casual farm laborers, lumbermen, Western miners, etc. It was among these men that Veblen in fact found the saucy irreverence and political intransigence he admired.

in reality a projection of his own multiple alienation, as immigrant's son, farmer's son, unsuccessful husband, and itinerant barely-tolerated scholar; but it was this alienation which put him far enough from our society to view it, for long suspended stretches, as a curious mechanism.

And yet I do not feel that Veblen's intellectual achievement can be reduced to the tangle of motives that produced it. (And I must remind the reader that I can only surmise what these motives were; to be surer of my ground I would need to know much more than I do about Veblen, his parents, his many siblings, his whole development.) In what follows, therefore, I shall proceed without further speculation as to Veblen's personality but take as given what Dos Passos too readily called "the sharp, clear prism of his mind." There will be no absence of ambiguities, but they will be those of Veblen's published thought, not the ambivalences of his inner life.

THE INSTINCT OF WORKMANSHIP

If there is a basic entity in Veblen's system, it is the "instinct of workmanship": an assumed human propensity for activity tailored to the efficient achievement of a goal. The instinct represented for Veblen the constructive element in human life, and his book entitled *The Instinct of Workmanship and the State of the Industrial Arts* (published in 1914 but mainly composed earlier) was said to be his favorite. It is the only one not largely immersed in the destructive element—emulation, business chicane, imperialism, the corruption of universities by businessmen, and so on—or professionally preoccupied with demolishing the assumptions of other economists (a genre referred to by Max Lerner as Veblen's "dispraise of economists").

In the opening pages of the book, the instinct of workmanship is sketched out as a tendency towards craftsmanship as an end in itself, and towards the accomplishment of constructive work—that is, by its very nature, it guides both ends and means, and may lead to confusion between them. As a tendency towards craftsmanship for its own sake, the instinct of workmanship may be thought of (though Veblen himself never put it quite this way) as a manual equivalent to a second Veblenian instinct, that of "idle curiosity," as he termed a playful surplusage of interest in the world, beyond pragmatic requirements. And in its other aspect, as a concern for useful workmanship in the interest of the species, the instinct of workmanship may be linked with still another Veblenian instinct, the "parental bent," a kind of generalised solicitude not only for one's own young but for the future of mankind.

These very linkages show that the instinct of workmanship, in Veblen's usage, is not oriented to specific goals but is diffuse, as much an assistance to other instincts in effectively reaching their ends as a definite drive. The instinct thus enters into all human activity in Veblen's view, even into activity running counter to its ulterior end of species-advancing construction. Thus, had Veblen lived long enough to read Stephen Potter's satiric books on "Gamesmanship" and "Lifemanship," he might have observed how the maneuvers of Potter's heroes deploy the highest arts of workmanship in precisely the sportsmanlike, invidious, and emulative manner Veblen most despised; indeed, he was already inclined to think that the British gentleman was the planet's noblest flowering of effortful, workmanlike futility. But the instinct of workmanship, though periodically defeated by its own zeal, is not wholly at the mercy of whatever conventional, pragmatic, and foolish ends a society may hold dear; it serves at once to accomplish and to alter those ends, for it is an active force —something like "intelligence" in John Dewey's system, or the "strain to consistency" in Sumner's—tending to bend men's activity away from mere habitual and mindless activity towards the (as Veblen saw it) natural ends of production and of concern for the young.

By calling workmanship an instinct, however, Veblen emphasized conscious human purposes less than biological drives, and cultivated purposes less than "natural" or inherited ones. And by stressing the ways in which custom could channel workmanship into the use of self-defeating means, he was selecting Sumner's more pessimistic as against Ward's or Spencer's more optimistic Darwinism. More often than not Veblen appears in the role of a debunker of exhortations to men's reason or of historical predictions resting on the predictor's notion of what it would be rational for men to do (such as Marxism). Yet, taking his system as a whole, Veblen was less inclined to stress the irrational than many others of the instinct-habit school. The very fact that he uses "instinct" loosely and often metaphorically—students differ as to how many instincts he postulated—saves him from an excessive reductionism. Then, too, his instincts have a bent to succor man rather than destroy him.

Veblen faced analogous problems in deciding between an emphasis on the wholeness of human behavior and an emphasis on compartmentalization. He differed from apperceptionist psychology in insisting on the purposeful *activity* of human beings, and the same line of thought led him to underline the *Gestalt* in behavior. In *The Instinct of Workmanship*, he declared (p. 40):

". . . in all their working, the human instincts are . . . incessantly subject to mutual 'contamination,' whereby the working of any one is incidentally affected by the bias and proclivities inherent in all the rest."

This must be so because the human organism is of one piece, and what it does in one department of life under the dominant aegis of one instinct, will affect its behavior in all other departments. Further, the instincts themselves are not separate biologically. Veblen asserted (ibid., p. 11):

"the common run of human instincts are not to be conceived as severally discrete and elementary proclivities. The same physiological processes enter in some measure, though in varying proportions, into the functioning of each. In instinctive action the individual acts as a whole, and in the conduct which emerges under the driving force of these instinctive dispositions the part which each several instinct plays is a matter of more or less, not of exclusive direction."

But as he grew older and more bitter, Veblen's emphasis on the rationality and wholeness of human behavior grew less and less. Symbolic and partly productive of this change was the increasing influence upon him of Jacques Loeb, a colleague at Chicago mentioned earlier. Loeb was a brilliant biologist who accepted the instinctivists' approach, retaining the associationist view that consciousness was an epiphenomenon and need not be involved in scientific study of psychology. His influence appears, for example, in Veblen's description of revolution in *Absentee Ownership* by the title of one of Loeb's books, "Forced Movements, Tropisms, and Animal Conduct."

THE REASON OF CURIOSITY

In what has already been said, it becomes evident that Veb-len vacillated in his view of the role of reason in human affairs. Instinct theories in general tended to give reason a low place, as Sumner on the whole had done (McDougall included scientific wonder among his list of instincts). For Veblen, reason sometimes appeared in the wavering purposefulness of workmanship, but was more fully embodied in his instinct of idle curiosity, to which men are indebted for an explanation of the universe. It was in an Enlightenment spirit of aristocratic curiosity that Veblen dissociated himself from pragmatism, which he regarded as the commonsensical manipulation of conventions for utilitarian ends.

Yet this dissociation was, as I have already indicated, at best a partial and intermittent one. For instance, between the chapter on "The Higher Learning" in *The Theory of the Leisure Class* (1899) and the book by that name (1918), Veblen's attitude towards the institutionalization of curiosity in scholarship as over against vocational training seems to have changed decidedly. In the former book he is on the side of vocational training, treating scholarship only as a furbelow to the gentlemanly life and a hazard for truly useful work; thus, he says that the quasi-theological and foggy trappings of academic ritual originated in the university and spread from there to the lower and vocational schools (pp. 369–370). In *The Higher Learning*, however, he insists on the segregation of the pure research of the university from the contaminating practical bent of the vocational school. He now contrasts the instinct of idle curiosity with *both* workmanship (or industry) and predation (or business)—usually, as we shall see in the next chapter, he makes a very clear dichotomy between workmanship and predation. In *The Higher Learning*, that is, both workman-like and predatory activities are lumped together and condemned as unduly practical. Moreover, when in this book Veblen decries the standardization of curricula and teaching procedures as an invasion of learning by mechanical techniques of piece-rate and statistical accounting, he is setting his face against methods of control which are native to industry, not to business—methods which he elsewhere upholds against the slipshod and personal conduct of business. That is, though Veblen's culture-hero was the engineer, he was to be kept off the campus: Veblen seemed to want to protect the universities against the "vulgar" modern mechanism for which he was ordinarily the spokesman. But the very concept of idle curiosity, which forbids a functional role to the instinct, prevented Veblen from rationalizing the higher learning as part of a defensible division of labor between instincts or between institutions. Failing to develop a theory of play, curiosity, and other "surplus" motives and activities, he was forced back on a traditional conception of the life of reason as a thing in itself, a residual category largely divorced from art and action.

Yet this passionate defense of idle curiosity against all comers makes *The Higher Learning* for me one of Veblen's most attractive, if not most original, books. Blithely he portrays university research as entirely without intended practical value (there may of course be unforseen practical applications of a scientific discovery), and in the course of his discussions squarely confronts the practical man's question: What is the use of this learning? Veblen magnificently responds (p. 200):

> "Benjamin Franklin—high-bred pragmatist that he was—once put away such a question with the rejoinder: What is the use of a baby?"

The bearing of children too, Veblen says, was once viewed from a utilitarian standpoint, and girl children were put to death—as Veblen puts it, "the investment was cancelled"—as economically useless. Now civilized men have come to regard the bringing of children to life as intrinsically good, and so, Veblen asserts, will they someday regard scholarship and science.

ENTER EMULATION

These three instincts—workmanship, idle curiosity, and care for the young (parental bent)—are for Veblen, then, not only a substratum of human nature but a source of moral absolutes. By means of these instincts Veblen goes to some pains to preserve the distinction between ends and means: these three activities are or can be ends in themselves, while all other lines of action are pragmatic, directed toward some ulterior end. Beyond that, what the three Veblenian instincts have in common is a turning outward from the individual to nature or society, a merging of the individual through work, observation, or solicitude in the processes surrounding him. The instinct of idle curiosity and the instinct of workmanship (in its aspect of pure craftsmanship) involve what Veblen calls a "non-reverent sense of aesthetic congruity with the environment" (*Theory of the Leisure Class*, p. 333), or again "the sense of communion with the environment, or with the generic life process" (ibid., p. 334). Workmanship for the sake of serviceability, and the parental bent, merge into this sense also, though with the emphasis on the human environment and the human life process—a revised Kantian imperative.

Veblen's decision to regard as most fundamental these three instincts, sharing one common quality—at a time when many psychologists were positing a dozen or more instincts—was not only a concealed moral choice. It was also the product of his immersion, along with the most enterprising social scientists of his day, in the evolutionary methodology of Darwinism. A fundamental tenet of this methodology was that the environment exercises a most rigorous selective pressure upon the organisms within it, and that only organisms perfectly adapted to the environment can survive. Now if man's genetic make-up was fixed in his pre-history, when his competitive struggle was presumably at its grimmest—and Veblen believed this was the case—then human nature could have afforded, so to speak, only those constituents most conducive to the survival of the species. The instinct of workmanship was therefore a brute biological necessity: "As a matter of selective necessity, man is an agent" (ibid., p. 15). Man could not have survived had he possessed compelling needs catering to his individual welfare at the expense of the species: such needs were luxuries which could develop only as, in the course of history, men created wealth enough to make them secure in their environment. But Veblen did not regard these late-coming attitudes, such as pugnacity, as "really" instincts—though once in a while he loosely uses the term—he rules them out with the Pavlovian argument that man had not been conditioned to their exercise for a long enough time: only the primordial trinity were "natural." In his essay on "Christian Morals and the Competitive System," Veblen argued that the Christian attitudes of serviceability and brotherhood would survive the late-coming attitudes of competition and emulation because closer to man's instinctual base, and because they are older and more thoroughgoing in terms of historical habituation.

But there was still another reason Veblen had for thinking workmanship would win out over the late-comer, wastemanship, namely his Puritanical and ascetic feeling that the surplus men could produce would never be great enough to permit them to survive in the face of wasteful, futile, and destructive conduct. As Darwin took over Malthus' perspective of a bitter race between man and his means of subsistence—leading Darwin to overemphasize the adaptation of organism to environment and the stressful, Spartan efficiency of natural selection—so Veblen along with many other Social Darwinists underestimated man's ability to survive in the face of many unproductive, "unreasonable" activities. No matter how bounteous the productivity of the nineteenth century—a century which in the West seemed to want to prove Malthus wrong—Veblen seems to have strongly felt the precariousness of existence, and hence held a tragic view of the consequences of productivity. As I have implied, it is his pessimism which attracts many people to him today.

Veblen saw history as a process by which man, through workmanship, at long last created the surplus wealth which made him for the first time moderately secure on the earth. But this same surplus, like Eden's apple, permitted a group of new, self-regarding motives to come into being. Emulation entered: men found their pleasure in invidious distinctions at the expense of others. The primitive balance of production and consumption gave way, in Veblen's view, to a world which by his time consisted on the one hand of countries like Germany and Japan where "too much" productivity put a military surplus in the hands of bellicose dynasts, and on the other of countries like England and America where "too much" consumption involved all classes of society in a meaningless chase of superfluities for emulative display. In either case, as he was wont to put it, the common man paid the cost.

Now it was paradoxical for Veblen to deplore man's advance beyond the struggle for sheer survival. For the whole point of the activist psychology, as developed by Peirce (under whom Veblen had studied at Hopkins), Dewey and William James, was to lay stress on man's free will and capacity for self-development. Veblen, moreover, had begun by interpreting adaptation as adaptation of the environment to human activity, rather than the reverse. In his first published essay, "Kant's Critique of Judgment" (1884), he paraphrased Kant as follows: since the knowledge provided the human organism by its perception is fragmentary and unorganized, the organism, which at any given moment is acting as a whole in one or another direction, *adapts* its perceived knowledge into an organized whole: "the principle of adaptation says that the particular things do belong together, and sets the mind hunting to find out how."

But Veblen does not fully share James' muscular, unruly sense of human freedom (nor the excesses of James' moral athleticism); to the extent that he does, he is afraid of what men do with their arbitrary power. And so his apparently whole-hearted acceptance of the Jamesian psychology is always qualified and finally overborne by the desire to bind men to a minimal, near-biological routine, in which, if nothing spectacular is accomplished (except in the harmless, out-of-the-way paths of idle learning), no great destruction is wrought either.

Similar fears seem to govern Veblen's attitude toward the joy of work. He shared William Morris' feeling that work should be a central and delightful activity: in *The Theory of the Leisure Class* he speaks of "the impulse of self-expression and workmanship" (p. 356), and in his essay on "The Instinct of Workmanship and the Irksomeness of Labor" he attempts to refute the opinion that it is natural for men to look on work as disagreeable by showing how invidious cultural definitions of work as demeaning lead men actually to feel it as such. Moreover, in various places and particularly at the end of *The Instinct of Workmanship,* Veblen states in the strongest terms that human nature is not suited to machine industry, having been genetically fixed in the vastly different societies of prehistory. And yet it is hard to think of a writer who has done more to domesticate the machine, or who has welcomed it with more enthusiasm as a tutor which will make men sober, factual, and peaceable. It would appear, taking all of Veblen's work together, that he regarded the machine as compelling an orientation to the external environment, impersonal as nature itself, capable of creating in men a "second nature" entirely methodical and workmanlike, rid of the exuberant animistic projections that might be stimulated by more creative or more artisan-like work. Men would suffer under this tutelage, but they would be safe. They would be led back, by a new road, to the old pre-emulative ways. Indeed, we see here, as we shall see again, a dialectical note in Veblen, inconsistent with his conscious anti-Hegelianism and straight-line evolutionism.

It should be clear, however, that there is lacking in Veblen any glorification of the machine—an attitude probably more common among French auto-fans and Italian poets than among comparable Americans. To glorify the machine would be to substitute one superstitious animism for another; Veblen wanted machines, like people, to be treated with solicitude, but not looked up to. He wanted people to be aware of living in a cold, impersonal world that cares not for their hopes and responds not to their anthropomorphisms. But again without glory. Machines are machines, nothing more; men are men, nothing more. And in this sense the emphasis on machines served him as a way of reducing the differences among men: as Freud made them submit to their sexual Daemon, and Marx to History, so Veblen made men submit to equalization by making them small, in the face of machinery and of the Darwinian flux.

Adam Smith had worried in one way about the consequences

of mechanized work for the individual; Carlyle, Butler, Ruskin had worried in still other ways; few sensitive intellectuals have been less worried than Veblen. For one thing, as a farm boy he did not look back on hand labor with nostalgia; for another, he did not have a very exalted idea of what life could be like at best—he himself asked for little enough. But whatever the personal sources of his view, it was productive and challenging to insist that machine work, while it may go against the instinctual grain, does not brutalize the worker, but trains him in a mechanistic rather than animistic kind of intelligence. Like his great contemporary Frederick Taylor, though with a different attitude towards the worker, he wanted to see means efficiently adapted to ends, without waste motion—and without waste emotion.

THE CONTAMINATION OF THE COMMON MAN

Veblen spoke of mixture and combination of motives as "contamination" (Freud uses the terms "repression" and "sublimation" in a similarly loaded way). For the surplus of motives which economic abundance made possible and inevitable was for Veblen, on the whole, a seduction.

The analysis of contamination is chiefly worked out in connection with the instinct of workmanship—the most diffuse, generalized, and plastic of Veblen's instincts. The parallel transformations of idle curiosity are, by and large, treated as mere reflections of changes in occupational discipline. For instance, the world outlook of early modern times, according to Veblen, expressed the work experience of the hand craftsman who acquires "natural rights" by mixing his labor with nature's raw materials, and whose God likewise shapes his raw material, the universe, towards self-willed ends. Indeed, Veblen's understanding of the ways in which technology develops out of animism and then turns against it is very suggestive. In *The Instinct of Workmanship* he describes how primitive man, by unscientifically assuming the nature of plants and animals to be like his own, gained a measure of real understanding; that is, his first technology came about through animistic identifications. But as this technology developed, it became increasingly matter-of-fact until it came to constitute in itself an "environment" which demanded impersonal adaptation for its mastery. The ever-present pressure to be serviceable, which is one aspect of the instinct of workmanship, thus led men by a round-about route from lore to science, forcing men away from their original animistically-guided technology to a mechanistically- and logically-guided one.

In another sense, of a bent towards craft for craft's sake, the instinct of workmanship is contaminated by emulation, technology's Manichaean foil. In Veblen's view the earliest societies, small and workmanlike, proffered prestige only for particular pieces of work, and to the man who made them only insofar as he was a workman. But as society became larger and private property made its appearance, workmanship was subordinated in two ways. In the first place—so Veblen tells the story—in a large society people could not know intimately each one of their fellow-citizens, so that in place of an appreciation for the actual work a man had done, some more external valuation had to be substituted; in modern society money, the ostensible end of work, and the goods which money will buy, serve this purpose. But this meant that a man's prestige no longer lay in his specialized capacity as a worker, but that a general potency was attributed to him; this attitude was sedulously cultivated by those who, through force and fraud, came to form a ruling class, and reached its full flowering in the concept of the divine right of kings. Beyond this, according to Veblen, there was a second factor working to put down workmanship in its old-fashioned and homely functioning: the incoming of private property and economic inequality placed a prestige value upon leisure, as a symbol of wealth, and work was correspondingly denigrated. That is, Veblen saw the origin of the leisure class in the possibilities for falsification and myth-making offered by bigness, by populations of a certain size, and in the possibilities of aggrandizement and escape from toil provided by private property.

In the leisure-class society, however, workmanship is not simply subordinate to emulative uses of leisure, but persists in a perverted (contaminated) form. For, as some faint sense of the serviceable bearing of workmanship still persists in the not completely myth-ridden underlying population, the wasters of the leisure class must deck out their wastemanship as somehow useful to the community at large. Further, the craftsman's feeling for purposeful accomplishment conditions even the pursuit of waste, which is entered upon with a grim efficiency. As Veblen wrote in *The Theory of the Leisure Class* (p. 33):

> "That propensity for purposeful activity and that repugnance to all futility of effort which belong to man by virtue of his character as an agent do not desert him when he emerges from the naïve communal culture where the dominant mode of life is the unanalysed and undifferentiated solidarity of the individual with the group with which his life is bound up. . . . Under the régime of individual ownership the most available means of visibly achieving a purpose is that afforded by the acquisition and accumulation of goods . . . the propensity for achievement—the instinct of workmanship—tends more and more to shape itself into a straining to excel others in pecuniary achievement."

We can go so far as to say that much of Veblen's work consists of an effort to examine physical artifacts, systems of thought, and individual lives in order to see the interplay of instinctual motives "frozen" in them, much as Freud saw a physical symptom as the frozen evidence of a psychological conflict. Thus, Veblen looks at classical economic theory to disengage its workmanship from its more or less elegant wastemanship, or he looks with quizzical wonder at the British or American gentleman, with his ability to be brilliantly incompetent in all industrial matters, effortfully idle, and calculatingly extravagant. Still again he will make what we might term a "content analysis" of particular objects in search of workmanship entwined with waste; as he writes (in *The Theory of the Leisure Class*, pp. 100–101):

> "Even in articles which appear at first glance to serve for pure ostentation only, it is always possible to detect the presence of some, at least ostensible, useful purpose; and on the other hand, even in special machinery and tools contrived

for some particular industrial process, as well as in the rudest appliances of human industry, the traces of conspicuous waste, or at least of the habit of ostentation, usually become evident on a close scrutiny."

This "content analysis" of objects and theories quite obviously proceeds on the basis of a theory of unconscious motivation in their human makers and users. Men, according to Veblen, conceal from themselves what they feel and do: they rationalize as decorously wasteful the activities that actually serve the common good, for to be useful has often become as demeaning as being "in trade" once was.

Conversely, and perhaps more typically, they find some utility, even necessity, in actions that serve primarily to keep them in the pecuniary race of intrepid expenditure or the occupational race of avoiding work of servile imputation. That they do this, even when the activity in question appears senseless to the culturally insensitive eye, testifies in Veblen's judgment to the strength of the human propensity to lead a meaningful existence. In other words, rationalization is the ever-recurring symptom of our desire to be reasonable. In seeing that the collision between human instincts and cultural pressures produced compromises both in motivation and action, Veblen was working in the spirit of the discoveries in the field of psychoanalysis that Freud was simultaneously making. In fact, whereas Freud tended to assume that the latent, the hidden motive was the real McCoy, Veblen had a less dogmatic view of the process of disentangling a mixture of motives: it was in each case a question of evidence to determine whether the overt or the latent factors predominated, and things might occasionally be what they seemed.

IT HAPPENED IN HISTORY

To psychological states in which one or another motive predominates, there correspond in Veblen's system different societies and different periods of history. Some indication has already been given of Veblen's picture of prehistoric culture. In the beginning there was savagery, the kind of society characteristic of Neolithic times: small, peaceable, sedentary, industrious, and protected by matriarchal goddesses of like temper. Women were equal to men. Veblen's evidence for the existence of such a Golden Age was, as he half-confesses, scanty; it was partly derived not from ethnology but from psychology by way of analogy between children and primitives. Veblen, like Kropotkin, was presenting a useful corrective to the prevalent competitive versions of Social Darwinism in his time.

The "fall" from savagery comes about, according to Veblen, for any one of a number of reasons, most of them involving an increase in wealth; but it may not in Veblen's view come at all (as the Eskimo and Pueblo * witness)—in contrast to Marx, Veblen can be commendably undogmatic on this point. The disruption of savagery and the shift to the next and "higher" stage of barbarism is marked by the development of patriarchal religions whose fierce gods symbolize the new order of status and dominance. The three good instincts which gave savagery its tone must now share dominance with the quasi-instinct of predatory emulation.

Barbarism itself passes through two stages, roughly equivalent, in European history, to the Dark Ages and feudalism respectively, and is in turn succeeded by the "handicraft era" of early modern times (this designation was one of several concepts in economic history that Veblen may have taken from Werner Sombart; the stages themselves, regarded as steps in a naively progressive series, can be found in Fourier). Veblen conceives the handicraft era as a period in which man's instinctual heritage, never wholly extinct in the underlying population which happily remains more savage than barbarian, again comes to the fore and takes the lead in shaping the general institutional situation.

For Veblen as for Marx and Engels, technology was the prime mover in these transitions from stage to stage. True, technology was mediated through the social relations of production, but these were bound sooner or later to catch up with technology;

---

* I am inclined to agree with those skeptical ethnologists who have recently shown, e.g., by dream analysis, that some of the cultures Veblen thought were survivals of peaceful savagedom—such as the Pueblo Indian groups—are not wholly composed of such happily peaceable people.

Veblen, like Marx, interpreted socialism as an effort on the part of the rest of the culture to catch up with the machine-made industrial revolution. In a way, Veblen was more technology-minded than Marx. The former saw invention as self-generated by the instinct of workmanship, with occasional unintended assists from idle curiosity. From this standpoint, what matters in history is not men's consciousness, their alienation or their effort to remove it, not even struggle, but simply work in accordance with instinctual drives. All else is waste, to be cut out or caught up sooner or later.

William Fielding Ogburn, who moved from economics into sociology, has since made the concept of "cultural lag" familiar, and indeed Americans are often more than ready to grant that their religious, political, and other "peripheral" doings are behind-hand in comparison with economic and technical advance. The very term "lag," which Veblen uses, implies a value-judgment in spite of itself, since to delay, linger, and wait is in the American idiom a sign not of sound conservative judgment but of backwardness. Yet Veblen repeatedly disclaims making such a value-judgment: he insists that he is merely speaking from an economic point of view and that from some other point of view, such as an aesthetic one, one might value precisely what was laggard. Much of *The Theory of the Leisure Class* is in fact devoted to a brilliant examination of the snob appeal of the outdated and the antique—of what is economically useless—as compared with the negative prestige carried by knowledge of the new, the useful, the mechanical. The leisure class itself, Veblen argues, is a laggard class, enabled by its wealth to remain in the backwash of economic development, hence a brake upon the wheels of progress.

For in spite of his disclaimers, Veblen does ally himself, more or less unequivocally, with the progress-minded thinking of the 19th-century rationalist. He envisages a society cleansed by the machine and its presumptive accompanying cast of thought of all ritual, reliquary, and rite. The problem of how such a society, if conceivable at all, would hold together never seems to bother him. Take, for example, his attitude towards the belief in luck, to which he devotes some interesting passages in *The Theory of the Leisure Class.* In his rationalist view that the march of technology would extirpate the belief in luck, because a true scientific determinism and such a belief could not coincide, he overlooked the possibility that it is the belief in luck which allows technology to be accepted by men whose jobs and skills it so drastically rearranges. In ruling out the belief in luck as superstitious, Veblen assumed a more predictable lot for individuals than an industrial system can assure them—and ruled out, too, as he did in other parts of his system, the compartmentalizations that allow magic and science, ritual and technology, to exist in the same individual. One could argue, moreover, contrary to Veblen's view, that gambling is socially useful in serving people as a paradigm of their fate in the larger social universe, balancing off their unluckiness if they win, "proving" it if they lose—in either case serving to keep people, and the "system," going. Veblen seems to have taken for granted an instinctual social solidarity resting on the instinct of workmanship and the allied parental bent, but the notion, so clear in Durkheim, that religious rituals might actually be the source of economic energies and scientific advance was quite alien to Veblen's aggressively economistic thinking; it was no accident, of course, that Veblen referred to himself as an economist and to his books as economic theory, and did not identify himself as a sociologist.

Nevertheless, he qualifies the simplistic concept of lag in two significant respects. In the first place, his notion that basic human nature is peaceable, only overlaid by a short-lived experience with pecuniary and barbarian predation, implies that certain kinds of lag or regression to this earlier more "natural" substratum will actually constitute a social advance. This leads him to an ambivalent view of Christianity: on the one hand, as a patriarchal religion of futile subservience to extravagant earthly representatives of a leisure-laden heavenly hierarchy; on the other hand, as a religion of brotherhood and abnegation at odds with pecuniary culture. Indeed, the leisure class itself plays a similarly ambivalent role. In the main, it is the fortress of conservatism, predation, and organized futility—to attain the prestige of which is the goal of the combatants in the economic arena. But by its very nature as a backwater, the leisure class serves to protect survivals of the non-invidious, non-predatory aspects of life. Its women, the most sheltered, are the most eager to exchange a life of fatuous vicarious idleness for workmanlike activity and social usefulness; it is their reversion which makes them reformers. Thus, it is only survivals of the recent past which Veblen considers genuinely laggard, and as soon as one reverts to the primitive savage culture one comes into contact with those *Ur*-human traits which are at the same time the face of the utopian future.

Veblen's second qualification of the theory of lag is related to his notion that technology is the first aspect of culture to be borrowed in a diffusion process. This gives an advantage to a late-coming (laggard?) society, which could borrow the fruit of another society's technological work without taking along the encrustation of irrelevant and interfering habits which had grown up around the technology in its place of origin. This important idea Veblen once put as follows (*The Instinct of Workmanship,* pp. 135–6):

"In the origination and indigenous working-out of any given technological factor . . . elements of imputed anthropomorphism are likely to be comprised in the habitual apprehension of these factors, and so find lodgment in the technological routine that has to do with them; the result being, chiefly a limitation on their uses and on the ways and means by which they are utilised, together with a margin of lost motion in the way of magical and religious observances presumed to be intrinsic to the due working of such factors . . . Now, when any given technological or decorative element crosses the frontier between one culture and another, in the course of borrowing, it is likely to happen that it will come into the new culture stripped of most or all of its anthropomorphic or spiritual virtues and limitations . . . ; since the borrowing is likely to be made from motives of workmanlike expediency, and the putative spiritual attributes of the facts involved are not obvious to men who have not been trained to impute them."

Veblen had doubtless observed how his father, coming as an immigrant to the United States, had perforce left behind a good many habitual agrarian practices of the Norwegian village, while accepting eagerly the developing machine technology of the American wheat belt. Moreover, his father accepted this technology without learning Yankee words and ways—much as Thorstein Veblen himself became rapidly acculturated to the international sciences of philosophy, philology, and economics without adopting the complex of customs maintained by the Yankee guardians of the higher learning.

Much in the same way, Veblen regarded German and Japanese imperialism as the product of a borrowing of English machine technology without English empiricism, libertarianism, and wasteful consumption. These predatory empires, still socially and ideologically feudal, having borrowed technology "clean," won an advantage over the Western democracies whose productivity had already been dissipated in an emulative race for idle and luxurious living. This advantage, however, would only be temporary; sooner or later, the machine would not only derange German and Japanese feudalism but also—a curious inversion of the "lag" theory—drag in its wake the very wasteful consumption practices that surrounded it in its Anglo-Saxon home of origin. Hence Veblen advises Japan (in 1915) to strike fast if it wishes to conquer and in *Imperial Germany and the Industrial Revolution* (also published in 1915) he suggests that Germany may have struck too late.

There is much that is paradoxical in all this for Veblen's own theories. If Germans and Japanese are now the hard-working people who have not yet learned how to act like dilettante gentlemen, should this not also make them peaceable, as other industrious folk have been throughout history? Veblen's not wholly satisfactory answer is that the dynasts have adopted technology but have not yet been domesticated by it, and when hard pressed, here as elsewhere, he falls back on racial explanations in which he only half believes. The fact is that, while Veblen's instinct of workmanship can be read as his puritanical paean to hard work, he only intermittently thought men lived by work alone (witness his concept of idle curiosity) and hence he did not feel compelled to admire the industrial late-comers for their vaunted "efficiency." Rather, despite or even perhaps because of their obedient workmanship, he regarded them as barbarians—so much so that passages of *Imperial Germany* might have been written for Lord Northcliffe's agency by an Oxford don, and were actually picked up by the Creel Committee as usable anti-German propaganda when America entered the War. (Even more clearly, and with an ethnocentrism reminiscent of "Yellow Peril" ideology, did Veblen regard the Japanese as barbarians; in *The Nature of Peace* he implied that a Japanese-German alliance meant providing a "drunken savage" with a machine gun.)

To be sure, Veblen's ill-disguised and quasi-racial dislike of the Germans may have less intellectual roots than here suggested: it may go back to hostility between German and Norwegian Lutheran groups in Minnesota and Wisconsin. But this does not explain, except in small part, why Veblen liked the English and especially the French despite the obsolescence of their technology and the ardent wastefulness their leisure classes had attained through centuries of practice (Dorfman states that the last intellectual project Veblen planned was to go to England in order to find out how such decency and kindliness could flourish in an imperialist state). We are brought back, not only to the ambiguities lurking in Veblen's concept of lag, but also to those lurking in his major concept of workmanship, with its character both as an end—which permits a judgment of the beneficence of a social system as a whole—and as a means—as to which judgment can only be in terms of efficiency.

All these subtleties in Veblen's thought, however, were to be submerged by the Russian Revolution, after which the Soviets stand out as justified both by socialist ends and ruthless means. In his Chicago period Veblen had been moved by Carpenter's "Towards Democracy," but in the 20s the poem had become meaningless for him and a few months before his death he stated that the best hope he saw was the Communists (Dorfman, p. 500).

SOCIALIST DARWINISM

In Veblen's mind, Darwinism was the suitable philosophy for the coldly impersonal experience of factory production, where men draw, not so much on the fruits of their individual labor, as on a pool of machinery and technological resource provided them by the society as a whole. By Darwinian emphasis on behavior conducive to the welfare of the species, Veblen wanted to emphasize that the accumulated industrial arts should not be appropriated by one part of the species as against the rest; there was no more "right" to do this than for a fish to appropriate the water in which it swam. Much of Veblen's work was devoted to belittling the Captains of Industry who thought themselves responsible for American productivity, whereas they merely engrossed the instinct of workmanship of the race, charged mankind for what, as a body, it already "owned," and wasted what others had produced in a frenzy of extravagant, usually vicarious display.

So often does Veblen harp on this theme that it seems fair to say that the conflict between workmanship and wastemanship is almost obsessive with him. Karl Anderson and John Gambs are right to stress that Veblen's dichotomy between constructive and destructive human tendencies appears in his analysis of all spheres of behavior (Gambs draws an analogy with Freud's split between Eros and the death instinct). In order to be moderately sympathetic with Veblen's nearly exclusive concern with economic production, and the passionate hatred for luxury that his irony cannot hide, we must go back to Rolvaag, Dreiser, Norris and other turn-of-the-century writers to remind ourselves of America as a neglectful country where people could starve. If we read Veblen literally, it would seem that he did want man to live by bread alone, provided Consumers' Research had studied the ingredients and no middle man had made a profit on the loaf.

This concentration on scarcity is what gives economics the name of the "gloomy science," and in Veblen's case it gives his system, to use his own slang against him, a certain one-eyedness. So exclusive an attention to activities beneficial to the species as a whole must leave out of view the whole range of more differentiated and individualized human motives. Of course, Veblen was commendably attempting to reinstate work and sympathy as natural human motives, much as D. H. Lawrence strove to restore to sex its rightful importance. But both men confused the alleged naive dominance of these motives among primitive tribes with the necessarily more subtle, "contaminated" part they can play in modern societies. Surely the middle-class citizen against whom both Veblen and Lawrence raged is more than half right in cherishing his exemptions from the round of procreating and maintaining the species. Dress and polite manners, which Veblen mocked, can be, like that "mental" love which Lawrence scorned, a means of establishing personal identity; although of course they can be and often are adaptations to conventional expectations, as Veblen and Lawrence claimed. We have already drawn attention to the fact that Veblen himself ducks away from utilitarianism in the field closest to home, that of university research and instruction, and stands out for the life of learning as an end in itself. He gets around the fact that instruction is a socially useful activity by welcoming it only as a necessary complement to research, in that it stimulates the instructor and trains up future researchers. Indeed, Veblen's whole treatment of the instinct of idle curiosity may be seen as something of a protest against the insistent pragmatism implicit in the instinct of workmanship and the unremitting condemnation of waste. Leaving aside what shelter it may have offered him in dealing with his efficient and impersonal father, we can see that this "tenderminded" motive held for Veblen a salutary corrective to the exclusively "toughminded," workaday preoccupations of the world around him. Yet by simultaneously enjoining the worker not to mourn his lost craftsmanship but to make his peace with machine production, Veblen was prescribing for others what he refused to accept for himself.

This is a pretty basic paradox for a man whose whole bent of thought and life was to deny any distinction to persons or among persons. Veblen did not want anyone to make anything of *his* person, which would have tied him down to *being*, to being a person, as against making something of his work, from which he thought he could disengage himself. So, too, he obviously thought that the university professor bore the same relation to his means of production—laboratories, journals, books—that the factory worker did to his, that is, an impersonal, detached, self-disregarding, unostentatious, nearly invisible connection. Certainly, no one has so trenchantly satirized the false pretensions of the educated. This admirer of engineers came to the opposite conclusion from the great engineer, Vilfredo Pareto, concerning the role of elites: Veblen thought the common man would be better off without them, Pareto that elites were simply recruited anew from uncommon common men riding on the backs of their fellows.* Yet it is again paradoxical that Veblen, who made the term "common man" his trademark, time and again expresses contempt for common sense, which he thought invariably lagged behind the facts of life: no iconoclast of his day was surer that the received opinions of the multitude were wrong. Perhaps the paradox can best be reconciled by recalling Veblen's view that ultimately the productivity of the machine depends on disinterested scientific theory—yet in trying to get rid of all aristocratic and privileged elements in thought and scholarship, he ended up entrusting theory to hard-bitten engineers, no likely vessel.

THE BIOLOGY OF HOPE

In all this, it is important to underscore the fact that Veblen's system of social science is as much biological as historical. This is true of the evolutionary methodology which Veblen took from Darwin and also of Veblen's heavy reliance on the concepts of instinct and race. In 1952 we need not labor over the limitations in Veblen's particular handling of the instinct-habit methodology. Likewise, most of what Veblen said on the subject of race is now beside the point; as he himself observes, this theory could be

* Dr. Lubin has told me that Veblen read Pareto, and had a considerable respect for him, as a scientific and engineering-minded economist. In Lubin's view, Veblen was more aware than his writings let on, of intellectual positions contrary to his own; he admired workmanlike craftsmen in his own field, even when they differed from him.

equally well stated in terms of learned habits. Yet covert assumptions with respect to race often crop up in Veblen's work, and enable him to rigidify his distinctions between classes, nations, and periods of history. His irony scarcely conceals an ambivalent respect for the "Dolicho-blonds" and in his very last bit of writing he speaks with wistful, partly racist admiration for the high illegitimacy rates among the Scandinavian peoples. There are times when his talk of race and instinct, in combination with his ascetic Puritanism, his desire to prune back culture to its savage beginnings, his hatred for middlemen of goods or ideas, make him sound like a sexless D. H. Lawrence or an unpoetic Ezra Pound. When, late in life, he stated that the next generation of economists could do without theory, or when he laughed at Malinowski's work which was then appearing, he was in effect turning his back on the very intellectual pursuits which had once excited him; he was almost ready, with the Nazis, to say: "When I hear the word 'culture,' I reach for my revolver."

However, all this talk, as with any thinker, needs to be put into a context. Compared with much of the writing on race in his lifetime, Veblen's treatment emphasizes nurture more than nature. Paradoxically, his more or less racialist hatred of the Germans sprang partly from his contempt for German racial boasting. Most of the time, Veblen is closer to the progressive biologistically-grounded assumptions of Lester Ward than to the Social Darwinists who assumed that their race, their kind, were the most fit to survive. And again and again he insisted that mixed races, hybrids, stood a better chance than "pure" ones, especially if, like the emancipated Jews, they also bore a mixed cultural inheritance. Finally, it is hard to blame a man who had suffered as much as Veblen had in the cause of scholarship if he lapses occasionally into anti-intellectualism, in his own complicated form of midwest Philistinism.

What is more important is that Veblen's emphasis on race and instinct at times led him to see institutions really as excrescences with the main dramatic tensions being located among the instincts, and between them and social life as a whole. As a conservationist in spirit, preoccupied with biological subsistence as the fundamental human problem, he tended to be unsympathetic to the institutions which men have built and inherited to give stability, channeling, and interpretation to life—especially, of course, when these seemed to get in the way of subsistence. And since Veblen recognized, with brilliant insight, that institutions often create the needs they serve, he concluded that they were largely exploitative. Thus he saw at the end of the human road a society devoted to industrial workmanship, free of anthropomorphic illusion, of emulation, waste, and war—a society which did not give other meaning to the universe than that blind play of cumulative forces studied by Darwin; a society in which men admitted their insignificance, their kinship with other animals, and their helplessness in the slow working out of the evolutionary drift. As a society without lag and friction, in which men served each other because instinctually bound to do so, not only the state but all other "superstructural" institutions would wither away.

It is of a piece with this biologistic thinking that Veblen never seems to have asked himself how species-serving workmanship could be so readily contaminated by the desire for approval, nor does he ask in what way emulation can result in workmanlike behavior. His system does not include a social instinct (along the lines of gregariousness rather than solicitude), nor does he try to explain how the very nature of group life may lead a culture to prefer other values to the workmanship which this descendant of peasant Lutherans took too much for granted. One senses that Veblen, in his methodology as in his life, sought to disregard those aspects of human nature which make men vulnerable to the judgments of their fellows—and this despite the fact that his writings abound in illustrations of such vulnerabilities.*

* See, e.g., *Absentee Ownership*, pp. 115–117: "Men are moved by many impulses and driven by many instinctive dispositions. Among these abiding dispositions are a strong bent to admire and defer to persons of achievement and distinction, as well as a workmanlike disposition to find merit in any work that serves the common good. . . . It is in these cases a matter of distinction, of course, with no hint of achievement, except such achievement as a loyal deference is bound to impute. . . . Men like to believe that the personages whom they so admire by force of conventional routine are also of some use, as well

One result is that, as against Freud's instinct system, with its irreconcilable conflict between love and destructiveness and its contradictory demands on love itself, Veblen's is an optimistic system, at least in the long run—optimistic, that is, in terms of one who asks of life only that it be peaceable and provident. The three instincts he regarded as native to man were all beneficent. Until the end of the first World War, Veblen seems definitely to have felt that somehow man will strive to right the balance of motives to the greater use of his own good sense and constructive rather than destructive propensities. While a King of France may let himself be roasted to death because he could not himself perform the menial office of displacing his royal body from before the fire, in general the common man—and much more surely, the common woman—is spared such distortions of workmanship and allowed to lead a life of slightly less strenuous absurdities. In this pre-war period Veblen believed that the gradual recrudescence of whole and natural ends, the slow erosion of futility, and the patient labors of idle curiosity, might bring things out all well in the end; revolution was not required, only a free play for the instinctual impetus inherited from Savagery.

VEBLEN: ANTI-INSTITUTIONAL ECONOMIST

This strand of qualified optimism in Veblen reminds us that he never made contact, so far as his writings show, with the pessimistic theories of society that were being developed by his great European contemporaries: Max Weber, with his emphasis on the "iron cage" of modern industrialism and bureaucracy; or Pareto, with his cynical notion of the "circulation of elites"; or Michels, with his analogous "iron law of oligarchy." The concept of bureaucracy which, under the influence of these men (and others, such as Mosca and Bentley), has become part

---

as of great distinction,—that they even somehow contribute, or at least conduce, to the material well-being at large. Which is presumably to be set down as one of the wonders wrought by the instinct of workmanship, which will not let men be content without some colorable serviceability in the personages which they so create out of nothing-in-particular." It seems pretty clear in such passages that Veblen is not the prisoner of his instinct-theory, but is using it as an ironical and polemical device. But the passage just quoted is out of his bitter late years.

of the working equipment of modern social science, remained for Veblen—as for many laymen today—simply an epithet.* His thought moves characteristically from a concern with individual motives or "instincts" to the largest aggregates, such as "the underlying population" or "the vested interests." In between lie his type-characters: the Captains of this and that; the Engineers; the denizens of country towns. For this so-called "institutional economist," institutions seem not to have had a very full-bodied existence—and when they did, he spent his time attacking them for being institutions. So, too, one could get from his closest study of an institution—*The Higher Learning*—the idea that current academic struggles were mainly between the faculty and the administration, and fail to see, within the faculty, any of the vested interests of "field" or method, any of the bureaucratic tendencies in recruitment or in judgments as to what was and what was not to be counted as "research." **

In a way, Veblen gave the vested interests too much credit,

* In his essay, "Some Neglected Points in the Theory of Socialism," Veblen does take account of Spencer's condemnation of socialism as bureaucratic, but he answers the charge by saying (1) that since capitalism is so wasteful, socialism can afford to be somewhat inefficient, and (2) that there are other alternatives, such as the possibility of a constitutional economy analogous to a constitutional democracy, to a regime of contract or of status. It seems to me from this argument that Veblen never met head-on (nor, for that matter, did Spencer and other laissez-faire advocates) the possibility that all large-scale societies would inevitably be bureaucratic, would suffer from hardening of the institutional arteries—and hence greatly resemble each other, whatever the label.

** In view of all this, it is perplexing that, in histories of thought, Veblen has been dubbed an "institutionalist." To be sure, as we shall see in the next chapter, Veblen's contrast between the state of the industrial arts and the system of pecuniary control, while reducible to a contamination of instincts, is certainly amenable to discussion in terms of institutions. Moreover, as a teacher he told other economists to study such institutions as advertising or banking rather than their predecessors' theories, and (as Clarence E. Ayres well emphasizes in *The Industrial Economy*, p. 25) insisted on the historical and hence relative nature of pecuniary patterns of thought. Some of his disciples took him up on all this, and turned from theory to statistics or to studies of particular industries' price policies or union practices in a way Veblen himself never did. "Institutional economics" thus includes some very different breeds of men: econometricians like the late Wesley C. Mitchell, irreverent critics of institutions like Ayres and Walton Hamilton, and some men, of whom the late John R. Commons is the outstanding example, who studied capitalist institutions outside the Veblenian entourage.

in supposing that the world was run in accordance with their whims and wishes—any absentee owners I have known have found themselves terribly frustrated by the "vested interest" of the officials (bureaucrats) through whom they had to deal. Likewise, he gave the university presidents too much credit; doubtless, when the latter in conclave assemble, they bemoan the intractability of their faculties, their comptrollers, their deans, their buildings and grounds superintendents—all of whom are vested interests, and all possessed of the (I would almost say) "natural right" of sabotage.

In one domain at least, Veblen realized this. He saw the AFL as a petty vested interest, copying the delaying and obstructive tactics of its business betters. But again he laid this to the leadership, and exempted, in conventional radical fashion, the rank and file; his recurrent attacks on the "aristocrats of labor" were simply part of the leftist line of those years, a line which greatly underestimated Gompers and Green because of alleged lack of ideological militancy. But this does not amount to a recognition of vested interest as an essential conservative force in society, let alone to a recognition of the usefulness of bureaucracy as a method of handling recurrent large affairs with despatch, impersonality, and some marginal control on the basis of set principle—"red tape" being the best substitute for the shedding of red blood yet found in civil affairs. And this is connected with the residual farm-boy in Veblen, who distrusted the central government, resented the income tax and the national debt, and hankered, in spite of his cosmopolitanism and belief in mechanization, for a handicraft age of small affairs. To be sure, hardly any of us escapes a similar ambivalence towards the modern world in which we live, or fails at some time to glance backward at our image of a Jeffersonian America.

CHAPTER THREE

BUSINESS VERSUS FULL PRODUCTION

The farmer spends his time in the fields, the laborer at his machine, and the businessman at meetings. . . . The object of a meeting is not, as the very young believe, to solve the problem at hand, but to impress the people there. And for this purpose, of course, the larger the meeting the better. . . . You will soon learn that the heart, the very lifeblood of modern business is the interoffice memo. If you're a good man with a memo you have small cause to worry. The memo, like the meeting, is concerned only incidentally with its apparent subject. . . . The waste is staggering. One authority feels that if one in ten falls on target, or is at least partly read, the mission is accomplished. . . . Address them to the highest officer who might be even remotely connected with the subject, especially the man who is in charge of those you are trying to impress.

Shepherd Mead, *How to Succeed in Business without Really Trying*

WHAT is the source of Veblen's power over us? His cavalier quality, the irony which permits him at once to embrace and to fend off life, these make him "modern" and we read him when we no longer read Henry George (unless we are fanatical single-taxers), Henry Demarest Lloyd, Ignatius Donnelley, and others whom Daniel Aaron has termed the "men of good hope." Moreover, the crash of 1929 and the fact that in the same year Veblen had died lonely and neglected have led many people to accept the astringent and derisive verdict he passed on capitalism and its culture. For, as Freud has observed, when we suffer misfortune we feel guilt—especially if we have earlier let die someone who played upon our shortcomings. An illuminating instance of these reactions is provided by John Cummings, an economist who reviewed *The Theory of the Leisure Class* with pedantic hostility when it first came out, and who, two years after Veblen's death, wrote a letter (quoted by Dorfman) which is filled with *mea culpas*, for instance the following:

> "I have often wondered how I could have been so blind. In the years since we have all seen the accumulating evidence of the widespread influence of Veblen's analysis of social and economic behaviour, as set forth in his *Theory of the Leisure Class*. . . . I was a product of the gay nineties. My economic thinking was in conventional terms of academic training . . . Veblen was cubistic and for the time incomprehensible."

Cummings' letter adds that if one has friends to dinner, whether or not they have read Veblen, they will "say something about the conspicuous consumption in these hard times of unemployment" —and it is plain that Cummings feels guilty not only for his criticism and specific injury * to Veblen but also bears a generalised middle-class guilt for being well-fed and employed. Cummings typifies our widespread uneasiness about "conspicuous consumption"—something which is, to be sure, not Veblen's doing alone, though he has greatly contributed to our vocabulary of misgiving and self-deprecation.

Our willingness to let Veblen punish us for our sins is

---

* Veblen's reaction to Cummings' review shows that he was grievously wounded. Veblen answered him—his only direct reply to a critic—in a full-length article, "Mr. Cummings's Strictures on 'The Theory of the Leisure Class,' " which starts off with an elaborately bitter apology for having written so clumsily as to be misunderstood by Cummings. The article contains an item-by-item rebuttal whose cake-walking style reveals the hurt it was intended to hide. Cummings, however, in the letter quoted in the text, doubts "if Veblen took my review of his book very seriously. . . . In my academic conventionalism I was just another interesting specimen for observation and analysis. . . . He knew he was eternally right, and if others did not know it, that was no affair of his." This, of course, is what Veblen wanted people to think, the pose he assumed in order to beat such early enemies as Cummings to the punch. But it hardly needs be stressed here that very few are that self-confident (recall that William James made his brother Henry doubt his best work, or that D. H. Lawrence almost drove Bertrand Russell to suicide by attacking him as bloodless)—Veblen least of all, ever unsure whether he was good for much.

heightened by another stylistic device of his. As in a morality play, he dramatically sharpens the conflict of good and evil by personification: in academic life, the good guys are the faculty, the bad guys the president and trustees, just as in the economy generally, the good guys are the engineers and skilled workmen, the bad guys the businessmen, the bankers and lawyers. Since we the readers are never quite so bad as his villains—and seldom so rich—we can deflect his shafts as directed at those other fellows; our guilt is then based on our admiration for the latter, or our ambitions, and can be assuaged by shifting our admiration to Veblen's heroes. Veblen can achieve this result because, underneath his detachment, he is really a very topical writer: *The Leisure Class* (1899) reflects the splurging and fake gentility of post-Civil War America; *Business Enterprise* (1904), the formation of trusts and the rise of finance capital to industrial hegemony; *Imperial Germany* (1915) and *The Nature of Peace* (1917), the first World War. Certain articles, such as "The Army of the Commonweal" (1894), are still more topical, long before Veblen began his short career as a weekly journalist on *The Dial*.* To all these issues of the day, Veblen applies his dichotomizing moralism, looking everywhere, as I have put it above, for the conflict between workmanship and wastemanship. And as this conflict runs through our individual lives as well as through our social order, we assist Veblen by our ability to internalize the voices of his dramatis personae. He obliges in turn by his own ambivalence towards his moralism.

As the price he pays for his power, Veblen may win acceptance today because we have hurt him or because we have been hurt as Veblen has been hurt, or because we have been untouched in a world where the news of misery is widespread. Moreover, since he abstracts from topicality through his dramatizations, there is the danger of overapplying him to an altered situation—a danger less pressing in writers of a more intransigent concreteness. I have concluded that I can best set forth what Veblen taught, and at the same time criticize it, by reapplying his

* Even within the field of technical economics, Veblen's articles and reviews deal with the current "news": with the rise of the German and Austrian schools, with marginal utility theory, with socialist deviation from Marx.

doctrine to the contemporary scene: to business, to academia, to politics, to economic theory, and to consumption; this is the purpose of the chapters that follow. My own biases, in terms of value judgment and of limitations of knowledge, will I trust be in sufficiently plain view. Unlike Veblen, I make no pretense not to be a moralist.

BUSINESS ARTFULNESS VERSUS THE INDUSTRIAL ARTS

In the movie "The Big Carnival" a man is pinned in a cave by falling timbers. For a cynical newspaperman, his plight is a "find" and he proceeds to "mine" the man out by drilling through the top of the mountain in which the cave is located, rather than going in through the direct, commonsense passage which would extricate him too soon and spoil his news monopoly—and spoil also the carnival-like monopolies of hawkers and other prehensile folk who are making a good thing out of the crowds who come to watch the drilling. In the course of these businesslike proceedings, a matter-of-fact and experienced engineer-artisan appears, and asks why they don't go directly after the trapped man, who all this time is suffering and is further tormented by the pounding drills overhead. But the interloper lacks the gift of gab and control of communications channels (the "state" is in on the deal, in the person of a blowsy sheriff who hopes for re-election from the publicity; so is a corrupt contractor who has close ties to the politician), and after making his point into the mike, the engineer is fended off by astute questioning—industry succumbs to business. (Compare Tom Sawyer's cave experience, and the role of the artless Huck.) But in the end business succumbs too; the trapped man dies, and as the Vested Interests have a falling out, the newspaperman loses his monopoly, and is shot by the dead man's rapacious wife.

The whole tale may be thought of as a Veblenian parable. The Carnival is business, blithely carrying on its sabotage of the life process, while pretending to be helpful and industrious, and diverting the paying customers by means of clamor and glamour. But it, too, perishes in the end, having pushed its control of industry to the point of strangulation. And the Vested Interests in the case, being predatory, not only succeed in killing the very goose they depend upon, but also fall upon one another, in a paradigm of modern war-making.

In fact, a content analysis of Veblen's writings would, I think, reveal that the idea which appears with the most frequency and intensity, early and late, is that there is an inherent, developing conflict between the state of the industrial arts and the system of ownership and control by which they are applied under modern capitalism. These arts, the usufruct of the race and its long cultural history, are the cumulative product of idle curiosity and matter-of-fact handling of the impersonal processes of technology; they are by nature cosmopolitan, drawing on the stock of all industrial peoples; their mastery depends on a mechanistic view of the world and in turn they nurture such a view among their devotees. By contrast, the system of business enterprise is the usufruct of a much briefer history—its pedigree hardly goes back further than 18th-century mercantilism, though it draws on animistic attitudes towards nature, and predatory attitudes towards man, which are of course much older. Business enterprise, moreover, comes increasingly in conflict with technological needs, as the scale of operations widens and the Captain of Solvency, such as J. P. Morgan, takes precedence over the Captain of Industry, whose eye was less on the main manipulative chance and more on the engineering problems of production.

Veblen dramatised this historic encounter in terms of a polarizing distinction between engineers and their allies—the class of men skilled in technology, including skilled workmen and scientists—on the one side—and absentee owners and their allies—the class of men skilled in chicane, including accountants, bankers, lawyers, politicians—on the other. These two groups had different roles in the processes of production: the former to produce, the latter to interfere with production on behalf of profits and inflationary credit transactions.

The "racist" streak in Veblen led him to suppose that hereditary factors might have something to do with the difference between the two groups; in *The Engineers and the Price System* he flatly states that engineers are "endowed with something more than an even share of the sense of workmanship" (p. 80). In the main, however, Veblen held that each group was formed, in its habitual orientations to life in general, by occupational experience; while inheritance played its part by affording each group some of the attributes of the other. Thus, engineers were not entirely immune from predatory and animistic preconceptions, especially if they had grown up in the pre-Darwinian days when "natural rights"—Veblen's great *bête noire*—held sway; and, conversely, even bankers were saved from a total commitment to unlimited predation by the instinct of workmanship, the desire to be serviceable in some way, and to win the plaudits of the underlying population—a population nearly but not quite ready to grant that profits, however won, were the sole test of worthwhile devotion to the community's interests.

This concession, however, did not lead Veblen himself to see anything benign in the Captains of Finance who were responsible for the turn-of-the-century trusts and combines—trusts and combines that were the topic for one of his famous courses. It is perplexing why he did not think, as did Bellamy, that these men had done a useful job in integrating business, making it easier for a syndicalist regime to take over. However, Veblen allowed no constructive role whatever to the financiers—if they did anything not wholly predatory it was because of some surreptitious return of the repressed instinct of workmanship; they were good only for persiflage and sabotage. We may suppose that Veblen was, at heart, an anti-truster, fearful of great and towering credit combinations, just as he was a free-trader on the national frontiers. Here, as elsewhere, he seems to have shared more with his despised classical economists and their 19th-century model of competition than he would have dreamed he could—so haughtily did he look down at this model as passé.

THE MACHINE AS TUTOR

Among "engineers" or "technologists," Veblen included both engineers proper and skilled workers. Of the two, the workers are slower than the engineers to adapt their thinking to the machine, for the machine discipline "falls upon them blindly and enforces an uncritical acceptance of opaque results, rather than a theoretical insight into the causal sequences which make up the machine process" (*Theory of Business Enterprise,* p. 312). But as Veblen shrewdly noted, the standardization of both wages and prices untrains the worker for pecuniary dickering. And the mobility required of the worker by modern industry may prevent him from acquiring property in the form of a home and its appliances, plus the metaphysical aura that such ownership brings.

Moreover, the machine takes its toll of conventional habits of thought even when it works less directly than this. All classes of the community are affected by having to live with machines, even the most archaic occupations such as army and clergy, so that, although the industrial and pecuniary groups become less and less able to understand each other, still the locus of the whole social discussion shifts steadily onto mechanistic ground. This is because the advent of the machine transforms not only the processes of production, but a much larger concatenation of activities which, despite lag, must become more standardized, more precise time-wise, and so on, to keep step with the machine.

Veblen proposed this picture of the machine and its operators as a counter to both Marxism and to the prevalent view of the time (as in Ruskin) which feared that the machine was rendering the worker stupid and delinquent. As to Marxism, Veblen held that in distinguishing between classes on the basis of property rights, Marx was thinking in terms of an outmoded legal fiction; for Veblen it was habits of life, and above all habits of work, which set apart different social groups.* Noting the growth of a salaried "white collar proletariat," Veblen ventured one of his brilliant prophecies: this group, although legally in a position identical with that of the factory proletariat, would continue to think in largely conventional terms because its work

* Veblen was being somewhat unfair to Marx here, failing to recognize that Marx, too, was concerned with the psychological consequences of having different roles in the processes of production: Marx is more of a theorist of economic experience and less a theorist of economic interest (in the sense of ownership or not) than Veblen and many others, both critics and superficial followers of Marx, have regarded him. Veblen, in fact, constantly tends to exaggerate the pre-Darwinian "datedness" of Marx.

was still of a pecuniary rather than a mechanical type (*Theory of Business Enterprise*, p. 351 n.).* The other belief, that the worker was brutalized by the machine, Veblen combatted as the one-eyed projection of men familiar only with animistic thinking, and hence unable to conceive of a mechanistic kind of intelligence. The worker's intelligence was changing, Veblen said, but in the direction of a new kind of intelligence, not toward stupidity.

Veblen in all probability had very little direct knowledge of factories—in any case, in my own view (as against his), it is not so much direct experience with the factory as the personal and cultural interpretation of experience which dictates attitudes. Where, then, did Veblen get his sympathy, so unusual among intellectuals, for machines? I have already noted that his father was unique among his group of Norwegian immigrants in mechanising his farm operations. It is quite conceivable that this Thomas Veblen sat for the portrait which Thorstein Veblen, years later, drew of the engineer. Moreover, Veblen as a farmboy who didn't like farming, or doing by hand anything a machine could be invented to do, was almost completely free of the rural yearning or nostalgia of many enemies of the industrial revolution. Furthermore, his uncommonly sharp eye for leisure-class patronizations perceived that those who sighed over the passing of the peasant and the artisan of earlier times were gulled by a feudalistic aesthetic, which preferred keeping the lower orders in their orderly places; against this, he counterposed his own functionalist aesthetic, which preferred, to the helpless naivete of the isolated artisan, irreverent skilled workers who knew the industrial score and could make machines produce.

Even today, Veblen's view is a rare one among the educated. True, the latter sometimes attribute a whole set of desirable human qualities to "the workers," seen in the image of the Soviet

* Cf. the recent development of this approach to the white-collar worker in C. Wright Mills, *White Collar* (New York, Oxford University Press, 1951). It is an open question what Veblen would say today about those office workers whose tasks have been altered by complex business machines. Perhaps he overestimated the ability of machines to create, so to speak, their own social climate, apart from countervailing factors.

Pavillion at the World's Fair as both more strong and more sensible than the bourgeois. But Veblen never lumped "the workers" in this fashion, which he would have regarded as a new leisure-class sentimentality; he made his point only about the skilled worker, the active machine-tender, not about the great masses of unskilled workers whom industrialization had also brought in its train.

My own very limited observations of factory life, and reflection on the observations of others, inclines me to the view that Veblen was right, those who feared the machine wrong: in the long run, industry does tend to make men rational, and herein lies hope for the world. Even the so-called unskilled workman frequently knows more about industrial processes than he is given credit for (though this is not generally true of working women, who ordinarily have the most repetitive jobs *). But the source and quality of this know-how remains an open question. For Veblen, it is the result of exposure to machines, to clocks, to complex industrial lay-outs, whereas I would suggest that it is also the result of exposure to other men confronting machines— exposure to urbanization as well as to industrialization. Other cultures react to machines with attitudes quite different from those typical in America—in France and Italy, for instance, often with more romanticism; industrialization does not invariably dictate the particular "vulgarities" and matter-of-fact, unanimistic and impersonal ways of thought Veblen attributed to skilled workers as such. As pointed out in the preceding chapter, Veblen tended to ignore social relations at work—he is more a contemporary of Frederick Winslow Taylor (about which more hereafter) than of Elton Mayo—and perhaps he saw the worker in the factory in terms of his own withdrawn mode. Then, too, his Gestaltist approach kept him from making a sufficient allowance

---

* James Worthy's studies at Sears show that women have almost universally better morale than men, in industry and office work. Is this because they are more, or less, matter-of-fact? This is reversed where men are a minority among women—there, they have better morale, whereas of course when women are in a minority among men, they have better morale. It would appear that the emotional relationship to the industrial plant itself may be secondary to sexual and cultural factors.

for compartmentalization: the ability of a worker to be mechanistic in one domain of his work and animistic in another—he spoke too soon in seeing industrialism, as Marx saw capitalism, as an uncontrollable fire that would burn out all feudal, pecuniary, nationalistic, and mystical ways of thought.

What has just been said needs, however, to be qualified in one important respect, one in which Veblen made a considerable advance over Marx and other socialists who, ignoring what Veblen ironically termed "psychic income," thought workers had nothing to lose but their chains. For Veblen realized that workers off the job were not under the educative influence of the machine but the (as he thought) stultifying influence of leisure-class ways of life. Indeed, as the standard of living rose, consequential upon industrial advance, more and more men and women gained the wherewithal to enter the leisure class, which Veblen saw as extending from the lace-curtain Irish who strove for gentility at the expense of comfort, all the way up to the absentee owner who frenetically manipulated and sabotaged industry so that he could compete effectively, if vicariously, in the invidious arts of consumption. It must have troubled Veblen, though he never said so outright, that consumption could not be mechanised and socialised as production was—he was as annoyed as any schoolmarm that school doesn't last all day and that its lessons can be undone in the home. Especially so since, despite growing American abundance, Veblen still thought, as we saw in the previous chapter, in terms of a Malthusian scarcity, so that playing hookey on the part of some meant not only the loss of educative hours on their part but starvation and misery on the part of the still less fortunate.*

---

* An ironical light is cast on Veblen's proposition by the repeated experience of industrialists that full production is often the result of the workers' "succumbing" to leisure-class standards, and working hard and long to get the wherewithal to meet them, in preference to a more casual set of work habits based on a lower standard of living. Thus, a British Labor Party member writes as follows, in answer to the question as to how the nationalized coal mines may be made to produce more:

". . . the social traditions of the miners make it difficult to devise adequate inducements [for increased output]. In the first place, their spending habits are based on depression standards and inadequate

HOW WASTEFUL IS WASTE?

Indeed, a major portion of Veblen's work may be seen as the effort to show the variety of ways in which a pecuniary culture sacrifices the industrial arts of production to the invidious ones of consumption. Such sacrifice is direct, as when resources are devoted to the production of superfluities—including such intangible superfluities as advertising, sermons and prayers, most learning, the services of porters, hotelmen, retailers, college presidents, and prostitutes. Such sacrifice is indirect when businessmen sabotage production in order to get the something for nothing they require in order to consume that something conspicuously—and when they withdraw their wives from the productive process to turn them into vehicles for display. In addition, there are other, more complex chains of sabotage. For one thing, the poor, forced down to a subsistence minimum to sustain the frivolities of the rich, lack the energies which would enable them to become capable machine-workers and citizens of industrial democracy; and even if they rise a bit above the subsistence minimum, their energies will be again liquidated in the race to imitate leisure-class modes of life. And these modes, as Veblen insists over and over, are inimical to industry, which comes to be regarded as vulgar and demeaning. Veblen thought "Society" repressed any awareness of the industrial means by which it lived much as Freud thought it repressed any awareness of the procreative means. Veblen concluded by estimating that the brake on potential production resulting from pecuniary sabotage in all forms ran between half and three-quarters of the total.

---

social equipment. Miners' wives do not normally indulge in the kind of social rivalry that expresses itself in fur coats; and often they cannot buy electric washing machines, because their houses aren't electrified. Thus, a rise of wages tends to be converted into more leisure rather than an improved standard of living. . . . Today by far the most important inducement offered to the miner is the high priority in new housing given to mining areas. Raising the miner's standard of housing will help to bring his spending habits more into line with those of other communities, and so make him more responsive to opportunities for higher earnings." Mark Benney, *Spotlight on Coal* (London: Bureau of Current Affairs, 1947), pp. 15–16.

Veblen's belief in increasing sabotage as productivity increased (with consequent unrelieved misery) resembles Marx's view of the increasing misery of the proletariat; in both cases, revolt was looked for as conditions became increasingly intolerable, although both men gave at least lip-service to the conceivable alternative of chaos. Both men lived to see their prophecies patently disproved: the workers did not get more miserable after 1848 but on the contrary living standards rose all over the Western world; and American production, despite, or perhaps because of booms and busts, went on expanding until Veblen's death in 1929. It would seem as if both men overestimated the power and ill-will of the "enemy": Marx of the capitalists and Veblen of that segment of capitalists who were absentee owners. Veblen, for instance, underestimated, in my opinion, the constructive role which Morgan and his confrères played in the rationalization of the American rail and industrial system, and saw mainly the looting; and while he granted, in *Absentee Ownership*, that credit inflation might give business a psychological boost, and thereby lead to expanded production, he somehow felt this wasn't right, wasn't solidly grounded, and wouldn't last: he went so far as to say that the American industrial plant, in 1923, was actually withering physically, and less able to support life than before World War I. Curiously enough, these misgivings about the economy resemble those of many conservatives today. The latter believe that production resting on inflated dollars and a huge Federal debt cannot be "real."

It is worth dwelling for a moment on this paradox. Veblen never wearied of attacking classical economics for its focus on physical assets, on land and production goods, whose importance in the modern world Veblen thought dwarfed by "intangible assets," that is by all the networks of influence, credit, persuasion which gave the Captains of Solvency pecuniary power over the market and over production itself. Likewise on the consumption side he emphasized psychic income, the prides of class and nation, of invidious distinction, which got distributed without constructive alterations of the economy's physical plant. Thus, he kept telling the economists: look less for the pea under the shell, or the shell itself, and look more at the charismatic face of the conjuror and the metaphysical expectations of the observant "underlying population." And he saw that an economic science which was preoccupied with physical exchanges was parochial, was still in the handicraft and artisan stage. Yet in failing to develop his insight that credit inflation might indirectly lead to an increase of physical plant through its effect on the psychological climate of business decision, he cut himself off from precisely the psychocultural economics for which he was campaigning, for he might have gone on to think of businessmen as victims of their own shell-game, their own, quite literally "confidence men," compelled by psychological pressures beyond their grasp to favor plant expansion (a theme we shall return to on pp. 162–6).

Thus Veblen's theory of crisis differs significantly from two which are closely allied to it, those of Schumpeter and Marx. Schumpeter saw crisis resulting from the emergence of new industries—railroads around 1850, chemicals and electricity around 1900—which attacked the profitability of older industries; Marx seems to have believed that crisis resulted from the competition of firms within each industry. In each theory, the crisis was functional: Schumpeter viewed it as a catharsis for the economy, eliminating unfit entrepreneurs; Marx accepted it as an unavoidable step in the march toward that concentration of each industry in the hands of a few firms which prepared the way for socialism; in different ways both men held that crises resulted from production. But for Veblen, crises were a phenomenon wholly distinct from production; they sprang not from the objective requirements of nature or of the machine process, but from psychology, from the cumulative effects of greed, misplaced optimism, and fear. In Veblen's eyes every stage in the genesis of a capitalist crisis, from the speculative watering of a new corporation's stock to the panicky unloading of securities on a falling market, was unnecessary, wholly unworthy of human beings—best compared to the magical rites by which a primitive tribe destroys a good harvest under the willful incantation of priests.

In a way it is an advance over Marx to see that crises need not result from the impact of only tangible factors, but may have psychological, "intangible" roots. But if we ask why Veblen did not carry his own theory further, we are struck by the possibility that his own buried parochialism and moralism—the very traits he attacked in the classical economists—got in his way. He did not want to see that the waste he so abhorred was not in the American system a mere excrescence, but in complex and round-about ways an essential element in full production. In his artisan's hatred of salesmanship, he could not allow it any constructive role either, even if production as well as consumption goods were sold by other than research engineering standards. More-over, though he insisted on their *industrial* incompetence, he probably exalted the cold pecuniary shrewdness of his Captains of Solvency, much as a farmer sees a "city slicker" as more slick than he really is. As a Populist, he had perhaps less of a sense than Marx that capitalists were victims rather than villains. His books treat the Captains of Solvency, Erudition, and so on after the fashion of John Bunyan, without individuation but as types; I have suggested above that this abstraction is one source of his fascination, but it also may make his work appear scientific and detached, though it actually fans exaggeration, making it appear that the Captain willfully sinks the ship he commands. In seeing businessmen as saboteurs, he again reminds us of today's con-servatives who fear that labor agitators or Communist spies will stop the wheels of American industry.

Exaggerations aside, however, he and the conservatives are both aware of one fundamental truth: the inescapable inter-dependence of a modern economy. To recognize that interde-pendence at a time when many of his countrymen still thought in local and traditional terms was one of Veblen's achievements. The very urgency of his view that business was strangling industry was prophetic in the sense that he saw that, economically, we had become one world, unable without utter chaos to return to mer-cantilist autocracy. Populist though he was in other respects, he was never an economic isolationist. If he shared many of the moral simplicities of Jacksonian America, he was never one to believe in a return by some legislative legerdemain to a farmer and artisan society. He had a sense of what it took, at least ma-

terially, to supply a modern urban population with the means of
life and livelihood.

MARCH OF THE ENGINEERS

"When Wells was young, the antithesis between science
and reaction was not false. Society was ruled by narrow-
minded, profoundly incurious people, predatory business
men, dull squires, bishops, politicians who could quote
Horace but had never heard of algebra. Science was faintly
disreputable and religious belief obligatory. Traditionalism,
stupidity, snobbishness, patriotism, superstition and love of
war seemed to be all on the same side; there was need of
someone who could state the opposite point of view."

George Orwell, *Critical Essays*

As Veblen aged, his belief that business was a parasitic
growth on industry became more and more an obsessive theme
with variations, such as the one linking politicians with businessmen in a conspiracy against the full use of the industrial arts. His
last published article, "Economic Science in the Calculable Future," written in 1925 as a kind of testament to his fraternity,
plays on the same notes, dividing economists into two groups: a
dominant majority who study business practice and train students
in polite chicane and salesmanship, and a minority of younger
men who (with the same advantages of coming late on the scene
he assigned to Germany and Japan) had escaped the 19th-century
preconceptions of hedonism, natural rights, and belief in progress,
and who will study technological practice where "monopoly is
mere waste." This latter crew "go quite confidently into their
work of detailed inquiry with little help from general principles,
except it be principles of commonsense, mathematics, and general
information." Thus, these men, Veblen's ideal children, will be
in effect the engineers of economics, hard-bitten, untheoretical,
no-nonsense folk—though he sees them, much like the engineers
in industry, suffering from discrimination at the hands of the
academic engrossers of differential gain. Presumably, his econo-
mist-engineers of the future would study neither price theory nor
philosophy.

This is, to be sure, not the first time that a man raised in
the classical culture has asked his disciples not to read the books

—as he thinks, the useless books—which helped shape his own outlook. Veblen had read enough Kant to know that there is no such thing as an untheoretical mind—that his engineers were theorists, too; yet he deluded himself into believing that he could rid them of myths and preconceptions, partly by making them illiterate.

Undoubtedly, a few economists and engineers—and not only in the Technocracy movement of the 30s—have not been unwilling to be flattered by Veblen that they were the original hardheaded characters, who knew what life was *really* like. My own not too extensive experience with engineers has been that they often do think they *know*, let us say, what women are capable of as factory operatives—know because they are engineers—when in fact they are no less bigoted and blinded by cultural definitions of reality than the lawyers and bankers Veblen detested. It is romantic to suppose that engineers are uniquely freed rather than frozen by their calling, a point increasingly recognized by the engineering schools such as MIT and Carnegie Tech which are seeking to acquaint engineers, partly to make them more suave, but partly for more genuine reasons, with the non-technological dimensions of existence.

Engineers, Veblen believed, work with things, not with people; they cannot be successful unless, so to speak, they work with rather than against the grain of current natural science outlooks, which require of them impersonality, objectivity, and coldness. (Lawyers, Veblen similarly believed, work with dogmas; they engage in negotiation, manipulation, and publicity—they are therefore "dated," due to disappear in the course of evolution in an industrial age, barring at any rate a movement of social regression.) But it is, of course, a matter for careful empirical study, not for a priori speculation, to find out how various occupations shape and are shaped by the men in them and drawn to them.* For one thing, there is no such occupation as that of "the" engi-

* It is interesting to see, in Cottrell's book, *The Railroader*, that the clerks may be "more rational" than the operating men, or even the mechanics; the clerks are more cosmopolitan, less constricted by hidebound customs of how to do things than those who appear to be closer to what Veblen would call the matter-of-fact.

neer, but a congeries of occupations, sharing only certain very general elements of training and experience—and this training and experience is capable of a still wider variety of idiosyncratic interpretations. Veblen was mistaken—he fell for a stereotype—in supposing that there was one good type of engineer, riding the wave of the future: cold, unenthusiastic, unimpressed. Engineers (and other people) can be good at their job, in an objective sense, even if they don't fit this preconception of their role, provided the preconception does not itself so influence them and others as to give them no chance at all to perform.

Veblen fell for a Populist and still popular stereotype, too, in supposing that lawyers were invariably wordy, abstract fellows, given to chicane in aid of business sabotage. And this judgment seems today particularly ironic since a good argument could be made that Veblen's contemporary influence owes more to lawyers than to any other single group. It was Brandeis who, in *Other People's Money*, popularised some of the conceptions set forth in *The Theory of Business Enterprise* and who, in his address on "Business—A Profession," sought to turn the eyes of businessmen away from irresponsible pecuniary maneuvers and towards the trained, responsible, efficient use of the industrial arts. He and other lawyers of Wilson's early brain trust framed the Clayton Act to combat monopolization based on purchases of industrial assets. And the whole renewed fight against monopoly by the Anti-Trust Division under the New Deal was led by lawyers whose view of the economy as operating better without the yoke of monopoly owed much to Veblen's writing. Not only, indeed, to his writing on monopoly but to his criticism of "natural rights" thinking in his brilliant chapter on the law in *Business Enterprise*, a chapter which might be read even today as a charter of the new legal "realism." Thurman Arnold's witty demolition of *The Symbols of Government* and *The Folklore of Capitalism* is gay and amusing where Veblen is bitter, but no one seems to me to have done more (unless it is Stuart Chase in *The Tragedy of Waste*) to indoctrinate the New Deal generation with an irreverent view of the rituals of law and ownership. The Technocrats made noise but not much else, while the Veblenian law teachers brought up the ablest legal minds with a disrespect for the sanctity of property rights, a pragmatic attitude towards legal forms, and an awareness of the coercions implicit in "free" contract—attitudes crucial for the creative role of leadership these lawyers played in the New Deal, in OPA, and in other war agencies.

It was probably Veblen's isolation from government service (an isolation not substantially altered by his Food Administration days) that led him astray here. There was in him nothing of the Fabian—the man who hopes to translate his ideas into the working equipment of civil servants, and who is forced to learn that ideas do not "naturally" get translated into laws. Whereas Lester Ward spent much of his life in Washington bureaus, and John R. Commons wandered back and forth between academia and government work, Veblen remained more literary and less "practical" than these men. By the same token, he was saved from the "contamination" that many of the Fabian type suffered who put too much faith in an improved civil service, an improved code of laws—too ready in the zeal of Wells' *New Machiavelli* to throw out the warnings of Spencer and Sumner as old hat. And, not being distracted by the hopes and fears engendered by temporary and contemporary incidents of legislation, he was freer to penetrate to fundamental tensions in the economy.

In fact, my own observations bear him out on one very important point: there is a great deal of animosity on the part of engineers against the "home office," the air-conditioned brass, bankers, and lawyers who have a veto power over corporate decisions. This is not because the brass represents the vested interests and the engineers the common man—as Veblen half-saw, engineers are by and large ferociously conservative politically and socially—but because of a much more general tension between the man who has the work in hand and the outside critic. And whereas Veblen saw the engineer as victim in a pecuniary culture, with sabotage as the prerogative of businessmen, it is actually a two-way affair: the man on the spot, the engineer or plant manager, often says something is "impossible"—and then proves it; innovation as in any field comes often not from the insider but from the outsider. Just as Veblen wanted to abolish university presidents and "return" the universities to faculty government (as we shall see more fully below)—failing to appreciate the degree to which faculties can be stuffy and need to be prodded from out-side—so he wanted the government of industry and, beyond that, of the country, to be in the hands of the insiders. In each case, he put his finger on undoubted tensions and resentments against outside interference, but in each case he signally failed to appre-ciate the social values of these inevitable conflicts.

His was, in fact, the dream of an administered economy, culture, and society which in another variant dazzled Marx and Engels and many men before and since—men who, belligerent as they may be in their writings and personal dealings, may (perhaps for that very reason) imagine a conflictless society, a society without politics and politicians, run by technicians along the "obvious" or "natural" lines. A comment in one of Veblen's post-war essays is revealing—he says that the present nations of the world should give way to a world economic system, divided along "neutral" boundaries for purposes of administration; by "neutral" he means that there would be (apart from the Vested Interests) only geographical and perhaps linguistic problems of deciding on regional subdivisions. While the notion of widening the market and getting rid of tariff barriers, taken by itself, is both sensible and prophetic (as we can see when we consider contemporary efforts, such as the Schuman Plan, to create a united European market), Veblen's hovering image of a world society purged of all friction based on history, association, and culture seems a Technocrat's illusion. Whereas, during the course of Veblen's life, a number of socialist economists concerned themselves with the managerial problems involved in a planned economy, ask-ing, for example, what measures could be substituted for price as clues to the cost of one resource use as against another (or how pricing could itself be used), and concerned too with the divi-sion of annual product between consumption and re-investment, Veblen ignored all such issues as blithely as Engels had done in writing (in *Socialism: Utopian or Scientific*) that in the classless society "the government of persons will be replaced by the ad-ministration of things"—a formula that has historically meant that persons will in fact be treated as things. Each intellectual discipline, like each race or nation, creates its own type of arro-gance; but those disciplines, such as Veblen's economics, that pretend to be "natural" sciences (rather than tentative sciences of nature) have something about them anticipatory of *Brave New World.*

To be sure, there is a certain unfairness in reading history backwards to discredit Veblen (or Marx) by reference to our contemporary brutalities; intellectuals are especially prey to this form of historicist grandiosity, since it puffs their own trade, which is that of words and ideas, even in the process of denouncing their enemies' influence. We must read Veblen in his own context and use what has happened since (none of which *had* to happen, on his or any other thinker's account) simply to help us focus on implications which might otherwise escape us. Thus, for example, we have learned to be wary of schemes of thought which divide the working force of a country into the useful men (workers, engineers) who produce tangible goods and the parasites (bankers, merchandisers, politicians, lawyers) who produce nothing, for Hitler and the Communists have used variations upon this Populist, indeed age-old, dichotomy for their own cruel purposes.* (As we saw above, Veblen, less anti-intellectual than many Populists, in his book on *The Higher Learning* exempted the scholar from the charge of parasitism, on the somewhat paradoxical condition that the scholar be *not* engaged in any useful work, but rather in the exercise of his function of idle curiosity. How he felt about artists, assuming there were any who did not cater to leisure-class dilettantism, he does not say.)

* In reading Veblen in our time we must not forget that bankers and merchants rated more highly in his day than in ours. Then the Captain of Industry was often an arriviste, whereas today it is the merchant and distributor generally who suffer from the disesteem of new money and lowly class origins as well as the disesteem of not "producing." A study of steel warehousemen and brokers by Louis Kriesberg, a graduate student at the University of Chicago, shows that the further one is from the actual making of steel, the more uneasy one is apt to feel concerning the justifiability of one's economic role. How far we have come in this direction we can remind ourselves by recalling that in 1863 J. P. Morgan and a young associate ostentatiously sent gold abroad to depreciate the currency and raise the market for gold they still held—while their purchased substitutes fought in the Civil War. Frederick Lewis Allen's biography of Morgan, wherein this story appears, does not indicate that the speculators had any moral qualms. Veblen's work is one reason their successors would have such qualms—indeed, would not be permitted to speculate!

As in all such relentless schemes, moreover, it is clearer what Veblen wanted to get rid of in the technocratic future than what he wanted positively to accomplish—in fact, he said approvingly of the Bolsheviks that they had introduced no new ideals, only destroyed old ones. He would get rid of all the parasitic occupations (amounting, as we shall see, in the case of the country town, to seven-ninths of the total population); correspondingly, this would get rid of the "superstructure," the legacy of habits of thought and conduct, associated with the pecuniary or non-mechanical employments. Thus, in every culture, according to Veblen, there exist side-by-side a body of workaday rules of thumb growing out of the common man's labor, and a more speculative philosophy, not to say mythology, typically produced by those at one or more removes from vulgar employment. This philosophy necessarily has a non-utilitarian, ornamental character, slowly if at all responsive to changes in the community's technology, and such an outlook would presumably perish with the parasites who harbored it.

Veblen's economist disciples do not like to think of him as a Technocrat, and were quick to disavow any close ties between him and Howard Scott—much as Marx's disciples mostly disown Stalinism. But in both cases it is important, if discomfiting, to see where the master's thought does give some basis for the disowned affiliation. In the thought of both men there *are* elements of ruthlessness, of an inhuman scientism, of vindictiveness disguised as moral indignation in the one case and irony in the other. Perhaps Marx had more of a sense of the past than Veblen did—he viewed the coming of industrialism with much more ambivalence and he surely had more of a sense of the future as an arena for unalienated men in control of their fate; indeed, it was just these "natural rights" and philosophic traces in Marx that Veblen criticized. It would be inconceivable for Marx and Engels, though less so for St. Simon or Comte, to put the engineers at the pinnacle of social virtue, but Veblen could have lived, I fear all too comfortably, in a brave new world where all consumption would be guided by Consumers' Research, all production by Technocrats, and living itself by a kind of Fordism, a code of simple and invariant rigor.

CHAPTER FOUR

SCIENTISTS VERSUS CAPTAINS
OF ERUDITION

Step by step Burgess and his lieutenants built up the liberties
of the School of Political Science. They got the Board of
Trustees to accept the principle of the absolute freedom of the
scholar to pursue the truth as he sees it, whatever the consequences; the principle of absolute equality of the faculty members; the principle that no scholar might be added to the
faculty without the unanimous consent of the faculty. The
principle was established that the president and trustees could
intervene in the affairs of the faculty only through the power
of the purse. President Seth Low, regarding himself justly as a
recognized authority on administration, sought admission to
the meetings of the faculty. He was turned down. A university
president could not conduct himself as an equal among equals.

Alvin Johnson, *Pioneer's Progress*

IN *The Higher Learning in America: A Memorandum on the
Conduct of Universities by Business Men,* Veblen applied
to academic life the set of distinctions we have already traced.
Only this time it is the scientists and scholars of the graduate faculties who represent the industrial culture—the "highly sterilized,
germ-proof system of knowledge, kept in a cool, dry place" (p.
7)—whereas the analogue of the Captain of Solvency is the university president, or Captain of Erudition, a politician-poltroon
given to salesmanship and publicity—and consequent sabotage of
impersonal science on behalf of the trustees, the absentee academic
owners. True, Veblen distinguishes at times between scholars,
sponges of the culture of the past, and scientists, governed by
"mechanistically effectual matter-of-fact"; but on the whole he
sees both groups as allied against any effort to turn the universities
to practical account, either as finishing schools for the wastrel

99

adolescent, or as extension services for the backward adult, or as vocational training stations for the hopeful aspirants to pecuniary wiles—in other words, against vocationalism and utilitarianism in education, under whatever aegis. And he sees both faculty groups as seekers of "esoteric knowledge," or a "higher learning," being "actuated by an idle curiosity, a disinterested proclivity to gain a knowledge of things and to reduce the knowledge to a comprehensible system." Thus, they stand united against the university administration's desire to use knowledge and intellectual distinction as a counter in inter-academic competition—in order, that is, to recruit students, donors, and the intangibles of eminence and repute.

This, along with *The Theory of the Leisure Class*, seems to me Veblen's wittiest book, the one where his shafts of satire, based on the closest observation of every scabrous detail, penetrated furthest; as an effective caricature of academia it has not been equalled (unless, perhaps, by Mary McCarthy's novel, *The Groves of Academe*).

While Veblen gained his knowledge of business and of factory life at second hand, through the reports of the muckrakers and of various investigating commissions, he had grandstand seats for some of the most characteristic academic games of his time. He was an undergraduate at Carleton in the heyday of the church-dominated school, pretty closely tied to an ethnic group, and could see the inauguration of the process by which most such schools have sought to reach a wider market without losing their original monopoly on ministers for a particular sect and on money from a particular flock. He was at Hopkins as a graduate student shortly after President Gilman sought to domesticate the best German university models; he went on to Yale at the time when, as Richard Hofstadter describes matters in *Social Darwinism in America*, the faculty was just fighting free of theological guidance —Veblen himself studied Kant there, under Noah Porter, President, philosopher, and friend. He had another spell of graduate work at Cornell, a land-grant college, in one of its high points. And his book itself took shape during his University of Chicago days, when William Rainey Harper, that "Great Pioneer," was, as Veblen puts it, "reshaping American academic policy." After that came Stanford, the "Harvard of the West Coast," luxurious, elegant, and controlled. The book was finally revised during Veblen's spell at the University of Missouri whose President, in defending and befriending Veblen, could not make up to him for the felt ignominy of teaching in a minor league—and one dependent on the Chamber of Commerce provincialism of the small-town Midwest. Veblen, in other words, did "field work" for this book as a "participant-observer"; this appears to be reflected in the effectiveness of the attack.*

It was, as we have seen, Veblen's habit of dramatic abstraction which led him to write the world-history of predation, seeing in each age a different group of men notably gifted in exploit, or in the selling of specious but respectable intangibles. He worked his scheme of succession both forward and backward, describing for instance a period of Viking history as "An Early Experiment in Trusts," or painting the modern minister as the lineal descendent of shamans or Egyptian hieratic practitioners. Often, such comparisons were more witty than revealing. But the idea that a William Rainey Harper is "really" a Dan Drew of education— that is a discovery of some moment in understanding the nature of entrepreneurial activity in American life. For today it would seem that the heads of non-profit institutions—cardinals, university presidents, foundation directors, the heads of charitable agencies and research organizations—have taken over much of the spirit and drive of the early Captains, whereas the present business heirs of the latter are apt to be as cautious and anemic as direct heirs frequently are. To be sure, Veblen saw this process as an unequivocal victory for business enterprise, whose methods, morals, and models were thus able to capture all the culture's "holy places." But one might also view the matter as a case of academic (or priestly) resistance to business (in Harold Lasswell's term) through "partial incorporation" of the business model—much as the Counter-Reformation Jesuits resisted Calvin by copying him.

* These remarks should not be taken as a one-eyed attack on my part against "arm-chair" research in comparison with field-work for I am considering here only the dialectic between the two modes in terms of Veblen's own career.

While in Veblen's day it seemed to some overly cynical observers that the University of Chicago was simply one more of Mr. Rockefeller's false fronts, it probably seemed to Mr. Rockefeller that he was victimized by Harper's ability as salesman—an ability acquired by many non-businessmen in a business culture.

FRESCOES FOR MR. ROCKEFELLER'S UNIVERSITY

In fact, the University of Chicago was in Harper's day and has remained something of a promotional tour de force. As Harper raided a good part of the faculty at Clark University, right out from under its famed President G. Stanley Hall, in what seemed at the time like an academic "Chapter of Erie," so Robert M. Hutchins took away most of Columbia's nuclear physicists to build the atomic bomb, the same method of "fabulous" salaries being used. Though not directly influenced by Veblen, Hutchins' book on the Higher Learning bows to Veblen's title, and his hatred of vocationalism matches Veblen's own. In fact, in divorcing undergraduate teaching from research, and in divorcing the university as a whole from football, active fraternities, and preparation for the humbler careers, Hutchins seems to have carried out many of the essentials of a Veblenian program. No doubt Veblen would have jeered at Hutchins' fondness for St. Thomas, and for dialectic generally; would have thought his "great books" courses for adults an unwarranted concession to community entertainment or service; and might have felt him to be too much a preacher and reformer. Probably he would also have found Hutchins too concerned with the classical culture to be a true devotee of vulgar technology and the industrial arts. But these theoretical differences between Hutchins and Veblen are minor in comparison with what would really divide the two men, namely the fact that Hutchins, like Harper, by his very creative energies, took power and prestige away from the faculty and (whatever his personal selflessness) made use of it in the national market for students, funds, and veneration. At times in *The Higher Learning* Veblen talks as if the presidents of universities, by sheer energy and effrontery, had subverted a company of scholars who were once devoted acolytes of science and quiet gatherers of incunabbula—as if he himself had witnessed the passing of an academic golden age, in which Harper's fearful example had become standard university practice.

The subtle differences between Veblen and Marx appear at their sharpest here. Marx was inclined to attack all academia as "superstructural," as more or less seemly covers for class exploitation—it would not have occurred to him to suggest reforms, even drastic ones. Far from having praise for objectivity, moreover, he would have regarded it as a bourgeois escapism: "idle curiosity," is something one could afford only after the revolution. Indeed, what is so striking in *The Higher Learning* if one reads it today is that Veblen seems to speak for the past, as an academic conservative, preferring if he had to choose, a musty Oxford to a bustling, vocationalist American state university. He has more in common than he might have recognized with Matthew Arnold's defense of the classical culture in "Literature and Science."

And of course Veblen is gloriously impractical in all this. The University of Chicago has had to live on high-pressure promotion because, in competing with the great endowed universities of the Eastern Seabord, it could not count on loyal generations of alumni who part with their sons and draw their testamentary trusts on the basis of unshakeable tradition. (In private, A. Lawrence Lowell of Harvard could be a very effective salesman of tradition.) Rather, Chicago and other come-lately institutions have had to appeal to "new money" like the elder Rockefeller's— and to do so must advertise, name buildings, and do all the other things university Vice Presidents for Development can think up to attract favorable notice. Veblen himself half-realized this, and concluded his essay with the pessimistic thought that, barring a revolution against the Vested Interests, no significant reform of the academic world was conceivable; monopolistic competition and its egregious publicity devices made it necessary for anyone to do what the others did—just as commercial advertising (so Veblen argued, in *Absentee Ownership*) benefited no one, but could not be dropped by any one company. Hence, Veblen thought that even a good and honest scholar, once in the president's seat, would shortly be as corrupt a salesman of "ponderous vendible intangibles" as any small-town banker, delegated by the board of trustees to give the institution an "efficient, businesslike management." In fact, a certain note of pity creeps into Veblen's discourse here, marking his recognition of the unfortunate role of the scholar-president, caught on the margin between God and Mammon, between science as a collective heritage and the business culture as a growing nastiness.*

A FACULTY IDYLL

But this admitted lack of a "solution" or "constructive measures" is surely not the true impracticability of *The Higher Learning*. Rather, it is Veblen's insistent assumption that an autonomous faculty, free of any bureaucracy, would return to a primal state of disinterested, generous, and collective pursuit of idle curiosity. Veblen writes as if the vested interests in scholarship are primarily pecuniary ones: he glorifies the colleague group as in other writings he glorifies the engineers (as in fact, here for once the engineers, like businessmen, all too practical and incapable of idle curiosity, are *not* glorified). Yet even in this flight of gratifying fancy, he covers himself—at times. He refers in a footnote to a particular faculty as "in the main an aggregation of slack-twisted schoolmasters and men about town" (p. 167); and he notes his suspicion that academic people mind somewhat less than they say they do the processions and other frippery ceremonials which drag them from their research and link them with their wives in a yoke of perfunctory and emulative dissipation. Nevertheless, he concludes that this form of amiable sabotage of science would not come to much without executive leadership, though with such leadership "current academic life is calculated to raise the question whether make-believe does not, after all, occupy a larger and more urgent place in the life of these thoughtful adult

---

* At the time Veblen was writing, presidents were increasingly chosen from the professoriate rather than, as earlier, from the clergy. Faculties, becoming stronger, were becoming more outspoken and critical. Pressure against them from the business community was thus in part a response to their increasing power. See Richard H. Shryock, "The Academic Profession in the United States," *Bulletin of the American Association of University Professors,* vol. 38, pp. 32–70 (1952).

male citizens than in the life of their children" (p. 169). Veblen has sufficient faith in the instinct of workmanship and the spirit of idle curiosity to believe that, but for the distortion worked by business pressures and motives, the academic personnel would not be seduced from the single-minded pursuit of research.*

Thus, it is apparent that Veblen sees the Captain of Erudition only in one of his roles: his salesmanship of the university's intangible assets in the marketplace and, conversely, his efforts as face-lifter within the academic walls in order that there be something to sell. He is, therefore, the principal channel by which business values enter the university. Mainly, what Veblen fails to appreciate here is the possibility of the president's playing a double game: fostering scholarly research as an intra-academic leader, and protecting rather than jeopardizing such research by his public relations work vis-à-vis the trustees, the alumni, and the community at large. That a president or other administrative officer might employ his parental bent in fostering scholarship rather than in sabotage of it seemed as unlikely to Veblen as that a businessman might foster rather than sabotage the industrial arts. And, just as Veblen would not grapple with his own realization that credit inflation might actually lead, through a boom mentality, to an increase in production and real income, so he could not, in *The Higher Learning*, grant that non-scholarly morale factors in the control of an academic administrator might lead to an increase in genuine research: for Veblen, good could never issue from evil.

In other words, Veblen did not admit the need for leaders as essential renewers of the vitality of institutions; in fact, as we have seen, he did not want institutions to be vital, but to die. Accordingly, he thought the universities could run themselves, once outside interference were removed, precisely as he thought the economy could run itself, as a technical engineering problem, once the

---

* Commenting on this passage, Dr. Lubin has told me how Veblen knew enough about faculty politics to help maneuver a fellowship for him at Missouri; Lubin was surprised that a man who seemed so remote was yet in gossipy touch with what went on. Plainly, Veblen's belief in the innate seriousness of faculties was to a considerable extent assumed as a polemical device to sharpen his attack on presidents and governing boards.

vested interests were liquidated. Here again, he fell back on a kind of Rousseauistic "state of nature" thinking, of the very kind he so bitterly attacked, viewing scholars as a breed, so to speak, of "scientific man," single-mindedly pursuing the truth that lies at the margin of the already known, and not requiring any institutional support in that pursuit. As the popular song says, "it's nice work if you can get it!"

Where, one might ask, do students fit into such an idyll? Veblen did not seem to mind if the young were taught, but he refused to accept this teaching as among the functions of the university; students should be permitted there only after adolescence and in the role of apprentices, and instruction should be carried on just so far as it aided the work of research. It followed, moreover, that students could be endured on the premises only if they were motivated by the same curiosities as the faculty: to train students for business or legal success seemed to Veblen a desecration of scholarship. Perhaps the Institute for Advanced Study at Princeton comes closest to Veblen's ideal.

THE ACADEMIC BOHEMIAN: MODEL-T VERSION

In this domain, by all accounts, Veblen practiced what he preached; we have already sketched some of the arts he elaborated for putting students off. In every conceivable way, he sought to spend as little of himself as possible in class, although he could be generous to students privately, and often enjoyed at Chicago walking and talking with them. He seems to have been more willing to carry the research-advancing drudgery of editing *The Journal of Political Economy* (a post he held while at Chicago) than the slightest drudgery connected with the curriculum. Dorfman reports that he would read and work between eight and two in the evening; perhaps he was one of those men for whom academic hours are intolerable.

But it would be closer to the truth to say that any hours were intolerable which were not geared to his own whim and pace; against inner resistance, he could not master the energy to cope with the diurnal routines of teaching, any more than, in his later years, of housekeeping and the most elementary attention to his own affairs.

One reason for his usually negative reaction to students may have been his uneasiness in the presence of the energies of adolescence, whether these were devoted in the more typical fashion of the day to football and dissipation or to an idealistic search for the true, the beautiful, and the good. It was during adolescence that he himself had been decisively set apart from his fellows, both on the farm and at Carleton College. Hence it is perhaps not simply a coincidence that a man who liked children (at least in small doses), hated and feared adolescents, and admired those who had put childish things away—that this man should also develop an historical sequence in which savagery comes off well, barbarism is lampooned as the all-too-prolonged adolescence of mankind, and the industrial society which is free of adolescent muscularities, rivalries, and illusions is seen as the shape of the mature future.

That Veblen was a big and powerful man physically did not prevent him from shrinking in the presence of the hale and hearty. By the same token, unlike more intrepid colleagues, he never fought back openly, never crossed students or authorities directly, never spoke in faculty meeting or joined in moves of protest. At best he could conduct himself as an academic Wobbly, a slyly effective saboteur of Registrars, Deans of Students, and other officials. His savage book on *The Higher Learning* may be seen as a stand-in for savage conduct: like many men who are withdrawn in personal intercourse, his emotions could flow more readily in absentia. Seeking to avoid all drama by mousy behavior, he ended by becoming an academic legend.

This legend, based both on his career and on his books, has had a not inconsiderable impact on the American academic culture. Every profession, as Professor Everett C. Hughes has often pointed out, has ambivalent feelings towards its clients—needs and hates them at the same time, feels and fears the constraint of their demands. Veblen vocalized and rationalized the teacher's uneasiness vis-à-vis students, his desire for an "ideal" student who would be all help and no trouble to anyone. But he did more, in his insistence on a one-function university. For every institution is vulnerable to a call that it should return to the outlook of its founders, vulnerable to an insistence that it should serve a single function only, and not a multiplicity—that churches should prepare for salvation and do nothing else; that businesses should make money and sell goods, and nothing else; that doctors should practice medicine and nothing else. Academic people, too, readily succumb to the notion that they should only do research, not counsel the young or reform our cities or engage in academic politics and publicity. Life is simplified if one's "calling" has only a single voice. The fact is, however, that every viable institution (again, a point repeatedly made by Professor Hughes) serves a congeries of functions, some of which may be "accidentally" linked by history, without any logical connection; thus, most universities which have survived have catered both to would-be scholars and professionals and to gilded youth seeking appropriate *rites de passage.*

But it is also true that in any gamut of functions thus brought together in an institution, some operations will have a higher prestige value than others; some will be "dirty work." Though it appeared to Veblen that academic bluffing and busywork brought prestige, he himself helped tweak an academic conscience that has increasingly given the highest status to research, the lowest (as in the national scene more generally) to "bureaucracy" and "politics." His belief that a university bureaucracy is not really necessary still hangs on, much as the analogous Manchesterism hangs on among opponents of "government intervention"; the result is to create a lot of obstacles to the doing of routine tasks needful in any large enterprise, and to build up fierce suspicions at the least signs of a parental bent on the part of university administrators.*

All in all, it is my impression that the Veblen legend and the Veblen book have helped give us many guardedly inefficient academic Bohemians, proud of their inability to preside at a meeting, or to turn in grade lists on time, or to remember appointments and the names of students, or to write memoranda not tainted by

---

* It is my observation that those university deans to whom Veblen has helped give a bad conscience, simply on the ground that they are no longer scholars, are likely to envy those of their colleagues who are still scholars and therefore to hamstring them unconsciously—whereas if they felt that their share of the total multiplicity of university functions was not inferior, they could afford to be more generous and helpful.

irrelevance. To be sure, such a cult of incompetence is in part a reaction against the earlier type of Philistine businessman who had no use for anyone who had not "met a payroll"—a reaction against the strident joviality of many vulgar, still-adolescent men who were adepts of academic intrigue. To this extent, Veblen's book served to encourage a useful counter-style. But the irony is that, while Veblen thought the universities were succumbing to businessmen, the reverse was beginning to happen even during his own lifetime: university careers were becoming increasingly attractive for purposes of social and career mobility as an alternative to business; their growing competitiveness and loss of gentility was due less to their conquest by trustees chosen from the ranks of the fatter vested interests than to the fact that young men were beginning to find a career in natural or social science rather than in banking or wholesaling. In fact, it is the greater prestige of universities which has lured the young seeking prestige —and at the same time has allowed them to pose as gentlemen amiably superior to businesslike conduct both within and without the ivied walls. Thus, in spite of his own hatred for snobbery, Veblen has ended by supporting, at least to some extent, certain current academic snobberies: the offensively superior attitude to the business world; the extra meed of honor given those who don't teach at all, or who teach graduate student males as against those who teach in secondary schools, or teach women, or teach extension classes. To be sure, these snobberies exist in many places, in England for instance, where Veblen's book is unknown—indeed, *The Higher Learning*, like most of Veblen's works, has had a small circulation. Nevertheless, it is my impression that themes and phrases from this book and from Veblen's other comments on education have helped in the United States, along with many more important influences, to nourish academic complacencies.

But a significant book, like a university, has more than one function, and more than one audience. It is its very success in some academic quarters that has made me enter certain *caveats* against *The Higher Learning in America*. It goes without saying that the book can still be read with profit as a guide to the subtle infiltrations of salesmanship into American academic life; as a critique of "pragmatism" and "vocationalism"; as a study in the ambiguity of the president's position; as a sardonic commentary on the pinched meanness of the academic proletariat, the white-collar Mr. Milquetoasts who must unite in one harried existence their own desire for scholarly achievement, their deans' desire for a fillip to notoriety, and their wives' desire to compete with the wives of the Chamber of Commerce. And, apart from such blessings, it is as I have said, a wonderfully sarcastic and witty book. It is true of Veblen, as of Samuel Butler, that "he remains one of the not very numerous writers who can make us giggle aloud in a crowded railway carriage"; * and perhaps it is also true of both men that their "satirical spirit will again become relevant in a new world of manageable misfortune." **

THE LEISURE CLASS AND RESEARCH

> Let us not take it for granted that life exists more fully in what is commonly thought big than in what is commonly thought small.
>
> Virginia Woolf, *The Common Reader*

Even if nothing much would survive of the *content* of Veblen's views which later decades would find markedly original, the range of his interests, in departing from what gentility and vested canons of "research" considered proper, would remain a liberating one—an independent contribution to academic freedom. For, as indicated earlier in this chapter, scholarship is always falling into an immaterial nepotism in the topics it considers worth sponsoring. Just to consider leisure was a step forward in an age of production. To an extraordinary extent Veblen studied matters which the university guilds had thought too vulgar or too trivial for notice. There were other men in the universities in his day who had a better sense, for example, of the place of leisure in the coming America of abundance—Simon Patten is outstanding in this respect—but no one studied the nuances of leisure-class behavior with Veblen's intensity. Who but Freud would have thought much could be made of the meanings of carrying a walk-

---

* Graham Hough in *The Listener,* vol. 47, p. 996 (1952).
** Philip Toynbee (on Butler) in *The Listener,* vol. 47, p. 1042 (1952).

ing stick, a topiç to which some brilliant passages of *The Theory of the Leisure Class* are devoted? What American, other than a few sociologists studying the American Negro, would have thought to trace the way in which a servant class spreads leisure-class styles among the underlying population at large? Even when Veblen studied more traditional subjects, such as Scandinavian history, he did not fail to have a look at the disreputable items, such as illegitimacy rates, which more conventional historians had let lie.

Moreover, his ironic detachment from all the "good causes" saved him from concentration on the matters his colleagues defined as "problems." They did not think such agencies as the YMCA constituted a problem but only lack of support for them—Veblen considered that these agencies supported a devout animism, a brutal sportsmanship, an honorific patronage of the poor, and were therefore a problem for a mechanistic industrial age.

To be sure, Veblen did not confine himself to finding significance in the esoteric or the disreputable, which would have simply established another snobbish hierarchy of research in place of the one he was undermining. Thus, he devoted an essay to the minuscule arts and crafts movement but also one to the headline-capturing Army of the Commonweal; and during the War he wrote on peace but also on the safeguarding of European scholarship. His hatred of distinction among persons was applied also to topics, with a salutary refusal to give priority to the study of the Colonel's Lady over Judy O'Grady, or vice versa.

Veblen to some extent shared the spirit of Zola and his American followers, and also the spirit of W. I. Thomas and other sociologists of the "Chicago School" who were plunging with gusto into the study of the life of the city, its immigrant swarms, its sexual deviations, its vagabond occupations. The turn of the century was the period of the great surveying expeditions by which literature and sociology took stock of the assorted peoples whom industrialization and urbanization had thrown together—expeditions to see, in Jacob Riis' famous phrase, "How the Other Half Lives." Yet there are great differences between Veblen and these contemporaries. In the first place, most of them, whatever manifestoes of "naturalism" might constitute their charter of work, were reform-minded. This is as true of Jack London, who combined a Darwinian premise with a vaguely socialistic conclusion, as of most of the sociologists and the later muckrakers. In comparison, Veblen's reform-mindedness was far more sublimated. In the second place, Veblen was too withdrawn, too "scholarly" in the classical sense, to enjoy first-hand contact with his objects of study: nothing could be more alien to him than the gusto of a Chicago novelist doing field-work in a shabby bar. The time Veblen most wanted to do field-work was when he applied for a grant, during his Stanford days, to make an expedition to the Aegean to study Cretan antiquities. And whereas W. I. Thomas late in life learned Yiddish so that he could read the advice columns in the Jewish *Daily Forward*—columns which he found rich in implication as to the shifts in attitude undergone by East-side immigrants —Veblen preferred to continue learning the dead languages, including Sanskrit, and to translate Scandinavian sagas.

It appears, then, that Veblen's term, "idle curiosity," goes far to describe his own focus of attention. It is "idle" in the sense of refusal to be committed to those "great issues" that his contemporaries took most seriously, in the sense of having nothing of the eager beaver about it, and in the sense of not giving an account of itself to any vested interest whether academic or popular. It is the curiosity of a bystander, who casts a cold eye, rather than of a rescue party or castigating moralist. It is playful, lively, inquisitive, unimpressed. That in Veblen's case it turned out to direct his attention to waste, trusts, socialism, imperialism, and many other unremittingly exigent issues, only indicates that he was human and that ivory towers are built by human hands for inescapably human purposes. Likewise, that Veblen's passionate moral sense sharpened his idly curious eye is also not to be wondered at; even our play and dreaming, as the Freudians have shown, express as well as relieve our workaday anxieties and inhibitions. And yet there is a real if impalpable freedom in play, which transcends the very human condition that shapes it—much as Veblen's concept of idle curiosity transcends his otherwise biologistically and economistically determined system. In the play of his irony, Veblen found a form for the manifold tensions in him—between his morality of reform and his morality of science, between his detachment and his fear and hatred of bullying and injustice, between his detestation of waste and his passive acceptance of Darwinian pessimism. In my judgment, his irony is as superior to the naturalists' grimness as Charlie Chaplin is superior to soap opera.

But having used this word "superior," I bring myself up with a startled realisation that Veblen would have rejected any such rank or distinction—other than one premised on his morality of waste. Plainly, I do not go along with him there but feel that some things are more worthwhile, more beautiful, more desirable than others. However, as a charter for research, the assertion that soap opera may be as significant as Chaplin cannot be gainsaid, and when anyone studies soap opera and other devalued products of popular culture he is making use of a freedom Veblen helped win: to proceed without reference to the boundaries between departments or between "important" subjects and "trivial" ones. We need this freedom, for even today, more than half a century after *The Theory of the Leisure Class*, there are plenty of Americans who think it somehow frivolous to study leisure, unless one has an eye to "improving" it, that is I suppose, making it more like work.

In fact, it is just Veblen's irreverence which we stand in need of in a day when total commitment is being asked of everyone. His effort to achieve disinterestedness appears all the more admirable in the face of Sartre's question "For Whom Does One Write?" or Robert Lynd's "Knowledge for What?" I would be willing to welcome a great deal of Bohemian irresponsibility among professors if that were the price of genuine detachment and unengagement. Increasingly, the conscience of academic people is hooked on to some social concern, some good cause or other, as against Veblen's desire to hitch it exclusively to Science. Whatever the theoretical shortcomings of his concept of idle curiosity, or of Science, and whatever the practical shortcomings of the model-T professor, I am not sure we have found a better concept or a better model. Though the details of the Veblen legend may be in error, he is surely, for these contributions, entitled to his place in the history of intellectual freedom.

CHAPTER FIVE

VEBLEN AND THE LIFE OF ACTION

I learned . . . it is not the men who do the work who can tell
the world about it. They are too familiar with it. It is the in-
vestigator from outside.

John R. Commons, *Myself*

VEBLEN found in the instinct of idle curiosity a kind of
biological platform for a skepticism which looked to many
of his contemporaries as not merely idle but irresponsible.
(The closest he came to real trouble, apart from recurrent academic scandals and precarious finances, was when the wartime
Postmaster-General banned *Imperial Germany and the Industrial
Revolution* as subversive.) Among economists he had much the
same reputation for being "unconstructive" that he must have had
among the farm folk of Minnesota. Only once in all his published
writing does he show any response to such criticisms of his alleged
negativism when, in *The Higher Learning* (presumably written as
early as 1906), he offers a "positive" proposal "partly out of a
reasonable deference to the current prejudice that any mere negative criticism and citation of grievances is nothing better than an
unworthy experiment in irritation" (pp. 270-271). He must at
times have regarded his whole life as "an unworthy experiment in
irritation" in an era when Teddy Roosevelt symbolized the general American prejudice in favor of "constructive," "virile,"
"hearty" action.

The proposal he makes in this instance—as we have seen,
that universities be run by their faculties alone, without the supervision of a president and governing board—is worth further
examination. Dealing as it does with the field closest to Veblen's
heart, that of university research and instruction, it may be taken

114

as the type of his subsequent moves towards reform in other institutions, that is, as the speech to his constituency of the man who later went to Washington.

Just as Veblen, in *The Vested Interests*, compares the nation to a corporation of which the citizens are the powerless silent stockholders, so in *The Higher Learning* he treats the American university as an overblown aggregation of dissimilar institutions, wherein the graduate school, the only true university, is administered as part of the same "trust" as the undergraduate college and the vocational schools. Just as the national state's only function, in Veblen's eyes, is its concern with the external affairs of diplomacy and war, so the administration of the American university, pointing up in the chief administrator or "captain of erudition," is seen to be serviceable only in publicizing the institution to the credulous laity. For Veblen the remedy in one field as in the other is syndicalist surgery. As in the nation at large affairs should devolve into the hands of a national resources planning board made up of engineers, so in the academic sub-culture each university and school should be run by its faculty. As he declares (*The Higher Learning*, p. 286):

> "As seen from the point of view of the higher learning, the academic executive and all his works are anathema, and should be discontinued by the simple expedient of wiping him off the slate; and . . . the governing board, in so far as it presumes to exercise any other than vacantly perfunctory duties, has the same value and should with advantage be lost in the same shuffle."

By the time *The Higher Learning* was published, in 1918, Veblen had already been lured, by the exigencies of international politics, out of his self-imposed aloofness towards reformers and reforms. He had returned from a summer abroad in 1914 with the naive feeling of the man who had been "on the spot"; he believed that he had first-hand evidence of German war-guilt, and he acquiesced in the proposals of friends to write books and memoranda on behalf of the Allies and, later, of Reconstruction. *Imperial Germany and the Industrial Revolution* was found inexpedient in linking Japan, an Ally, with Germany (as well as in its wryly sardonic comments on England), but its portrayal of German culture as wholly absolutist and aggressive conformed to the "line" of Allied propaganda—when Veblen deals with Germany, even his irony and his disclaimers do not conceal his violent animus. A measure of his wartime zeal is the fact that when the Bolshevik Revolution, which he was later to support unreservedly, occurred in October 1917, he deprecated it as weakening the Allies' strength.

He was glad to leave the University of Missouri in 1918 for a post in the Food Administration, and he seems to have half-believed that at last economic science was being called upon to aid the rational conduct of war mobilization. Of his daily work in this period little is reported, but there survive a number of memoranda which have been published in *Essays in Our Changing Order*. All of them make reform proposals—some, as we shall see, quite fanciful for their time, but others sober-sided enough. In the latter category is a paper on price-fixing for the staple food-stuffs which could well be a memorandum on New Deal agricultural policy; in fact, a number of the New Deal agricultural administrators (among them, Henry Wallace, Tugwell, Jerome Frank) appear to have been greatly indebted to Veblen's thought in general if not in this particular.

REVENGE ON HADLEYBURG

Mark Twain's boyhood in Hannibal, Missouri, left him with a very ambivalent feeling towards the small midwestern town. The Tom Sawyer books show the nostalgic side, though even they are streaked with bitterness, while "The Man That Corrupted Hadleyburg" and other later writings present Mark Twain's passionate sense of the meanness and pettiness of life in the country town, especially after the California Gold Rush had excited cupidity and left behind a trail of men who had missed the main chance.

The sort of nostalgia that led Mark Twain to hark back to a pre-pubertal, pre-Gold Rush age of innocence (so excellently portrayed in Dixon Wecter's *Sam Clemens of Hannibal*) could not lead Thorstein Veblen to take pleasure in his own boyhood; for comparable feelings of belonging, he had to hark back in his imagination to the days of Scandinavian innocence, the days of the Sagas, before his parents' coming to America. Veblen saw only the malevolent, grasping side of the country town, first as a Norskie boy in Minnesota, and later in what he regarded as his exile in Columbia, Missouri, where the State University is located. He thought Columbia the apogee of Chamber of Commerce thinking, at once vulgar and puritanical; as he later wrote in *Absentee Ownership* (p. 142):

> "The country town of the great American farming region is the perfect flower of self-help and cupidity standardized on the American plan. Its name may be Spoon River or Gopher Prairie, or it may be Emporia or Centralia or Columbia. The pattern is substantially the same, and is repeated several thousand times with a faithful perfection which argues that there is no help for it, that it is worked out by uniform circumstances over which there is no control, and that it wholly falls in with the spirit of things and answers to the enduring aspirations of the community. The country town is one of the great American institutions; perhaps the greatest, in the sense that it has had and continues to have a greater part than any other in shaping public sentiment and giving character to American culture."

Life in such a town, Veblen continues, is "a scheme of salesmanship, seven days in the week," marked by pusillanimity; as he continues (p. 159):

> "One must avoid offense, cultivate good-will, at any reasonable cost, and continue unfailing in taking advantage of it; and, as a corollary to this axiom, one should be ready to recognize and recount the possible short-comings of one's neighbors, for neighbors are (or may be) rivals in the trade, and in trade one man's loss is another's gain, and a rival's disabilities count in among one's assets and should not be allowed to go to waste."

To be sure, he admits that the country town supports churches and missions, but this, too, is not waste, but a frugal insurance premium and certified enterprise in "salesmanlike tact" (p. 162). So the country town "becomes a system of intellectual, institutional, and religious holdovers." Veblen hastens to add, of course, that no critique is intended, and that he cannot help it if, "outside of the country towns, where human intelligence has not yet gone into abeyance," the term "holdover" carries a colloquial sting (p. 160). All in all, he sees the denizens of the country town as more despicable than the big city magnates and politicians who at least have the virtues of their larger vices.

This, then, is the set of attitudes that Veblen brought to the problem of dealing with the farm labor shortage that loomed in 1918. After a tour through the Midwest for the purpose of gathering statistical data with his now-famous assistant Isador Lubin, Veblen prepared a report to the Food Administration on "Farm Labor for the Period of the War." The memorandum proceeds to its fanciful conclusion by a series of severely logical steps. It observes that the mercantile establishments of the country towns amount to great pools of wasted manpower, easily released for other duties if their functions could be taken over by a system of federally-administered purchasing and supply depots. These could be run through the post-office, and in cooperation with the large chains and mail-order houses.

Maintaining a straight face, Veblen calculates that seven-ninths of the work done in a typical country town in the farm belt is dispensable, for it either, like retailing, duplicates itself to no purpose—certainly not to lower prices or improve service—or, like banking and real estate, dry cleaning and other service trades, is nearly 100% waste; all this apparatus being in turn a breeder of further waste because of the need wastefully to service the servicers. All the government would have to do would be to enter as competitor at cost in buying from and selling to the farmer; the result would be a release of all but some two-ninths of the townsmen. And since the people so released are largely farm-raised folk who have fled manual labor in search of a pecuniary niche, they would inevitably return, without conscription, to the farms *faute de mieux*; and they would benefit, at least in muscle, from their enforced introduction—only, Veblen repeatedly points out, for the emergency period of the war—to more suitable and more patriotic work as hired hands. The memorandum also seeks to demonstrate that no alternative labor supply is available, for he insists that even hired work on a wheat-belt farm is skilled work, not to be readily recruited in the cities, or even from among Europeans or Chinese peasants without experience of the Great Plains.

Veblen was disappointed that his plan was not accepted or seriously discussed; he appears to have felt that the big packers controlled the Food Administration; his hopes dashed, he soon left the government. Reading the memorandum today, however, leads one to wonder whether Veblen ever intended it to be taken seriously. One could imagine that he was being cynical and sardonic—being sure he would not get a hearing and pulling the leg of the authorities by the scientific and statistical cast of his argument. Yet this cannot be the whole story. For the memorandum was written on the premise—which floated so many not dissimilar hopes among liberal war-supporters in World War II— that the war's outcome hung in the balance and that without drastic internal reforms military victory could not be assured. Veblen appears to me to have genuinely believed this, believed that the war opened up possibilities for a thoroughgoing change in basic institutions.

The memorandum, moreover, is only one of three he submitted—if they were all jokes, he was forcing a laugh pretty hard. Of these, one recommended a progressive tax on menial servants for the period of the war—both to provide manpower, and, in the alternative, revenue. The other proposed that the I.W.W. farm workers be freed from the prosecutions under the espionage act and local law they were then undergoing, and be brought into wholehearted cooperation with the war effort by being, in effect, enlisted into an industrial army under their own self-chosen leaders; Veblen promised—with what seems to me insufficient basis in experience *—that, under these conditions, they would give their best efforts as against the "conscientious withdrawal of efficiency" they were then practicing. Veblen liked Wobblies, and as a follower of Bellamy and William James he liked the idea of an industrial army; he hated menial servants and those to whom they ministered; and as we have seen, he hated the country town. Government service gave him the chance to be "practical" about these hates, just as, shortly thereafter, the invitation to submit a memorandum to the House Inquiry on post-war arrangements allowed him to suggest that the vested interests and the national frontiers which protect them be, forthwith, abolished.

In all these proposals for reform, Veblen was in one respect very much within the main current of American progressivism, for his unquestioned end was increased efficiency—efficiency of administration and of production. As Jacques Barzun has observed, America has had a long "romance with practicality," but of course has not called it a romance but a self-evident goal—and surely it has been self-righteously pursued. It is a goal which, as I have earlier indicated, Veblen took over from the businessmen who made it their nominal motto. He wanted, no less than the *New Republic* crowd did, to run a businesslike war—only for him business was not businesslike. For all these reasons, it seems to me that Veblen was at least partly in earnest in his wartime reform proposals, although his fear of rejection, of seeming stupid, led him to push his programs to such extremes that he could pretend that, of course, they would come to naught if in fact they did—like a person who seeks to cover an unintentional *faux pas* by clowning. At the same time, by deliberately demanding the "impossible," he managed once more to sabotage himself.

* Dr. Lubin recalls that Veblen was not so far off here as one might suppose today: the I.W.W. leaders were eager for protection against arrest and harassment, and would have responded whole-heartedly to a deal such as Veblen proposed. Dr. Lubin notes that Veblen admired the craftsmanship of many Wobblies, focussing, as he did with other workmen conventionally defined as unskilled, on axemanship, shovelmanship, and so on. As Veblen once wrote: "The 'common laborer' is, in fact, a highly trained and widely proficient workman when contrasted with the conceivable human blank supposed to have drawn on the community for nothing but his physique" ("On the Nature of Capital," in *The Place of Science*, p. 344).

He was aware of at least a doubtful reception: he remarks, in one of the farm labor papers, that he will be charged with "special pleading"—and he says, yes it is special pleading, for the grain, for the harvest; it is hard to know whom he thought he was deceiving.

ZUM EWIGEN FRIEDEN

Kant wrote his great book *On Perpetual Peace* during the wars unleashed by the French Revolution, wars towards which he retained detachment. Veblen's book, *The Nature of Peace and the Terms of its Perpetuation*, published in April, 1917, urged American entrance into the war in order to compel a peace in accordance with lasting peace aims. For, while recognizing the similarities among all modern industrial states (just as he recognizes the similarities among all classes in a capitalist society), Veblen sharply distinguishes between democratic and dynastic nations; and, positing that dynastic states, above all Germany and Japan, are incurably aggressive, he foresees only two alternatives for America, submission or victory, and with much show of deliberation of course selects the latter.

In this book, Veblen puts great emphasis on the need to formulate constructive proposals in advance of a crisis. He proposes a League of Nations, or, better, a League of administrative agencies grouped around "neutral" boundaries, once the dynasts have fallen. Here he appears to talk like a reformer, but his impatience with reformism comes out in his impatience with the details of reform planning. He terms his own scheme "peace by neglect," and he ridicules "ingenious and elaborate provisions of apparatus and procedure" developed by legal minds (p. 215). He seems unable to free himself from Sumner's dogma that "stateways cannot change folkways": on the one hand, he urges the necessity of planning because it is so difficult to bring about social change, while on the other hand, stressing the forces of patriotism and pecuniary advantage which sabotage efforts towards stable peace, he puts his reliance on the drift of things rather than on deliberate action.

His hope is in the (pp. 196–7):

"slow, random and essentially insidious working of habituation that tends to the obsolescence of the received preconceptions; partly by supplanting them with something new, but more effectually by their falling into disuse and decay. . . . The endeavours of the pacifists should suffice to convince any dispassionate observer of the substantial futility of creative efforts looking to such an end. Much can doubtless be done in the way of precautionary measures, mostly of a negative character, in the way especially of removing sources of infection and (possibly) of so sterilizing the apparatus of national life that its working shall neither maintain animosities and interests at variance with the conditions of peace nor contribute to their spread and growth."

This curious mixture of reformist zeal with conservatism is further indicated by the fact that Veblen opposed Wilson's introduction of a graduated income tax, and came out against the President's deficit spending and his creation of the Federal Reserve Board. On such matters, his attitudes resembled those of the more conservative Midwest farmers. Even his attack on governmental protection of foreign investors, in his memorandum to the House Inquiry, was deemed by him "little else than an unreserved extension of the principles of free trade, but with the inclusion of foreign investments as well as commercial traffic in the scope of this free-trade policy" ("Outline of a Policy for the Control of the 'Economic Penetration' of Backward Countries and of Foreign Investments," *Essays in Our Changing Order*, p. 381).

The Nature of Peace, however, read as a whole, is not a conservative's book. It is not gently ironic, but sharp and cutting —"biting." It opens the series of radical and reformist essays that continues with *The Vested Interests and the Common Man* and *The Engineers and the Price System*. Even so, it remains a gentler book than its successors. Seen, along with his other War proposals, in the perspective of the bitterness that followed their nonadoption, the book may represent the high point of the utopian and activist zeal that Veblen had so successfully sublimated in irony in his earlier writing and teaching. After the War he wrote, in a vein parallel with that of many others, that before 1914 the United States was moving onward and upward, towards the defeat of business and the victory of the common man and the uncontaminated industrial arts; the War came as a catastrophe to these hopes. And Wilson became, suddenly, not the man who was too slow to go to war but the one who was too quick, the betrayer of all of mankind's hopes; in a monstrous over-interpretation, Veblen claimed that Wilson, out of fear of Bolshevism at home and abroad, had planned it that way. Thus, in a savage review of Keynes' *The Economic Consequences of the Peace*, Veblen said that the author, in criticizing Wilson and the Versailles settlement, had missed the fundamental point that Germany was to be erected as a screen against Bolshevism, and that the indemnities against which Keynes protested would never be paid. On the contrary, Veblen maintained that the peace was not vindictive enough, that German wealth should have been confiscated: being absentee wealth anyway—"and there is no question as to the war guilt of these absentee owners"—this would not hurt the underlying population.

Here we see Veblen, who ordinarily gave individuals virtually no importance in the slow cumulative processes of historical change, making a decisive Satan out of Wilson, and likewise casting the German absentee owners in the role of aggressor the Kaiser had previously filled. In comparison with this, his book on Imperial Germany (1915), despite its anti-German chauvinism, is markedly detached, with the vested interests of America and Britain coming in for ironic deprecation along with the dynasts of Germany and Japan.

I think that it becomes clear, from the very virulence and undisguised bitterness of Veblen's post-war work, that he was, in spite of his vaunted detachment, part of that general movement of progressive cosmopolitanism whose hopes were frustrated by the seriatim shocks of the War, the Peace, and the aftermath. For his ideals were, after all, the 19th-century ones of material progress and scientific enlightenment (and the Kantian ideal of perpetual peace), so that his iconoclasm was vulnerable to that greater iconoclast—the War itself. This is not altered by the fact that, in a thoughtful essay written in 1906, he had speculated on a possible reversion of the social-democratic movement to patriotic bellicosity; he wrote:

> "It may be that the working classes will go forward along the line of the socialistic ideals and enforce a new deal, in which there shall be no economic class discrepancies, no international animosity, no dynastic politics. But then it may also, so far as can be foreseen, equally well happen that the working class, with the rest of the community in Germany, England, or America, will be led by the habit of loyalty and by their sportsmanlike propensities to lend themselves enthusiastically to the game of dynastic politics, which alone their sportsmanlike rulers consider worthwhile. It is quite impossible . . . to foretell whether the 'proletariat' will go on to establish the socialistic revolution or turn aside again, and sink their force in the broad sands of patriotism." ("The Socialist Economics of Karl Marx and his Followers: II," in *The Place of Science in Modern Civilization*, p. 442.)

As everyone knows, we may intellectually anticipate death and disaster without being emotionally ready to accept them; we hope against hope. And indeed, pessimistic predictions are often efforts, by naming the evils, to ward them off.

Professor Louis L. Jaffe of Harvard Law School, commenting in a letter on the foregoing, makes what seems to me a first-rate interpretation of Veblen's Washington experience; he writes:

> "Veblen was obviously unfitted for action: he was in a sense unmanned and his only protection was to belittle those who did act. People in this position are always humiliated by the action of others and particularly humiliated when called upon to act either because they cannot act or their action will be of the same order as the action which they have criticized. A man like Veblen probably had no sincerely held theory of action, partly because his view of the world was too selective, too special to provide any sound basis, and partly, I suspect, because his secret desire was that the world should

remain as it was. Such mastery as he had was based on his knowledge of its idiosyncrasies. He hated the thought that it might escape from the forms which he could despise to forms which he would have to accept. I suppose that Washington brought him uncomfortably close to his basic weakness of will and his ambiguity of intention."

CHAPTER SIX

THE COMMON MAN VERSUS
THE STATE

The analogy of the clam may not be convincing, but it may at least serve to suggest what may be the share played by habituation in the matter of national attachment. The young clam, after having passed the free-swimming phase of his life, as well as the period of attachment to the person of a carp or similar fish, drops to the bottom and attaches himself loosely in the place and station in life to which he has been led; and he loyally sticks to his particular patch of oose and sand through good fortune and evil. It is, under Providence, something of a fortuitous matter where the given claim shall find a resting place for the sole of his foot, but it is also, after all, 'his own, his native land' etc. It lies in the nature of a clam to attach himself after this fashion, loosely, to the bottom where he finds a living, and he would not be a 'good clam and true' if he failed to do so; but the particular spot for which he forms this attachment is not of the essence of the case. At least, so they say.

Veblen, *The Nature of Peace*

VEBLEN AND MARX ON THE STATE

THOUGH Veblen repeatedly criticized Marx's Hegelian metaphysics and dismissed as scientifically irrelevant not only his propaganda but also his more philosophical and speculative writings, he greatly admired Marx. He attributed hardly less hegemony than Marx had done to the way men get (and spend) a living; like Marx, he tended to regard politics, art, and religion, as "superstructural" aspects of society. To be sure, where Marx is indignant, Veblen is ironic; where Marx speaks of the bourgeoisie, emphasizing their productive, creative, but eventually exploitative role, Veblen speaks of the "kept

126

classes," emphasizing their passivity and lack of contribution to industrial advance; and where Marx speaks of surplus value—a "natural-rights" concept Veblen couldn't deride often enough—Veblen speaks of waste, a hardly less metaphysical category.

The Vested Interests and the Common Man is, in fact, as polemical, sardonic, and political as anything Marx wrote. It is full of such phrases as the following: "chicane of the gentleman-investors who have been managing the affairs of the civilised nations" (p. 31); "Back of it all is the nation's divine right to carry arms [while] the common man pays the cost and swells with pride" (p. 137); "These Balkan states . . . are simply a case of imperialism in the raw. They are all and several still in the pickpocket state of dynastic statemaking" (p. 145); "Commercial honesty, of course, is the honesty of self-help, or *caveat emptor*, which is Latin for the same thing" (p. 101). His remarks about the Irish nationalist movement are typical (p. 148):

"It is a case of the Common Man hard ridden in due legal form by the vested interests of the Island, and of the neighboring island, which are duly backed by an alien and biased bureaucracy aided and abetted by the priestly pick-pockets of the poor."

To be sure, unlike a Marxist diatribe, the book does not lack Veblen's trade-marked insistence that the terms he used implied no value-judgments; thus, he writes, after pages of denouncing the sabotaging engrossers of "free income," and the "self-help" of dollar-a-year men (p. 94):

"Now, these businesslike manoeuvres of deviation and delay are by no means to be denounced as being iniquitous or unfair, although they may have an unfortunate effect on the conditions of life for the common man."

Still more unlike Marx is Veblen's embittered recognition of the power of nationalism to defeat and delay socialism; as he declares (p. 126):

"The common man . . . has an undivided interest in the glamour of national achievement, and he can swell with just pride in contemplating the triumphs of his gentlemanly government over the vested interests domiciled in any foreign land, or with just indignation at any diplomatic setback suffered by the vested interests domiciled in his own."

And yet in the outcome Veblen and Marx are in agreement that national ambitions are inconsistent with the world economy created by steady technological advance (although both added the caveat that a regression and even another war were outcomes to which the kept classes might succeed in driving their respective sets of politicians). For Veblen, the nation itself—if not the nationality group "bound together by homebred affinities of language, tradition, use and wont . . . essentially based on sympathies and sentiments of self-complacency" (p. 147)—is as out-of-date as the priesthood and other instruments of ceremonial predation. The common man, he argues, has nothing to lose with the defeat of his nation, and indeed something to gain if the result is the liquidation of diplomats, armies, and other wasteful and unproductive consumers of the national income.

Hence, Veblen broke sharply with Wilson, even before the end of the War (the *Vested Interests* took shape as a series of lectures at Amherst in May, 1918), over the issue of national self-determination. This "right" appeared to Veblen as a recrudescence of the divine right of kings, now "taken over—at least in form and principle—by the people at large," but he added that "as 'democratic sovereignty' it has been converted into a cloak to cover the nakedness of a government which does business for the kept classes." The increase in the number of such governments, each with its own parade of honorific establishments, Veblen thought a total defeat for the underlying population: for him, the less government and the fewer governments the better. The Mazzini-type sentiment which regarded the nation as a spiritual instrument which could join a European concert of amiable orchestration is completely absent from Veblen's treatment of the state: for him, the state has hardly changed from the Baroque times "when the princes and prelates 'tore each other in the slime' " to the present.

Veblen is here applying a calculus of economistic utility to the affairs of nations: he treats national "honor" and "integrity" as intangibles quite comparable to the "good will" which the individual firm capitalizes upon as a symbol of differential advantage; and in both cases he sees the result as sabotage and waste. (Let us note in passing that, despite his praise for fact-mindedness, Veblen is greatly given to such highly abstract and often confusing analogies as he here draws between the nation and the capitalist firm—and that in fact these analogies are the source of much of his power and charm.) In a famous later essay, on "The Breadline and the Movies," Veblen goes further and argues that the kept classes are able to make the common man pay for the very opiates, the films, which keep him enslaved—an advance, he sarcastically argues, over Roman days when the rulers had themselves to pay for circuses as well as bread.

It follows that the Veblen who confronts us in his explicitly political writings is not only a "classical" economist horrified at all non-economic behavior ("waste") but a come-outer, who reminds us, alternately, of such radicals as Marx, Liebknecht, and Rosa Luxemburg. He wavers from a strictly Marxist position only in phrasing the class conflict as one between large and small owners, rather than between the propertied and the proletariat; apparently he does so in order to leave room in the revolutionary ranks for the small farmers who "have carried over out of the past and its old order of things a delusion to the effect that they have something to lose" (p. 167). (The same compromise, as Veblen knew, had already been carried out by the Continental Social Democrats and by the Bolsheviks.) The role of "a vanguard of dissent" Veblen assigns to the I.W.W., who "appear to grow increasingly sure" (*The Vested Interests*, p. 181); he continues (pp. 182–3):

"it is not that these and their like are ready with 'a satisfactory constructive program,' such as the people of the uplift require to be shown before they will believe that things are due to change. It is something of the simpler and cruder sort, such as history is full of, to the effect that whenever and so far as the timeworn rules no longer fit the new material circumstances they presently fail to carry conviction. . . . To these untidy creatures of the New Order common honesty appears to mean vaguely something else, perhaps something more exacting, than what was 'nominated in the bond' at the time when the free bargain and self-help were written into the moral constitution of Christendom by the handicraft industry and the petty trade. And why should it not?"

It is plain that Veblen here took the I.W.W. too seriously—as Marx took too seriously the stirrings of 1848. No doubt, Veblen took heart from the panic into which Bolshevism threw many articulately respectable Americans, but he seems to have greatly overestimated American working-class interest in, not to mention sympathy for, the Bolshevik as a fellow common man who has "faced the question: What do I stand to lose? and has come away with the answer: Nothing" (from "Bolshevism Is a Menace—to Whom?"). The Harding landslide must have greatly surprised him. Nevertheless, if one thinks how restless the farmers became in the days of the Great Depression, if one thinks not only of Roosevelt's four terms but of Truman's succession, one realizes that America even in Veblen's day must have been readier for change than many professional interpreters supposed. Veblen's sense of bitterness and alienation made it easier for him to foreshadow the future, as against the boosters who thought everything would turn out all right.

Yet, despite prophetic notes of this sort, it is hard for us today to be sympathetic with any writing, innocuous enough when it appeared, which praises violence and crudity on behalf of some vaguely specified, free-swinging New Order. As we like to appeal from the agitator in Marx to the philosopher, so in Veblen it makes sense to appeal from his praise for the Soviets to a comment he makes on earlier and Oriental despotisms in *The Instinct of Workmanship* (p. 168):

"these stupendous dynastic fabrics are as insignificant as they are large, and none of them is worth the least of the fussy little communities that came in time to make up the Hellenic world and its petty squabbles."

There, pretty clearly, Veblen indicates his allegiance to Western traditions of freedom and rationalism; on the whole, with aberrations, he no more admired the Eastern, the large and brutal, than he did the rural and the archaic.

WHY JEWS ARE UNCOMMON MEN

His attitude towards archaism is expressed in all his work, but nowhere perhaps with such poignancy as in the extraordinary essay he wrote concerning the nationalistic aspirations of Zionist city Jews to become again rural, archaic—and a nation. And here a gentler side of him appears, quite removed from the embittered Bolshevik who wrote *The Vested Interests* or *The Engineers*. Indeed, the Zionism of 1919 which he criticizes is itself gentler than that of 1949, and Veblen sees it as closer to his dream of "live and let live" than was the case of the other aspirants to nationhood. Still he finds in Zionism "a dominant bias of isolation and inbreeding," impracticable in the modern world of mechanical industry. Beyond that, and more important, he argues that what has made the Jews outstanding—the essay is called "The Intellectual Pre-eminence of Jews in Modern Europe"—has been what would today be called their marginality or alienation, resulting from their dispersion among the peoples of Christendom. The ghetto Jew, whose life is still date-lined "B.C.," makes no contribution; it is the Jew who mixes, racially and intellectually, with the host peoples, who does so; as Veblen declares (*Essays in Our Changing Order*, pp. 225–6):

> "It appears to be only when the gifted Jew escapes from the cultural environment created and fed by the particular genius of his own people, only when he falls into the alien lines of gentile inquiry and becomes a naturalised, though hyphenate, citizen in the gentile republic of learning, that he comes into his own as a creative leader in the world's intellectual enterprise. It is by loss of allegiance, or at the best by force of a divided allegiance to the people of his origin, that he finds himself in the vanguard of modern inquiry."

Veblen here favors cultural hybridization just as he thought genetic hybridization to underlie the economic progress of the European peoples.

This loss of allegiance, according to Veblen, is inevitable

owing to the dated nature of the Jewish heritage: "the clay vessel of Jewish archaism suffers that fortune which is due and coming to clay vessels among the iron pots" of "the mechanistic orientation" (p. 229). But at the same time the Jew "is not thereby invested with the gentile's peculiar heritage of conventional preconceptions which have stood over, by inertia of habit, out of the gentile past, which conduce . . . to blur the safe and sane gentile's intellectual vision, and to leave him intellectually sessile." Under these circumstances the Jewish "disturber of the intellectual peace" continues as "a wanderer in the intellectual no-man's-land, seeking another place to rest, farther along the road, somewhere over the horizon." He is not likely to meet strange gods by whom he will learn to swear—he is more likely to be sworn at, and interned.

It follows, Veblen argues, that, contrary to Zionist hopes, the result of a Jewish nation would not be a heightening of the Jewish contribution to the civilized world, but on the contrary regression to "a life of complacent futility at home" (compare Marx's cosmopolitan contempt for "the idiocy of rural life"), exchanging a new brand of Talmudic lore for a "free-swung skeptical initiative." And yet Veblen cannot quite bring himself to urge the Jews to continue "a thankless quest of unprofitable knowledge abroad"; he can only view with dismay that such a choice has to be made.*

* Elsewhere I have set forth my great sympathy with this essay of Veblen's, my belief that marginality is often constructive, as against the contemporary nostalgia for "roots." Here I should stop to note that Veblen is perhaps too charitable to the Jews in seeing them as insubordinate Wobblies of the intellectual world; true as this may be of Marx and Freud and a number of other great and courageous thinkers, there are many other Jewish intellectuals who have sought not knowledge but fame among the gentiles, and have found the road to fame paved by innovation; many of these men, moreover, were quite easily self-deceived in their desperate efforts to assimilate themselves to the gods among whose communicants they sought to move. As already suggested, the essay is partly projective: Veblen saw in the Jews something of his own career and fate. Save for a brief period during the first World War, he, too, was unable to identify himself with a host people, being at home neither among the God-fearing and theologically disputatious Norwegians of his youth nor among the Yankee goyim. (Cf. my article, "Some Observations Concerning Marginality," *Phylon: A Review of Race and Culture*, vol. 12, p. 113, 1951.)

GERMANS AND ENGLISHMEN

In his contempt for the provincialities and flummeries of nationalism, Veblen is in the Enlightenment tradition of cosmopolitanism which links such otherwise divergent figures as Condorcet and Marx. And, as I have said, if we can rid our reading of him from afterthoughts occasioned by the recurring notes of praise for a brutal New Order (as, with other leading writers, we must disregard an anti-Semitism which since their day has become less venial and idle), we will find that his contribution to this literature against Leviathan stands up well for wit and understanding. However, in seeing the state as the One Big Union of the vested interests, Veblen hardly moves beyond Marx's concept of the state as the executive committee of the bourgeoisie.

In *Imperial Germany and the Industrial Revolution* (along with a companion article, "The Opportunity of Japan"), Veblen transcended his Marxist models in developing a theory as to the particular aggressive potentialities precisely of those states that were *not* dominated by the bourgeois but had nevertheless managed to acquire the war-making facilities of the capitalist West.* As already indicated, Veblen's anthropological account runs in

* The reception of *Imperial Germany* would make an interesting chapter in itself. In World War I it was ambivalently received on several counts. To the virulent pro-Ally, it appeared too detached; its comments on the English gentleman as the highest flower of wastefulness, too unfriendly. To the liberal Walter Weyl, educated at German universities, it appeared too hostile to German *Kultur*, as to the bent of which Veblen took very much the line of the more aggressively patriotic Entente intellectuals. Moreover, as soon as Japan became an ally, the book's linkage of Germany and Japan as unscrupulous dynasties, effective because as industrial parvenus they had not paid "the penalty of taking the lead," become inconvenient to the Creel propaganda office. But this very linkage made the book (republished in 1939 with a glowing introduction by Dorfman) well received among Office of War Information officials in World War II, as if it had been written for an occasion when the Western democracies would meet these countries in combat. And beyond such expedience, it seemed to foreshadow the power of fascism, interpreted as a marriage of dynastic ambition with industrial late-coming efficiency. Henry A. Wallace wrote in 1940 that it "is probably the most acute analysis of modern Germany which has ever been written."

Yet the book is hardly at all, in tone and method, an "occasional" one: in the main, it exudes a patrician air of ironic detachment from contemporary

terms of borrowing, of diffusion, leading to his brilliant statement that when a mechanical complex diffuses from one culture to another it does so without the encrustation of mythological and animistic elements it had acquired in its original habitat. That is, Veblen sees the Germans and Japanese as picking up the machine culture from England in the late 19th and early 20th centuries without the crippling make-believes that culture was enmeshed in —much, we might say, as the Plains Indians picked up the European horse culture without the feudal attitudes which crimped ease of riding among the Spanish or the Anglos, until they relearned it from the Indians.*

The make-believe Veblen had in mind is manifold. It includes the British cult of the gentleman; the obsolete British railway system, maintained out of habit; the sports culture—"such a *tour de force* of inanity as polo" (p. 142)—with its "deadening of the sense of proportion"; the British prejudice against women working in the fields; and, among the working classes, "more of this mandatory expenditure on decencies, physically superfluous and commonly æsthetically obnoxious," than on the Continent. Even the insubordination and relative monarchical disloyalty with which Veblen credits the English is a drawback when it

---

events; indeed, it takes its leisurely start with a discussion of the hybrid racial character of the Germanic tribes, and it has much to say concerning Baltic antiquities. In his warm-up, Veblen is greatly concerned to rebut racist explanations of German and Japanese aggression; as he declares (p. 67):

"The spirit of 'duty' in these (German) people is apparently not 'nature,' in the sense of native proclivity; but it is 'second nature' with the people of the Fatherland, as being the ingrained traditional attitude induced by consistent and protracted experience."

While, in my opinion, this is somewhat chauvinist, in underestimating the "weakness for free institutions" harbored in many Germans of the Kaiser's Reich —Veblen in a footnote points to German folk tales as slight evidence of a submerged insubordination—in its insistence on cultural and environmentalist rather than racial explanations, it is superior to some World War II books which are still more disgracefully chauvinist and unscientific.

* Veblen oversimplifies the German case here, for Germany, unlike Japan, contributed from the beginning to the Western scientific and technological development; indeed, much diffusion occurred *within* Germany, as when Protestant Prussian industrialists brought their entrepreneurial zeal to the Catholic Rhineland.

comes to stripping down for war. Above all, the fantastic structure of credit and capital, erected on obsolete plant, makes it difficult for the British to modernise their industry.

These encrustations, both on the side of production and consumption, are in Veblen's view inevitable in the capitalist system, given time. He therefore anticipated that the German and Japanese Empires which, at the time he wrote, profited from the spread between the productiveness of their industries and the lagging "consumptiveness" of their societies, would before long be bogged down in the same rounds of futile expenditure as the British. Only for a short space could the dynasty absorb, for armaments and rivalrous display, the excess which the aristocrats and workers had not yet learned to waste in appropriate leisure-class futility. Hence, in "The Opportunity of Japan," Veblen advised the Japanese that they must strike now or never if they wished to exploit their temporary margin (in so "advising" the "enemy" as to its main chance, his work foreshadows the brilliant satire of Ignazio Silone, *The School for Dictators*, in which a would-be American Mussolini is advised how to go about his business of deceiving the masses.) In *Imperial Germany*, Veblen is inclined to think that the Kaiser and his military gang have waited too long, that their "net gain" over the other powers was at its peak a half dozen years before the War (p. 262). Among other things, the "specialists in prowess," as Veblen terms the army, were already succumbing to the archaisms of long-standing military establishments.

Throughout this account, Veblen appears to enjoy his role of Machiavellian calculator of power and destiny. Yet he is in the anomalous position of preferring the British, who allow individuals to waste the social product in the upkeep of polo ponies, to the Germans, who socialize dissipation in collective aggression. When forced to choose between a society which suffers from overconsumption because of the pace-setting maneuvers of a decadent leisure class, and one which suffers from overproduction because of the dynastic ambitions of its military junta, Veblen favors the inefficiency of peaceable waste to the efficiency so many have admired in the Germans and the Japanese which tempts the leadership to war.* And perhaps we can see here why Veblen was so smitten with the Bolsheviks who appeared in 1917 to combine a desire for ascetic efficiency as an economic program with a political platform promising cosmopolitanism and peace.

We must ask, however, whether Veblen is correct in his fundamental idea that national and cultural boundaries serve as filters which can transmit the modern industrial complex while retaining the "irrelevant" social habits that have grown up in the country of export. Certainly, the European "productivity teams" which have come since the War to study American know-how are in search of some cultural secret of high production, and not of blue-prints they can get in the mails. Likewise, the Point IV "missionaries" we send to "backward" countries seem to believe they must bring not only tractors but a set of attitudes which make tractors meaningful. Whereas in Veblen's eyes the Bolsheviks took over the economic advantages of industrialization without any of its political shams, my own guess is that the Russians are still dazzled by the America of Hoover and Ford and are doing their best to ape its industrial manners as well as its industrial plant—it is Veblen himself who was taken in by the make-believe change in title by which that plant became the property of the "people." However, even if it could be shown that Russian managers are as much like American captains of industry as they know how to be, it would still be true that the Russian masses have not yet been permitted to learn how to spend on the Anglo-American scale and that this gives the Politburo a war-making advantage of sorts. If they

* The following sentence presents one aspect of his anti-German slant (p. 172):
"Both German and English-speaking peoples make much of personal liberty, as is the fashion in modern Christendom, but it would seem that in the German conception this liberty is freedom to give orders and freely to follow orders, while in the English conception it is rather an exemption from orders—a somewhat anarchistic habit of thought."
As an island (like Iceland—Veblen's personal Eden) England was able to reach this condition because "exposed to the slow corrosion of peace and isolation" (p. 173)—note how Veblen tends to avoid any ideological or religious explanations.

read Veblen, they will be inclined to strike before this margin goes the way of individual dissipation. In pointing to the danger that "backward" peoples can acquire "forward" techniques, but not for long. Veblen does not help our unsteady nerves!

DID VEBLEN FORETELL FASCISM?

And yet none of this amounts to an understanding of totalitarianism, but only of old-fashioned militarism revved up by industrial advance. It does not even carry us too far in the understanding of modern Japan, whose loyalties are not to be summed up as simply flunkeyism (as we can see, for instance, in such a book as Ruth Benedict's *The Chrysanthemum and the Sword*). Veblen accepted without his usual skepticism the Entente explanation for the outbreak of the First War as German aggression pure and simple; he saw the Kaiser and the Junkers pretty much as Beasts of Berlin; and, as in the passages quoted, saw "the" Germans as given over to obsequiousness without any awareness of the complexities underlying the Wilhelminian regime. *A fortiori*, then, he did not predict the Third Reich, with its historically new developments in terror, resting on a mass base of fanatical SS recruits—a regime run not by specialists in prowess from the old Wehrmacht and Junker cadres but using these on behalf of a new elite of specialists in terror, propaganda, and organization, dominating people less because of ingrained flunkeyism than because of sheer strategic power coupled with mass insecurity.

Still, *Imperial Germany and the Industrial Revolution* gives us one important clue to the rise of Nazism. Consider in this connection the well-known fact that Goebbels and Co. (the Communists, too) went to school to American advertising men, and to World War I propaganda experts such as Edward L. Bernays; they applied techniques developed to sell goods to the sale of myths and ideologies and, in some senses, did "better" at it than the original American inventors who were less ideological and in most cases more scrupulous. It is in Veblen's spirit to see this as an instance of the "penalty of taking the lead," and the advantages of borrowing. Indeed, it is in Veblen's spirit to concern ourselves with "vendible imponderables" such as myths, for was he not, in *Absentee Ownership* and other writings, greatly preoccupied with the nature of the advertising operation? That Americans should now be frequently defeated by Soviet propaganda in the world idea-market is an irony Veblen would have richly enjoyed.

And it is just here, in his understanding of the continuing power of myths, even in modern industrial society, that Veblen departs most profoundly from Marx and other socialists in the Enlightenment tradition, and is closer to such modern prophets of irrationality as Freud and Pareto. The politics of *Imperial Germany* is a politics, and not a mere reflection of capitalist chicane; it marks perhaps the furthest reach of Veblen's awareness of the importance of non-economic influences on society. Nevertheless, the thesis, when examined more closely, does rest upon an economic interpretation of history, for it sees international rivalry as the result of differential rates of industrialization, giving each national group in turn, in its transition from dynastic to leisure-class consumption patterns, a single chance for hegemony over world markets and resources.

When Veblen came, two years later, to publish *The Nature of Peace* and, after that, *The Vested Interests*, he reverted to a straight Marxist (Hobson, Hilferding, Lenin) theory of imperialism as a struggle among capitalists. And, as we have seen, he took the side of the Soviets against the opposing states, in part we may be sure because the term "Soviet" led him to think that the State had indeed been abolished and an industrial republic ushered in.

VEBLEN AS A WOBBLY

But in judging this identification, we must never forget that, tough as the Soviet spokesmen talked, their enterprise was precarious at the start, and in terms of his own country in its Palmery days and of the world at large Veblen was siding with the underdog. In his successive political stages—and this is very rough, for Veblen never actually joined a political group or engaged in direct political activity—we may say that Veblen was a Cleveland free-trader, a Bellamy nationalist, a parliamentary Socialist, and a Bolshevik with syndicalist leanings. But throughout his career he had a compelling sympathy with the outcast: with immigrants, Jews, workers, farmers, Wobblies, primitive tribes, the small Scandinavian countries, the embattled Soviets, women, and cats (as against dogs). It is true that this sympathy for the outcast, as so often, was qualified by a certain fascination with the powerful and entrenched: the priests and princes, the captains of statecraft and solvency, the Harpers and Rockefellers, whom Veblen fought with his sarcasm which he pretended was science. The very fact that Veblen identified with the underdog carries the implication that his self-contempt would be projected onto the powerless ones; this helps explain the recurrent notes of disdain and impatience with which he observes the underlying population. Even so, he never allowed his Darwinism to put him on the side of Spencer or Sumner politically, and he was never tempted to betray the common man, or any of the weak and vulnerable people, to their quondam rulers.

Moreover, Veblen's image of the common man—and in this, too, he recalls Bellamy—is never an image of a herd, but of men of his own stamp, with a mechanistic turn of mind. Thus, in his description of "The Army of the Commonweal," Veblen writes that the men of the Army do not seek a lax anarchy but a government "aware that the entire community is a single industrial organism" whose integration disregards boundaries of class and place. And he sees them, despite misguidance by ethical and clerical economists and sociologists, as responding to the economic situation; they are "the product of the environment acting upon the average intelligence available." Here in Veblen's politics, as in his picture of work, men respond, not so much to each other and group contagions, as to the impersonal "environment"—that is, as atomistic individuals.*

* What Veblen did not take seriously enough, in terms of his theory of social change, was the fact that the Wobblies were mostly unskilled and casual laborers—not the highly skilled artisans from whom Veblen expected a radical outlook on things. The Wobblies, the radical longshoremen, the radical, land-hungry peasants of Russia and the Orient—these groups did not lead Veblen to re-examine his belief that it was the machine discipline that was the directly

Lincoln Steffens wrote that the Wobblies encouraged their members to commit sabotage with precision in order to preserve their sense of workmanship. And it was Wobblies and men like them who lined the streets of Seattle for Woodrow Wilson's visit in 1919 and who, as he passed, neither cheered nor swore but stood silently; that is, they behaved impersonally (this traumatic incident is said to have hastened Wilson's death). The Wobblies, insubordinate even to their own officials, wore no man's collar; they were the vagrants of the industrialised mines, forests, and farms of the West; like Veblen, they travelled light. In his Stanford days, Veblen appears to have known and liked some men of a Wobbly cast, and the free-thinking, free-speaking Harry George who lived under his roof at Cedro was (as Duffus describes him) a kind of a Wobbly among the graduate students.

To commit sabotage with precision is a highly skilled and individualistic thing. Perhaps it could be said that Veblen devoted much of his life to the art, as theorist and as practitioner.

---

revolutionizing force in the world. For similar reasons, his theory gave no place to the radical intelligentsia, other than engineers—did not explain why he himself, hardly a tutee of the machine, was radical. All this, of course, hangs together with the technologism discussed in chapter two.

Moreover, many Wobblies and longshoremen, like Veblen himself, were what he termed "home-bred aliens," not readily assimilable to the ethos of the country town. Veblen wrote (in *Absentee Ownership*, p. 440) that "Apart from any glamor of national prowess, in the way of blood and wounds, the nations have also a certain sentimental value as standard containers, each of its distinctive cultural tincture, very precious to persons of cultivated tastes in these matters," while of course "The industrial arts . . . have no use for and no patience with local tinctures of culture. . . ." Yet the articles of Daniel Bell and others in Donald Drew Egbert and Stow Persons, *Socialism and American Life* (2 vols., Princeton Univ. Press, 1952) indicate the extent to which radical movements in America, such as the I.W.W., have depended on "local tinctures of culture," whether among Jewish garment workers, Finnish woodsmen, or Welsh miners—their enclaves or "standard containers" being as often created as disrupted by the advancing industrial arts.

CHAPTER SEVEN

THE REFORM OF ECONOMICS

We believe that political economy as a science is still in an early stage of its development . . . and we look not so much to speculation as to the historical and statistical study of actual conditions of economic life for the satisfactory accomplishment of that development.

From a resolution at the first meeting of the American Economic Association, Saratoga Springs, 1885.

WHEN it came to reforming the American economy, Veblen exhibited the contradictions and ambivalences we have observed in earlier chapters: until the first World War, he insisted on playing the role of the disinterested savant and, far from asking his fellow-savants to endorse socialism, he urged economists to purge themselves of any desire to meddle in politics, and to rid their theories of assumptions involving the implicit acceptance of any society or any goals. But, by the same token, most of his working life was spent as a reformer of economics itself: for thirty years he bombarded the profession with reviews, essays, notes, and books proclaiming the irrelevance of classical economics and its latterday variants to the modern industrial economy and asking, as the famous essay "Why Is Economics Not an Evolutionary Science?" literally does, "What are we going to do about it?"

We might put it this way: when dealing with the formidable masters of wastemanship in the economy at large, Veblen was self-protective and hesitant, as befitted his picture of "massive vested interests moving in the background under cover of night and cloud"; but when dealing with the comparatively ineffectual doyens of idle curiosity, he was confident and direct, as be-

141

fitted his picture of scholars dealing impersonally and in a matter-of-fact way with phenomena. Economics, like the other learned professions, was still a craft—Veblen sometimes spoke of the "guild of economists"—and as we have seen, Veblen was personally drawn towards craftsmanship despite his judgment that its day was done in the face of mechanization. Whatever his criticisms of Lester Ward and J. B. Clark as overpreachy, he respected them as fellow-craftsmen and would certainly have defended them (as they defended him) from criticism outside the social science profession. When Veblen, under Bellamy's influence, decided to return from the Iowa farm to get more schooling, the discipline he chose to work in was theoretical economics; the alternative had not been practice as an industrial consultant, but other academic fields such as philology or philosophy.

Only much later, as part of the process of disillusionment sketched out in chapter five, did Veblen begin to identify himself with engineers—that is, with practical life—rather than with savants. In *The Engineers and the Price System*, he found a place for the economist only as an assistant to the engineer, as a "production economist" or "consulting economist" engaged in presumably statistical coordination and articulation of the work of engineers specializing in different industries. And only then did he abandon his life-long hopes of reforming an economic theory which he came to dismiss as merely (pp. 144–5)

> "inquiry into the ways and means of salesmanship, financial traffic, and the distribution of income and property, rather than a study of the industrial system considered as a ways and means of producing goods and services."

DOWN ON THE FARM

Veblen's earliest articles on economics dealt with the price of wheat (herein was one of the few places he used statistical material). In one of these he observed that "agriculture is fast assuming the character of an industry." In the section on the "Independent Farmer" in his last book, *Absentee Ownership*, he emphasized the farmer's "protracted habituation to a somewhat picayune calculation of the main chance" (p. 136). Thus it would seem at first glance that Arthur K. Davis is right when he points out that Veblen saw farming in the glare cast by industrialization and missed those more traditional aspects that have remained relatively immune to business and industrial values.* But in other passages of *Absentee Ownership* Veblen insisted that most farming in the civilized world had hardly changed since Neolithic times. Despite the growth of unit size and mechanization, "farm life is still a neighborhood life of homely detail and seasonal fortuities"; Veblen continued (pp. 244–245):

> "With the result, among other things, that the rural community is still shot through with prehistoric animism in a degree that passes the comprehension of any person whose habits of thought have been shaped by the technology of physics and chemistry. So it has come about that the rural community is still the repository of timeworn superstitions, magical, religious, and political, such as would do credit to the best credulity of neolithic man."

Perhaps Veblen could hold in his mind these disparate pictures of farming—at once as a kind of small business and a kind of pre-business life—because of his own only partial mobility out of the world of the farmer. While, like his brother Andrew, he entered academic life, he did not abandon the coonskin cap with which he had startled J. Laurence Laughlin at Cornell. And while, after teaching "agricultural economics" for a few years at Chicago, he left it for more theoretical and highbrow specialties, he retained to the end of his life a whole set of farmerish "down-to-earth" sentiments. I think we can point to certain parallels between his brand of economics and the "economic" experiences undergone by the Norwegian immi-

* Arthur K. Davis, *Thorstein Veblen's Social Thought,* Doctoral Dissertation in Harvard University Library (1941), pp. 25–26. (On the whole this thesis is a very clear presentation of Veblen and location of him in sociological perspective.)

grants among whom he grew up. In doing so, however, we must be very cautious. In principle, such ex post facto explanations, even "obvious" ones, are always open to question: they do not tell us how other farm-boys came to hold different views. Nor do I know enough about Veblen's early life to be at all sure what being a farm-boy meant to him, especially after he had done tours of duty at Hopkins and Yale as a philosophy student.

The Norwegian immigrants of the mid-19th century were "The Uprooted," to borrow an apt title of Oscar Handlin's: the first generation had few precedents to guide them in their cultivation of the dry, matted Western soils, or in their encounters with the dry, matted tangle of Yankee commercial practice. On the basis of a study of Norwegian language patterns, the historian Theodore Blegen concludes that some fifty percent of American agriculture was strange; and, as Western farmers in the latter half of the nineteenth century became increasingly dependent on the market, they were confronted with the uncertainties of a competitive economy—no less strange to them than competitive sports.*
At the same time, these farmers were becoming specialized in a single crop—in the Veblen family's area, wheat—on whose climatic and market fortunes a whole year's livelihood, and indeed an equity in an increasingly over-capitalized "freehold," might depend. Specialization and the American social climate encouraged the introduction of farm machinery as an additional complication for farm managers. But, as two of our most observant economic historians point out, more men probably went broke from over- than from under-mechanization.**

Thomas Veblen, as it happens, did not suffer from his unusual readiness to mechanize. But, as we have seen, he was victimized by being forced off his first claim by speculators, after he had built his home. It was only in the third generation that the folk of Veblen's community came to speak English freely, and to create a cadre of professionals who could mediate, as Yankees had exclusively done, between the farmers and the Eastern

* See Blegen, *Grass Roots History*, pp. 101, 106.
** Thomas Cochran and William Miller, *The Age of Enterprise*, p. 214.

"interests." For these farmers, the sharp-trading, fast-talking merchants and lawyers of the Minnesota country towns must have been as hated as the East Indians are in South Africa who bargain between Bantus and Boers, or the Chinese in Southeast Asia who bargain between colonial rulers and "natives," or the Jews in Eastern Europe who once mediated between landlords and peasants.

Thorstein Veblen, however, came to regard the country town and its denizens as a faithful, if slightly exaggerated, microcosm of American society at large—the small-scale version of all the other rackets and trickeries "made in America." It seems likely that his generalized bitterness reflected the sense of apartness of immigrants set off from indigenous ways of life not only economically, linguistically, and in religion, but also in attitude towards the land. The Norwegian peasant accustomed to seeing the same plot of land pass from father to son in endless succession was shocked by the American-style farmer who bought land, "wasted" it, waited for its exchange-value to rise as a community developed around it, then sold out and moved on. (Indeed, handbooks for immigrants advised them *not* to go to the frontier, but to buy land in more settled areas—advice not all of them could afford.) The selfishness the Norwegian saw in such conduct is well symbolized by Veblen's comment that the politician of the American country town does not "stand" for office, he "runs" for it.

Even farmers who were native-born encountered similar frustrations, and the movements known as Grangerism and Populism—in some ways, too, the Single Tax ideology—sought to interpret these frustrations and to retaliate for them. Despite his gift for abstraction and his sophistication, Veblen himself shared many Populist attitudes. As the figure of Bryan makes plain, these attitudes were strongly influenced by rural or fundamentalist Puritanism. Puritanism lingered among farmers for much the same reason (as Professor Shannon points out in *The Farmer's Last Frontier*) it originally arose among middle-class townsmen: to set them off from the self-styled "better" classes who lived luxurious and "immoral" lives. We shall see in the next chapter the extent to which Veblen's *The Theory of the Leisure Class* is a Puritan tract which idealizes the homely, simple life and ascetically derides the showy, expensive goods and services consumed by city people.

Likewise, Veblen's stubborn, empirical "show me" attitude is one for which urbanites have often mocked the farmer. The Midwest Norwegians, like other converts to Populism, had been sold many a gold brick, particularly railroad bonds and railroad promises; they took refuge in a radical suspicion and distrust of all promises—and thus, as invariably occurs, exposed themselves to new gullibilities. We may interpret much of Veblen's contribution to the economics of capitalism as an emphasis on promises, that is, on credit, coupled with an almost obsessive insistence on their insubstantiality.

We might even suggest that Veblen's theory of economic crisis, with its Populist preoccupation with the role of finance, is traceable to his farmer origins—though of course Veblen was too much the professional economist ever to be a Midwest money-crank. It is a theory in which capital, credit, interest, and price—the most significant influences on farm production—play the principle roles, while the category of wages, which plays so large a part in Marx's crisis theory, plays almost no part in Veblen's, any more than it did in the life of the 19th-century farmer. Just as Veblen saw the farmer's depression of the post-Civil War period as coming about through a fall in prices due to the introduction of machinery while capital costs on land and machinery rose, so he saw depressions in general as arising from overcapitalization and inflation. Indeed, his chronic emphasis on speculative inflation of capital values is prefigured in the belief among Western farmers—a very widespread belief according to Hicks' *The Populist Revolt*—that the Eastern trusts habitually watered their stock.*

We do not, of course, need to go down on the farm to look for origins of Veblen's life-long advocacy of free trade; save for

---

* Veblen, like so many Puritanical observers, missed the fact that apparently inflated values were more often than not rendered solid enough by the fabulous growth of American population and productivity—in some ways, the speculators and their willing victims had a better sense of the American future than did their minatory critics.

the forgotten Henry C. Carey, this was stock in trade among economists anyway, though possibly intensified in Veblen's case by a background of rural hatred for the high prices a tariff on imported goods permitted—a tariff set by a distant government with which no emotional identification existed. And is not the following characteristic passage of Veblen the kind of statement a Henry-George-reading farmer might make, who saw capitalist profits resulting from mere waiting for land values to appreciate, not from productive effort (*The Higher Learning*, p. 71)?

> "There is a homely but well-accepted American collo-
> quialism which says that 'The silent hog eats the swill.' . . .
> it happens that American conditions during the past one
> hundred years have been peculiarly favourable to the patient
> and circumspect man who will rather wait than work. . . .
> America has been a land of free and abounding resources;
> which is to say, when converted into terms of economic
> theory, that it is the land of the unearned increment."

Beyond the details and the metaphors of theory, Veblen's country-boy background would seem almost surely to have been an element in the kind of criticism he regularly makes of institutions. He takes a critical position which looks as if it were totally outside a given institution, but the values of his position are to some extent drawn from the very institution being criticized. Thus, when Veblen uses the canon of efficiency to attack business practice, he is actually using a canon businessmen themselves have developed—but he attributes it only to engineers and skilled workmen. Likewise, when he uses the canon of idle curiosity to attack the current academic scene, he is using a canon drawn from European graduate schools and perhaps Hopkins too. And, as we shall see, when he attacks economic theory he does so alternately as an insider and as an outsider. This constant shift of perspectives, which allows Veblen to claim a kind of innocent originality of view, reminds us of the boy who saw that the king was naked—but perhaps did not understand the symbolism by which the courtiers were saying the same thing.

Yet when all has been said about Veblen's rural background, what is striking about his system as a whole is his sophistication and his sensitivity to the industrial and corporate revolutions of his lifetime. His understanding of the techniques by which "good will" was capitalized is something one might expect in a financial writer like Henry Varnum Poor, but was an extraordinary achievement for a man of Veblen's background. Though he never lived in New York until his New School days, he had a better grasp of many Wall Street practices than the Populists did, and, as I have already indicated, he was thoroughly aware that the future lay with the newly-developing industrial America, which would be urban, and not by any remote chance with the pastoral.

INSIDE ECONOMICS VERSUS INSIDE U.S.A.

We still have to face the question why Veblen became an economist and spent his life exploding what he regarded as a collection of "received" homilies grounded in an archaic metaphysics. Perhaps the answer lies somewhere between the asserted relevance of economics to the most basic, the most elemental of human needs—livelihood—and the attraction of its rigorous intricacies. That is, both aspects of Veblen's "instinct of workmanship," as he defined it, must have found release in a discipline which on the one hand had pretensions to serviceability, but on the other was a monument to taking pains for taking pains' own sake. For Veblen was both a burned-up farmer's son and a man whose first job had been teaching that paradigm of idle curiosity, mathematics (the one branch of learning, incidentally, he thought to be relatively independent of technology); mathematics, in fact, was the field of his brother Andrew and his favorite nephew Oswald. Though he gave up mathematics (possibly, because accomplishment proved too difficult), he turned at various times in his life to pursuits equally "idle": to translating the Laxdaela Saga and to the study of Mediterranean and Baltic antiquities.*

* Commenting on this, Helen Singer has suggested that Veblen's archaeological and linguistic explorations were not "idle" wanderings for him but part of an effort to establish at once the origins of modern society and a kind of cross-cultural economic system without dates. Certainly he ground his axe on the sagas as elsewhere, but it is also true that at times system-building was lost sight of in immersion in the data for their own sake and without militant aims.

Yet basically he wanted to be serviceable, even if he did not care to admit that his father and rural neighbors were right in insisting, with hard-fisted rural thriftiness, on direct and visible serviceability. In choosing a career in economics, he managed at once to obey and to criticize his father's mandate. For by entering this career he gave up the rather resigned retreat his wife's Iowa farm had provided, and he sought to reform himself, economics, and mayhap America by detaching the discipline from practical, reformist concerns while attaching it the more firmly to the hard-headed, no-nonsense study of industrial and business practices.

Veblen argued that the temptation of economists to give practical advice inevitably led them into taking the *status quo* for granted; as he insisted (in *The Higher Learning,* pp. 186–187):

> "academic science as habitually pursued, is commonly occupied with questions of what ought to be done, rather than with theories of the genesis and causation of the present-day state of things, or with questions as to what the present-day drift of things may be, as determined by the causes at work. . . . It is usual among economists, e.g., to make much of the proposition that economics is an 'art'—the art of expedient management of the material means of life; and further that the justification of economic theory lies in its serviceability in this respect. Such a quasi-science necessarily takes the current situation for granted as a permanent state of things; to be corrected and brought back into its normal routine in case of aberration, and to be safeguarded with apologetic defence at a point where it is not working to the satisfaction of all parties. It is a 'science' of complaisant interpretations, apologies, and projected remedies."

This remedial or tinkering bias of economists Veblen attributed to a philosophical orientation dating from the 18th century, when the tinkering craftsman and the small businessman who furnished Adam Smith with his models were just passing their day of predominance. Veblen made the now-familiar criticism that classical economics assumed that each type of economic actor received a reward in rough proportion to his contribution, a neat trick accomplished by arbitrarily assigning quotas of work to income received without examination of the actual industrial process. As Veblen complained, the going economics (*The Engineers and the Price System*, pp. 27–28):

> "assigns no productive effort to the industrial arts, for example, for the conclusive reason that the state of the industrial arts yields no stated or ratable income to any one class of persons."

If one aspect of the "natural rights" approach to the distribution of income was this assumption of just desserts, another more general aspect was the economist's notion that the economy is balanced and harmonious, a machine, as Veblen put it, without "leak, lag or friction." This quasi-theological assumption allowed the economist to preoccupy himself only with those features of the going system which were in fact harmonious and to neglect those which disrupted economic solidarity. For Veblen these latter were pecuniary; he declared in "Pecuniary and Industrial Employments" (*The Place of Science*, p. 286) that in economic theory

> "Pecuniary . . . activities are handled as incidental features of the process of social production and consumption, as details incident to the method whereby the social interests are served, instead of being dealt with as the controlling factor about which the modern economic process turns."

Natural law thinking, according to Veblen, not only gave an 18th-century gloss to 20th-century capitalism, and not only saw productive order where pecuniary chaos reigned, but also reduced man himself to a mere passive creature, tending an economy headed towards some imputed harmonious goal. That is, if the economy is presumed to be heading somewhere, it acquires a kind of activism, while human action, being merely a means to the achievement of the grand purpose of society-as-a-whole, is regarded as inert raw material. Veblen's hope was to reverse this relationship assumed by economic theory; to see the behavior of human beings as active and teleological, and the "behavior" of the economy as simply cumulative, undirected process. As he declared in "Why Is Economics Not an Evolutionary Science?" (*The Place of Science*, p. 74):

> "The later psychology, reënforced by modern anthropological research, gives a different conception of human nature. According to this conception, it is the characteristic of man to do something, not simply to suffer pleasures and pains through the impact of suitable forces. He is not simply a bundle of desires that are to be saturated by being placed in the path of the forces of the environment, but rather a coherent structure of propensities and habits which seeks realization and expression in an unfolding activity. According to this view, human activity, and economic activity among the rest, is not apprehended as something incidental to the process of saturating given desires. The activity is itself the substantial fact of the process . . ."

As we shall see, Veblen did not always live up to his own mandate here—else he might have found "waste" itself a form of activity which human beings could choose as an outlet, whereas he urged men to confine themselves to just those activities that made rationalistic, economistic sense. However, this program opened a new direction for economic thought: since man was an agent, he must be considered as a whole, and by the same token all human activity, as part of the context, must be studied by economists if they are to understand narrowly "economic" behavior. It was this approach, as well as his desire to bring what he did within the walls of his chosen guild, that led Veblen to term his *Theory of the Leisure Class* a work on economics. Underlying the book is a very modern sense of the oneness of man's life in any given society: of the "pattern of culture."

Though Veblen was of course pre-Freudian in lacking any detailed awareness of the ways in which institutions and motives were linked together by the processes of socialization, he did have a very good intimation of the link between institutions and habits. (In that sense, if not in the senses discussed in chapter two, he is properly thought of as an institutional economist, especially if one bears in mind that for him such features of the economy as the price system, the corporation, absentee ownership, and the state of the industrial arts were all dubbed institutions.) As he declares (in a review of Irving Fisher, *Essays in Our Changing Order*, p. 143):

> "In economic life, as in other lines of human conduct, habitual modes of activity and relations have grown up and have by convention settled into a fabric of institutions. These institutions, and the usual concepts involved in them, have a prescriptive, habitual force of their own, although it is not necessary at every move to ravel out and verify the intricate web of precedents, accidents, compromises, indiscretions, and appetites, out of which in the course of centuries the current cultural situation has arisen. If the contrary were true, if men universally acted not on the conventional grounds and values afforded by the fabric of institutions, but solely and directly on the grounds and values afforded by the unconventionalised propensities and aptitudes of hereditary human nature, then there would be no institutions and no culture. But the institutional structure of society subsists and men live within its lines, with more or less questioning, it is true, but with more acquiescence than dissent."

From this point of view where all the facts of social life were relevant to economics, the work of the greatest of Veblen's contemporaries in the ranks of economists seemed anemic. Thus, he begins the review of Fisher's *The Nature of Capital and Income* by noting that it "is of that class of books that have kept the guild of theoretical economists content to do nothing toward 'the increase and diffusion of knowledge' during the past quarter of a century"; and continues:

> "What it lacks is the breath of life; and this lack it shares with the many theoretical productions of the Austrian diversion as well as of the economists of more strictly classical antecedents."

In his own work, Veblen insisted on defining his terms in the way he believed them to be actually employed in the market, and claimed to be drawing on no other facts than were generally known to the common man. He made extensive use of such documents as the Report of the Industrial Commission, and the Report of the Interchurch World Movement on the great steel strike which followed the first World War, much as Marx used the reports of British Parliamentary committees.

Correspondingly, Veblen attempted to view the economic process from within, to impose on it no other categories than those it created itself. It was this new point of view, not simply an effort towards more empiricism, which Veblen felt to be significant in his appeal to the "facts" of economic life. He began a preface to his chief economic work, *The Theory of Business Enterprise*, by stating this explicitly:

"In respect of its point of departure, the following inquiry into the nature, causes, utility, and further drift of business enterprise differs from other discussions of the same general range of facts. Any unfamiliar conclusions are due to this choice of a point of view, rather than to any peculiarity in the facts, articles of theory, or method of argument employed. The point of view is that given by the business man's work,—the aims, motives, and means that condition current business traffic. This choice of a point of view is itself given by the current economic situation, in that the situation plainly is primarily a business situation."

From the point of view of the "current economic situation" the luminaries of economics were tried and found wanting. One and all they seemed to Veblen to assume that the categories of the present economic system had existed eternally and would continue unchanged; with the result that economic history, on the one hand, and prediction, on the other, were alike neglected in favor of gratuitous advice as to "what is to be done." This was true, for instance, of Fisher, J. B. Clark, and Karl Marx. Feeling that Fisher treated interest, in his work on that subject, as a perennial economic category, Veblen objected: "The whole matter lies within the range of a definite institutional situation which is to be found only during a relatively brief phase of civilisation that has been preceded by thousands of years of cultural growth during which the existence of such a thing as interest was never suspected." More picturesquely, he makes the identical criticism of Clark's handling of marginal utility "so that, *e.g.*, a gang of Aleutian Islanders slushing about in the wrack and surf with rakes and magical incantations for the capture of shell-fish are held, in point of taxonomic reality, to be engaged on a feat of hedonistic equilibrium in rent, wages, and interest."

It is this cultural absolutism of Clark's, Veblen argued, which enabled him confidently to venture into proposals for economic reform. Of these Veblen commented caustically ("Professor Clark's Economics," in *The Place of Science*, p. 230):

> "The measures of redress whereby the economic Order of Nature is to renew its youth are simple, direct, and short-sighted, as becomes the proposals of pre-Darwinian hedonism, which is not troubled about the exuberant uncertainties of cumulative change."

Veblen's own model for economic theory comes out clearly in a footnote to this article on Clark. Economic theorists should aspire to the impersonality of the natural scientist, to his indifference toward the outcome of events or the respectability of their antecedents and to his consequent ability to seek for genesis and trend without emotion (ibid., p. 189, n. 6):

> "What would be the scientific rating of the work of a botanist who should spend his energy in devising ways and means to neutralize the ecological variability of plants, or of a physiologist who conceived it the end of his scientific endeavors to rehabilitate the vermiform appendix or the pineal eye, or to denounce and penalize the imitative coloring of the Viceroy butterfly? What scientific interest would attach to the matter if Mr. Loeb, *e.g.*, should devote a few score pages to canvassing the moral responsibilities incurred by him in his parental relation to the parthenogenetically developed sea-urchin eggs?"

Nor does Karl Marx escape whipping, despite the fact that

in countless ways Veblen was indebted to him: for Veblen spared those close to him in thought, like Marx, no more than he did those close to him in life, like his teacher Clark or his student H. J. Davenport. Marx's labor theory of value, according to Veblen, was no more than a demand for the full product of labor projected onto external reality; the demand itself Veblen held to be understandable at a handicraft stage of technology, but simply nonsensical when the accomplishment of a given produce flowed from the co-ordinated effort of thousands of workers. And Marx's dialectical logic of development Veblen viewed as just one more pre-Darwinian, teleological scheme of thought ("The Socialist Economics of Karl Marx and his Followers: I," *The Place of Science*, pp. 436–7):

"The neo-Hegelian, romantic, Marxian standpoint was wholly personal, whereas the evolutionistic—it may be called Darwinian—standpoint is wholly impersonal. . . . The facts were construed to take such a course as could be established by an appeal to reason between intelligent and fair-minded men. . . . The romantic (Marxian) sequence of theory is essentially an intellectual sequence, and it is therefore of a teleological character. The logical trend of it can be argued out. That is to say, it tends to a goal. On the other hand, in the Darwinian scheme of thought, the continuity sought in and imputed to the facts is a continuity of cause and effect. . . . The sequence is controlled by nothing but the *vis a tergo* of brute causation, and is essentially mechanical. The neo-Hegelian Marxian scheme of development is drawn in the image of the struggling ambitious human spirit: that of Darwinian evolution is of the nature of a mechanical process."

HOW "NATURAL" CAN ONE GET?

Even economists of the German Historical School, to whom (particularly Sombart *) Veblen owed a great deal and with

* Arthur K. Davis' doctoral thesis on Veblen discusses his debt to Sombart in detail. Veblen's characterization of the "handicraft era,' his notions of the origins of capitalism, for instance the emphasis on accounting and credit, his theory of crisis (a point Davis does not make)—all seem to derive to some

whom he had a good deal of sympathy, were scrutinized by him with an almost obsessive eye for partisanship; thus, in reviewing Schmoller, he praised his use of data from anthropology and geography, his evolutionary framework, and his factuality—but only insofar as he dealt with the past, for in dealing with current matters Veblen felt Schmoller succumbed to sloppy chauvinism.

And yet, as we have seen in chapter two, Veblen's own approach was itself much cumbered with culture-bound assumptions about what is "natural." He could not of course be aware how ideological was his emphasis on biology, on strict Darwinian analogies: he had a sense for the metaphorical nature of other men's work but took his own to be entirely grounded in literal fact. What, moreover, are we to say about his cultural relativism when an essay of his on medieval Vikings is entitled "An Early Experiment in Trusts"—especially when we realize he is not merely satirizing the trusts by putting them in ancient dress but is at least partly convinced he is telling us something about the Vikings, too? Likewise, when he attacked advertising as waste— some of the most scathing sections of *Absentee Ownership* are devoted to the economic costs and cultural crudities of ads—he assumed that people would "naturally" know what they wanted. And his view that people wanted to be serviceable to others, and needed no supervision by absentee owners—but that, presumably, their direction by engineers would constitute no problem—rested on his assumption of an "instinct of workmanship" and the associated attitude of social solicitude. To be sure, Veblen thought that only the younger engineers were relatively exempt from the predatory animus of an earlier day; but this very faith in the young as such, which runs through much of his work, is a faith in the "natural," the unspoiled. That is to say, Veblen had a view of "natural" human nature, when undistorted by emulation, not too different from that of some of the optimistic hedonists and eighteenth-century theorists he scorned.

---

extent from Sombart, as well as from the English economic historians. Veblen, as noted, does not specify his indebtedness in his books; in his lectures he expressed sympathy for Karl Marx and praised Marshall for his sense of process. Like other radicals, he seems to have used L. H. Morgan's work.

Moreover, in *The Engineers and the Price System* Veblen himself takes the soap-box in advocating a soviet of technicians: a more far-reaching reform, it may be noted, than the meliorative proposals of his academic opponents. And he permits himself to speak of the "end" of mechanical technology (p. 132), the "purpose" of the engineers who are to run the economy after the revolution (p. 141), and the goal which the new industrial order is "designed" to bring about (p. 142).

THE MARGINAL UTILITY OF INSTITUTIONAL ECONOMICS

That Veblen thus committed the sins with which he charged other economists should enable us to take a calmer view both of the "received economics" and of Veblen's contribution to it. It was easy for Veblen, as for many critics of his stripe, to miss the point that Locke and others who talked the language of social contract and natural rights were not so naive as they might appear; they were appealing to an imagined earlier state of society as Veblen himself appealed to more or less mythical cross-cultural comparisons; their pre-history was his anthropology. Much has happened since Veblen's day to renew our resistance to his concept of "value-free" science, and the cultural relativism at which Veblen aimed is either thoughtlessly denounced or thoughtfully transcended. But all the more, therefore, it behooves those of us who criticize Veblen's concept of science to grasp its achievements, and to understand that without the emancipation from theocratic and pragmatic leading strings that he and his allies fought for, we would not be privileged to take a less intransigent and more pluralistic view of the role of values in economics and in social research generally.

In Veblen's day economists were what might be called emotional mercantilists. Just as the sociology of the late nineteenth century was linked with socialism on the one side and with social work on the other, so the economists, though many had gone over to laissez-faire in their politics, never doubted for a moment that they should be concerned with policy, with the national welfare and the proper role of the state. If they speculated about the nature of rights, or markets, or monopolies, they did so with a conscious eye on practicality; their aim, if not their theory in its details, was utilitarian. In this sense, the great English economists, from Adam Smith through Marshall to Colin Clark or Keynes, have been *political* economists, advisers of state even where they told the state to keep hands off, and concerned with the consequences for a moral citizenship of the processes of getting and spending.

This pragmatic or publicist bent is ironically striking in William Graham Sumner, the teacher above all others whom, as we have noted, Veblen admired. In his greatly influential *Folkways*, Sumner insisted on a disenchanted, relativist view of human conduct: men are irrational prisoners of custom, which is in turn the residue of magical solutions which once happened to "work"; might makes morality; reason operates in history at best as a modest "strain to consistency" among the inherited folkways and mores; nothing is more idiotic than for reformers to set themselves up, by state action or otherwise, to change the mores—for instance, the time-honored subordination of the Negro in the South. Sumner was a former minister, and in this vein which he pursued with high courage he belongs with the other former ministers or minister's sons (Harold D. Lasswell, W. I. Thomas, Samuel Butler—the list is endless) who, in emancipating themselves, sought to free the intellect from theocratic tutelage. But there was another side of Sumner, in which he was a publicist for laissez-faire, against tariffs, colonialism, and government paternalism whether on the side of business or labor, the strong or the weak. So, quite in contrast to his anti-reformist bent, he appealed to reason to defeat the reformers who would shackle the economy and make it less of a free-for-all. Indeed, it is hard to think of a remembered American economist of Sumner's day—whether Ely, or John Bates Clark, or Fetter—who was not political in the sense of having a program for the country.

There can be little doubt—hard as it is to trace "influences" —that Veblen's criticisms of these thinkers took effect. Today, those economists who remain in the classical traditions do not pretend to be engaged in describing the real world of business; rather, they are building models or paradigms for which they make more modest claims. Thus, they might set up a model of "perfect competition" while granting that no such system was ever realized even in the heyday of Manchester; it is at best an approximation. Or, if they develop a theory of games, this too is consciously a paradigm, not necessarily to be superimposed on any given economic order. Moreover, these economists no longer take rational, hedonistic behavior for granted; they may insist that rationality is required if the competitive model is to work but, like Frank Knight, they may be reconciled to what they regard as man's basic irrationality—they may be pessimists. Often, they try self-consciously to set forth their own value premises.

Nor can it be doubted that Veblen's view was one of the factors that led to a shift in legal thinking about rights during the last three or four decades. Well-educated lawyers today realize that rights are not pre-existent but are the creations of a given social order, and that legal problems are therefore problems of social engineering. Veblen, of course, was not the only one to say this; Holmes did, and the early Roscoe Pound, and many others. Yet the movement known as "sociological jurisprudence" in its early days and "legal realism" in the 20s and 30s included many men—Walton Hamilton, for instance—who were either students or devotees of Veblen.*

This is ironical, of course, for if engineers in Veblen's eyes stand at the apogee of matter-of-fact at-homeness in the modern world, lawyers share with bankers his metaphysical hell of natural-rights nonsense and occupational practice compounded of chains of paper-work wholly (as he loved to say) irrelevant, immaterial, and incompetent for the machine process. It is the lawyers, taught the limits of their discipline, who often distrust logical argument

---

* Commenting on this point, Professor Willard Hurst of the Wisconsin Law School observes that a number of lawyers influenced by Veblen have had their attention directed to the importance of the lawyer as a builder of corporate and governmental structure out of the intangibles of human relations—this, despite the fact that Veblen himself as we have seen underemphasized the significance of institutions and especially the place of legal paper-work in cementing society. This is of course only one of many ironies in the reception of Veblen in quarters where he himself would least have anticipated being heard.

and who have, as Holmes put it, "an eye for the jugular," whereas engineers can easily get embroiled in logic and word-play.

And yet in spite of all this, it seems to me to be an open question whether Veblen and his intellectual allies have done much more than enforce a greater semantic sophistication on economists, a greater tightness of assumptions. Perhaps departments of economics remain refuges for men of wildly rationalistic drives, for men who cannot bear disorder—or who, like Veblen himself, cannot bear waste. Perhaps thinkers such as von Hayek or the late Henry Simons have not been forced to make any fundamental concessions to Veblen or what he stood for in their search for the leverage which would enforce a laissez-faire economy on business, labor, the farmers, the officials, and all the other power-wielding groups that have restored mercantilism with a vengeance. At best, Veblen may have left his mark in the way many economists talk, in their wariness and defensiveness, and possibly in the fanaticism with which some of them cling to what they may deprecatingly refer to as their model-building entertainments.

Moreover, while professional economists today "believe" in culture, they have gone on making refinements in price theory; and macro-economics, the analysis of national income, while often the work of Veblen's disciples, has studied behavior only in gross, statistically, without much curiosity as to motives and cultural trends. Only in the theory of the firm has there been any considerable attention given to the detailed context of economic activity and decisions, with such questions being asked, for instance, as whether executives may not prefer a big company for the sake of prestige, a small company to escape responsibility, making their decisions concerning plant expansion or market tactics on these supposedly non-economic grounds. Those academic wanderers, the economic historians, have profited more from Veblen than have the professional economists and, so far as I know, are the only ones currently pursuing research on the basis of observation in a particular company. The breath of life for economists (as for lawyers) tends to remain "theory"—that is, the theories of other economists (or other lawyers).

Veblen, on the basis of his paper on "Economic Theory in the Calculable Future," would have been disappointed but not surprised at this: he would have laid it to the influence of the vested interests and the cultural predominance of pecuniary (price) rather than industrial or technological concerns. He may be right to a small degree; he could also argue that "theory" has a leisure-class ranking above the direct observation of behavior; but I think these are not the essential points. In my opinion, economics suffers less from its vices than from its virtues: as the social science with the greatest achievements to its credit—and price theory, whatever the limits on its universal applicability, is one of them—it has had little reason to listen to newer sciences such as anthropology and social psychology which have accomplished less. (*Pari passu*, something of the same sort is true of the law.)

Moreover, Veblen talked about the economics of the common man (as Holmes talked about the common law from the point of view of the "bad man"), but like many program makers who urge intellectuals to get close to "life," engaged in no research of his own on the subject. To do such research beyond reading newspapers and reports is inordinately difficult. Suppose one does observe a group, for example, of small-town bankers over a period of time to see whether they are in fact as stodgily grasping and unproductive a lot as Veblen thought them to be (I think myself one might find considerable industrial creativity in the group). The problem of typicality would still face the observer—and he would for a while have been away from "theory" and its often prestigeful and mayhap stimulating makers. I think such research greatly worth doing, but can hardly blame economists for leaving it to sociologists or to the economic historians. The personal model economists follow is still a theorist in the grand style, a Schumpeter, a Marshall, a Keynes, a Veblen, and not a field observer.*

Another way of putting all this would be to say that Veblen

---

* Observation of individual consumer decisions and their roots in mass psychology now being done under George Katona had to wait for the development of polling.

wanted *his* field, economics, to be the master-science, embracing business practice, technological development, anthropology, and pre-history. His criticisms of the "guild of theoretical economists" testify to his ambitions for them: no less than to understand social evolution in relation to technological change. Once rid of moralizing, of pragmatic concerns, of rationalistic formulae, he thought economics could embrace all these territories in which he was himself keenly interested. But today this sort of imperialism among the social sciences has passed to some extent out of the hands of economics into the congeries of the more "social" social sciences, such as sociology, anthropology, and social psychology. Few non-economists, however, are sufficiently familiar with the ramified and well-worked terraces of economic theory to feel confident in studying market behavior, credit practices, and other matters which involve some technical aspects. The anthropologist is likely to regard economic theory as he regards legal theory, either with an ego-bruising awe which keeps him at a safe distance, preoccupied with child-training customs or myths or social class, or with the same contempt with which Veblen himself finally regarded it, as "a web of excessively fine-spun technicalities" (from his review of Böhm-Bawerk). But Veblen had learned those technicalities and penetrated them to arrive at the assumptions behind them: if he did not study the behavior of businessmen on the hoof he at least studied that of economists in journal and congress assembled. His work and his program both remain as reminders to all social scientists of the possibilities of a science of economic behavior preoccupied with culture and with change, that is, in his terms, "evolutionary."

CREDITS AND CYCLES

Veblen's affiliations in the economic field were, as has been noted, chiefly with the historical school. Less directly, however, he worked in the vein of subjectivism opened up by the theorists of marginal utility. The latter had opposed the notion of economic value as created by human desires to the classicists' presumption that value expressed objective inputs of labor. Veblen took this conception and applied it to production as well as distribution. Capital, credit, interest, wages—all these lost under his touch their old substantiality, and came to be seen as transactions, creatures of fancy; as, in fact, a sort of modern black magic deposited in the midst of the workaday industrial world.

His starting point is to dissociate the categories of "credit" and "capital" from any ulterior material facts to which they might be presumed to refer. This is the subject of two chapters (5 and 6) in *The Theory of Business Enterprise*, published in 1904, and of two articles, "Credit and Prices" and "On the Nature of Capital," which appeared shortly thereafter. In severely logical argument, he expands the assertion that an equivalence between industrial and pecuniary data is simply a "putative phenomenon warily led out from a primordial metaphysical postulate"; whereas the facts of economic life show that, for instance, an expansion of credit can raise prices without bringing new goods into the market; or that corporation securities commonly have an aggregate value two or more times that of the firm's physical plant; or that money is often made by restricting production rather than increasing it, or with no effect on material production at all (as in speculation, corporate mergers, the pecuniary appreciation of property not active in production, etc.). The efforts of conventional economists to derive monopolistic profits from "entrepreneurial wages," or watered stock from "good will," are exposed in all their feebleness. The fact is, according to Veblen, that capital in modern times is chiefly corporate securities, and that these became wholly divorced from the physical plant, being "intangible assets"; what this class of capital represents are capitalized differential advantages held by the firm in question in relation to other firms, monopolistic privileges in the way of patents, tariffs, franchises, and advertising, and "corners" on scarce materials, which add nothing to the community's aggregate stock of means of production. Moreover, these immaterial assets propagate their kind, for by mixture with securities based on material assets, they widen the range of collateral available for credit extension, which is to say, for the creation of further intangible assets.

This brings us directly to Veblen's theory of depression. The gist of it was this: the typical corporation capitalizes not only the value of its physical plant, but also the value which the presumed future earning-capacity of its intangible assets seems to warrant; by this extensive borrowing, it commits itself to a future level of earnings which will enable it to pay its interest; any succeeding prosperity will induce further capitalization, so that, in effect, every corporation commits itself to a continuously expanding economy; but this is unreasonable, since the profits of one corporation must be (according to Veblen) at the expense of another, and since technical innovations will result in a lowered price level, render debts unpayable, and thus bring on general liquidation and contraction of values. So massive and rapid is technical innovation in a modern industrial economy that depression, rather than prosperity, is the normal state of affairs (*The Theory of Business Enterprise*, p. 234). From this dilemma there are for modern capitalism only two possible avenues of escape: first, "some form of wasteful expenditures, as, *e.g.*, a sustained war demand or the demand due to the increase of armaments, naval and military"; or second, "an elimination of that 'cutthroat' competition that keeps profits below the 'reasonable' level"—in other words, monopoly (*The Theory of Business Enterprise*, pp. 210–11, 255).

Leaving aside for the moment the validity of this theory, its many points of contact with the work of Keynes and Schumpeter are striking—all the more so because of the immense temperamental and ideological gap that separates Veblen from the spirited, successful versatility of the men from Cambridge and Vienna. Schumpeter, it is true, explicitly rejected the Veblenian thesis of a primacy of pecuniary over industrial processes in capitalist economies (review of Wesley Mitchell's *Business Cycles, Quarterly Journal of Economics*, November 1930). But he is close to Veblen in holding that industrial innovation in a capitalist economy inevitably entails depression. For the innovation is typically brought onto the market by a new firm, whose establishment is accompanied by a temporary inflation—succeeded, however, to the extent to which the new process surpasses processes in use, by a forced financial retrenchment or liquidation of the older firms; hence eventually a purgative series of dislocations.*

Cf., e.g., "The Decade of the Twenties," *American Economic Review Supplement*, Vol. 36, May 1946, pp. 1–10.

If Schumpeter is akin to the industrial side of Veblen's analysis of depression, the financial side of it coincides in many ways with Keynesian economics. Keynes, like Veblen, had no implicit faith in the normality of prosperity, and abandoning any assumed equivalence between supply (goods) and demand (money), he was more aware than Veblen that wasteful expenditures, through their indirect effects, could revive a whole economy (as a cultivated balletomane, he did not share Veblen's horror of waste—including public works). But while Keynes's orientation was to the inducement of new investment in order to carry forward essentially sound existing investments, Veblen wrote in one of his first economic pieces that "the trouble lies not primarily with the rate of profit on new investments, as indicated by the rate of interest on money seeking investment, but with the rate of profit on property already invested and capitalised in the past" ("The Overproduction Fallacy," *Essays in Our Changing Order*, p. 110). Also, Veblen paid much less attention than Keynes to the productive repercussions which unproductive expenditures might have; that is (as indicated in chapter three, pp. 88–91), Veblen treated credit expansion as merely inflationary, explicitly disregarding "the indirect effects of a speculative advance in the way of heightened intensity of application and fuller employment of the industrial plant" (*The Theory of Business Enterprise*, p. 112 n.).

These instances do not exhaust the ways in which Veblen anticipated modern tendencies in economic thought. Long before Berle and Means he spelled out the divorce of ownership from management which the corporation entails; * and he attempted a theoretical treatment of monopoly, and the accelerated advertising it involves ("product differentiation"), at a time when the popular outcry against trusts had not yet been accompanied by a more sophisticated approach among economists.

In spite of all this, Veblen's economics is definitely dated. He took the passing phase of financial domination over industry to

* Veblen's animus, however, was to show the idleness, the unproductiveness, of the absentee owner, and not, like Berle and Means, to analyze the latter's disenfranchisement.

be an advancing trend (here his Darwinism would seem to have played him false). He overemphasized, not perhaps the role of pecuniary considerations in capitalist economies, but the independence of industry from pecuniary operations such as the extension of credit; in this he may be contrasted with Schumpeter, who claimed that large-scale credit came into existence precisely to finance industrial innovation. Within Veblen's own lifetime, Carnegie and later Henry Ford were among those who showed the way—which Veblen took to be a sporadic exception, an unsuccessful mutant as it were—towards the self-financing of industry.

There are two likely explanations for these deficiencies in Veblen's economics. One is that around the turn of the century the investment banker came into sudden prominence all over the industrial world, and many besides Veblen—for instance, Rudolf Hilferding, the Marxist—were led to exaggerate the significance of this type. The other is that the limitations of Veblen's analysis are in many ways the limitations of a farm-based economics as suggested earlier in this chapter. But to say as I do here that Veblen as a practicing economist did not greatly succeed in transcending his time and place is only to say that he was human. I suggest that he be read today, less to ferret out specific "contributions" to the stream of economic thought, and more for the stance he maintained towards the economy and towards his fellow-economists. His belief in a mechanical logic of cause and effect, and the false predictions to which this kind of extrapolation led him, are no longer inspiring. But his belief that the industrial economy, especially in its American variant, was potentially enormously productive—this belief seems to have been among the inspirations of the New Deal, a prediction which his own statement helped make come "true."

"FULL PRODUCTION WITHOUT WAR"

This is the title of a book by Harold Loeb, one of the economists of the "younger generation" to whose sort Veblen was appealing in his testamentary essay on "Economic Theory in the Calculable Future." What Veblen wanted was an economics of production rather than distribution, dealing with tangible realities rather than pecuniary symbols. Towards such an economics he made very little tangible progress during his life, relying mostly on symbolic exhortation, but in some early essays we can find a fleeting attempt to distinguish between economic concepts valid only for capitalism, and concepts which would hold good in any industrial society (presumably including socialism). Thus, writing of Böhm-Bawerk, Veblen stated that while wages is a category specific to capitalism, "the laborer's income, or earnings, and social capital both are facts intrinsic and fundamental to any theory of industrial society" (*Essays in Our Changing Order*, p. 135), and again, that Böhm-Bawerk's theory concerning the "roundaboutness" of production was really a technological notion, applicable to industry in general, not a theory of capitalist business traffic ("Fisher's Rate of Interest," ibid., p. 138). Further, Veblen's discussion of the misuse of natural resources in *Absentee Ownership* can be seen as an anticipation of modern concern with tangible problems of conservation; or his crude attempts to estimate unused capacity, wasteful production, and the like, by round fraction, as an advance towards national income statistics.

This last point about unused capacity deserves a further word. Marx, like the optimistic Samuel Ure on whom he drew, had had a sense of the Promethean productivity of capitalism, a sense of its heroic possibilities for expansion. In a feudal society, with aristocratic values, the capitalist was a revolutionary: however gross his motives or phony his libertarian rationalizations of them, these motives sparked social change. Engineer and entrepreneur were necessary allies (as the studies of Bert Hoselitz, Robert K. Lamb, and other economic historians have shown), whatever tensions might arise between them in managing the enterprise and dividing the spoils. And this was true even in 18th-century America, with its planter power tied to seacoast merchant and shipowner hegemony. But in post-Civil War America, with the feudal class and the feudal values long since overthrown, it was understandable that engineers and production men would think they could get along without financiers—just as it was understandable that Populist farmers would think they could get along without the usurer. Since production did not always expand but often contracted, somebody had to be holding it back.

Frederick Taylor responded to this awareness in one way, Veblen in another. Taylor, like Robert Owen before him, hoped that both workers and managers would rise to the appeal of self-interest, once he could get his hands on a model (as he did at Midvale Steel and again at Bethlehem) and show what could be done. To all who would listen, he preached the gospel of scientific management; like Owen at New Lanark, he had some effect, but nothing like what he had hoped for—indeed, he was fired from Bethlehem, though he saved them much money, as victim of a shift of cliques and of a dislike on all sides for expertise. Veblen, less close than Owen and Taylor to factory experience, took the Marxist path of looking for a "contradiction," and thought he found it in isolating the pecuniary classes as the saboteurs of productivity—a view which led him to incite the engineers to revolution. As we know, this call had no success.

And yet it would go much too far to say that Veblen had a smaller influence than Taylor on America's current mammoth productivity. For by convincing many New Deal economists, and others as well, that America's industrial might was at least twice as great as the figures showed, he doubtless influenced the climate in which planners told Franklin Roosevelt that America could make 50,000 planes a year, and beyond that, the general optimism about the economy which spurred on those actually influencing its direction. For the thinking represented in such books as Harold Loeb's helped put pressure on businessmen to expand and, in a cumulative process, broke one after another of the bottlenecks that consequently appeared. It doesn't perhaps matter very much whether this was the doing of engineers—it was, at least as often, the doing of lawyers, bankers, civil servants, and other non-experts—nor even whether it was the result only of war and preparation for war—it was also, to an as yet indeterminate extent, the result of a radically enlarged set of wants in the population at large. Veblen, though he feared America's capacity to consume, had faith in the country's capacity to produce and, by criticizing a performance which seemed to most the acme of possibility, led people to look for the sources of the lag, leak and friction that kept performance down.

Having myself seen something of American industry at its most allegedly efficient, I feel that it operates—like most of us as individuals—at about 30% of par. Our productivity, such as it is, often results from workmanlike inventions (frequently organizational rather than mechanical or technological ones) to circumvent our inefficiency and our lack of the instinct of workmanship. It would perhaps not be too farfetched to hold that, since such inventions often go beyond the mark aimed at, the sabotage and incompetence that stimulates them amount, in an irony Veblen would have enjoyed, to our secret weapon! However, the climate for nurturing and applying these inventions may again be changing, and there are some who think that the "let George do it" philosophy has spread so far that production is itself threatened by the political and psychological emphasis on distribution and consumption. Still, having seen how even Veblen's optimism about what a soviet of technicians could produce fell far short of what the War Production Board in the second World War actually did, it would seem the part of wisdom to say of the national income that we ain't seen nothing yet!

In any case, it may be that the "Veblenian diversion" in economics will have its greatest impact on the emerging theory of economic development. It is fascinating to notice how, in dealing with problems of Egypt or India, unimpeachably orthodox economists slough off financial categories, as in speaking of "saving" as unused physical resources or of "profit" as a physical ratio of consumption yield to invested manpower and materials. Likewise, in the attention paid to social costs a Veblenian emphasis on cumulative change and interrelatedness is evident. It would be a fitting triumph for the shambling immigrant's son if his guerilla warfare with the guild of economists, largely unsuccessful along the Hudson and Potomac, could help bring "fullness of life" to the banks of the Ganges and the Nile. His often (as he would have wished) invisible spirit marches on when such questions are raised.

CHAPTER EIGHT

LEISURE AND URBAN PASTORAL

One way of getting an idea ot our fellow-countrymen's miseries is to go and look at their pleasures.

George Eliot, *Felix Holt the Radical*

"ALL WASTEFULNESS is offensive to native taste." So Veblen declares in *The Theory of the Leisure Class* (p. 176). Against the fashions and furbelows of the Gilded Age, he sought to oppose a picture of primitive society extrapolated from the work of Tylor, Frazer, Boas, and other students. In this society, men did not (wastefully) file their teeth nor scarify their cheeks nor ornament their tools beyond functional need! Close to the soil, given over wholly to the arts of peace, making no distinction among persons or between the sexes, Veblen's "ignoble savages" give him an anthropological norm with which to criticize the "artificiality" of later cultures. Just as men for fifteen hundred years have been seasonally open to the model of the early "primitive" Christians, leading to periodic reformation movements, so, too, since at least the days of Montaigne men have recurrently felt their customs to be artificial and have sought to restore the purity of some "natural" mode. Veblen's critique of conspicuous consumption, along with other more directly moralistic attacks on late-Victorian extravagance, has had, it seems to me, a reforming impact on our middle-class culture. Save in Texas, which is for all impractical purposes not a part of the Union, the crazy millionaire is dead, and a subdued nonconspicuousness seems to be spreading over our leisure and consumption practices. Were Veblen alive today, I think he would be surprised at the impact views such as his have had on the educated rich themselves, for whom many of his phrases have been translated into what is virtually a set of sumptuary laws.

When published, as well as now, it has been customary to read *The Theory of the Leisure Class* as a programmatic book, a barely disguised frontal attack on late-19th-century extravagance. Thus, Dorfman points out that Howells, who gave it a sympathetic send-off in *Literature*, enjoyed it as a critique of "those other fellows," the aristocrats and parvenus against whom he was then directing his own novelistic bills of complaint. And, as I have just indicated, some of the rich, feeling themselves under pressure from many sides, took the book as its slogans filtered down into the popular conscience, as an agenda of what not to do. Indeed, such phrases as "conspicuous consumption" or "invidious distinction" are today so current in our talk, that for many readers the book has lost power to clarify the contemporary scene. I would like to send readers back to it with renewed interest, looking less for the low-down on the rich than for a mode of analysis of the mixed motives of consumer behavior. For the book needs to be read, not as a critique of how the rich act (though that is one aspect) but as a theory of how society acts. For in Veblen's view, hardly any American is so poor and benighted as to escape participation in the leisure class in his mode of life as well as in his dreams.

THE NATURAL HISTORY OF THE CORSET

Let us take, as an illustration, Veblen's brilliant analysis of the function of the corset as a device by which men display the unsuitability for menial work of their dependent wives. The very point of the corset, Veblen insists, is its discomfort: women prove, by donning this pecuniary casing, that they belong to a man (else they would not submit) and that he can afford their idleness. If *he* were to wear a corset, or dress with analogous restraint, he would be thought effeminate: as the superior sex, men prove their pecuniary capacity vicariously, without self-imposed suffering. But of course, menservants, like women, must wear outlandish and uncomfortable garb as proof of their master's prowess, and likewise priests must don vestments of corset-like power to incapacitate, as testimony to their service to a heavenly master rich and powerful enough to afford such chastised acolytes.

How, then, Veblen asks, are we to explain the corset-free classes of society? That he asks such a question shows his grasp of the "method of exception" in social science, the exceptional case being used, not to disprove but to refine and restate the rule. Veblen's reply disposes easily of the indigent groups where the corset is worn for holidays only: here women have to work too hard to afford the diurnal pretense of corseting. The real problem is presented by those wealthy classes which during Veblen's lifetime had emancipated themselves from the corset; he explains matters as follows (pp. 184–5):

> This rule [the corset's indispensability to "a socially blameless standing"] held so long as there still was no large class of people wealthy enough to be above the imputation of any necessity for manual labour and at the same time large enough to form a self-sufficient, isolated social body whose mass would afford a foundation for special rules of conduct within the class, enforced by the current opinion of the class alone. But now there has grown up a large enough leisure class possessed of such wealth that any aspersion on the score of enforced manual employment would be idle and harmless calumny; and the corset has therefore in large measure fallen into disuse within this class.

Veblen adds that women who have risen rapidly in the pecuniary scale tend to carry the plebeian canon of the corset, as a vulgar snobbery, along with them. For similar reasons, the less advanced industrial countries still fasten the corset on their small wealthy class. Thus the cross-cultural and cross-class trail of the corset serves Veblen as a kind of test for ascertaining the size and security of a country's leisure class. And his suggestion that the American upper strata have become sufficiently sizeable, and well interconnected through communication channels, to develop their own standards (not simply as counterpoint to the humbler masses) seems to me to provide a fundamental clew to the spread of the blue-jeans style throughout what Veblen would consider the reputable classes today.

Indeed, elsewhere in the book he observes that the very rich have recently gone in for "nature" in a big way, and for "crudely serviceable" contrivances as against ostentatiously expensive and discommodious ones. Much of this is fake, he argues, as in the rustic fences and expensively-bred cows that decorate many estates with a veneer of usefulness over a base of luxurious extravagance. But he is acutely aware that there is a divergence of taste between the upper strata and their more plebeian imitators in this respect; as he writes (pp. 136–7):

> To-day a divergence in ideals is beginning to be apparent. The portion of the leisure class that has been consistently exempt from work and from pecuniary cares for a generation or more is now large enough to form and sustain an opinion in matters of taste. Increased mobility of the members has also added to the facility with which a "social confirmation" can be attained within the class. Within this select class the exemption from thrift is a matter so commonplace as to have lost much of its utility as a basis of pecuniary decency. Therefore the latter-day upper-class canons of taste do not so consistently insist on an unremitting demonstration of expensiveness and a strict exclusion of the appearance of thrift. So, a predilection for the rustic and the "natural" in parks and grounds makes its appearance on these higher social and intellectual levels. This predilection is in large part an outcropping of the instinct of workmanship. . . .

This and similar passages (e.g., p. 140, pp. 186–7) are to be taken into account before *The Theory of the Leisure Class* is considered a dated memento of the 90s, for this kind of analysis of the mixed motives underlying class-based styles of life is as applicable now as then.

An excellent case in point is provided by developments in gardening among the English upper classes. The "tasteful" gardener of today avoids like the plague the nurseryman's plebeian creation of large, showy double blossoms, and instead cultivates the "cottage" flavor, the inconspicuous rock plant, the difficult bog flower. The high priests of good taste, like the Sitwells, prefer to find their pet plants in some forgotten village garden rather than in the hybridist's greenhouse, and take great pride in the austerities of the scree, where a maximum of labor is demanded for a minimal return of color.

Veblen's theory, then, sees the vulgar impressed by show, the "better element" by a conspicuous abstention from show in which hints to one's ability to withstand pecuniary competition are calculatingly scattered. That is, Veblen regards all consumption—and leisure behavior in general—as determined mainly by the desire to impress others, and only secondarily by the desire for sustenance, comfort, or thrift; in either case, the behavior is "economic" and individuals are the passive puppets, the corseted victims, of economic processes which they neither control nor comprehend. Veblen's theory leaves individuals no freedom to withdraw from the unceasing chase for pecuniary reputability, nor does he make room for consumer behavior which is whimsical and idiosyncratic, governed neither by the need for sustenance or the need for show. And this theory fitted not too badly an American scene in which millions of people, leaders and led alike, strove eagerly to absorb one fashion uglier than the last in an endless, fundamentally unmerry potlatch. The mother in the *Middletown* of the 20s who tells the interviewer that she cannot send her daughter to high school because she cannot give her silk stockings is simply a late testimonial to the cruelty of this game; a whole series of novels from *The Great Gatsby* to *Point of No Return* is another.

FROM BLUE-STOCKING TO BLUE-JEAN

Even in Veblen's day, however, there were gathered around the Unitarians in New England and the Quakers in Philadelphia groups less dominated by conspicuous consumption than New York and Midwest millionaires and their imitators. The Bostonians whom Henry James described in his novel of that name were not only plain of dress and sparing of display but also violated Veblen's rule (set forth in chapter 8 of *The Theory of the Leisure Class*) that the well-to-do are conservative forces in society, which he believed to be true not only because of their vested interests but also because of their sheltered removal from the dynamism of industry. To be sure, Veblen admitted that these sheltered ones, by virtue of their isolation, occasionally took part in philanthropic and uplift movements, but he thought that such amiable want of fraud and force would quickly eliminate them and their descendants from the leisure class in favor of more rapacious *nouveaux arrivés*. What he failed to see is that the *nouveaux* would allow themselves to be tutored by these same gentle mutants, and that, over time, the upper social strata would remain in the vanguard of the "modern" movements in art, culture, and politics. Indeed, reform in America owes much to those who are theoretically most sheltered of all—the leisure-class women—just as it is the women in *The Bostonians* who are the progenitors of change.

One reason for this may be that these women have time to read, and some freedom to agitate to bring the world closer to the heart's desire. The very accusation Veblen makes, that they are over-sheltered, has led thousands of young ladies of gentle birth to seek to "unshelter" themselves by cross-class adventures of one sort or another, from social work to anthropology to marrying Negroes to joining the Communist Party. For educated men and women, the blue-jeans uniform may symbolize a desire, not only to see as a tourist how the other half lives but to share that way of life in some fashion—often as their version of urban pastoral.*

It is this role of ideology, acting upon individuals *within* a class rather than upon classes as such, that Veblen, like Marx before him, disregarded. Marx believed that if the proletariat were brought into consciousness of their "actual" condition, they would unite to overthrow the bourgeoisie; he failed to foresee that they

---

* Even this "modern" development can be traced back to the 90s. Professor Richard Hofstadter has called my attention to a remarkable lecture by Jane Addams: "The Subjective Necessity for Social Settlements." Urban sociology, which gave people a good excuse for venturing into the slums, dates from this same period.

were in fact to be brought into consciousness of the Marxist press and parties, and that these parties and their ideology would constitute their "actual life-conditions." Similarly, Veblen believed that if men were brought into physical contact with modern machine industry they would increasingly tire of leisure-class posturings and pastimes; they would come to lead a natural, nononsense life. He failed to foresee that many individuals in the better educated strata would be brought into contact with Veblenism, and would learn from him a critique of their consumption which would in turn become part of their conditioning.

When my students in the College at the University of Chicago read *The Theory of the Leisure Class*, they are anything but shocked at its unmasking of bourgeois styles of life; rather, they act as if they had always known that. Several years ago, they insisted with vocal unanimity that nobody bought a Cadillac for any reason save show; the idea that a Cadillac might be comfortble or pleasant to drive they hooted down as a rationalization. (So widespread has this attitude become that the Cadillac Company is worried about it from the point of view of sales and is trying in current advertising to play down the note of conspicuousness—something the car itself, in some models hardly distinguishable from an Oldsmobile or Pontiac, already does.) So thoroughly are these students and others like them at some of our universities indoctrinated with Veblenism that they cannot allow themselves much pleasure of variation in dress: the blue-jeans garb accompanies them not only to class but to their evening folk-dancing dates—there was actually a strike at one girls' dorm when an attempt was made to enforce a rule that dresses be worn to dinner. Perhaps in this sense, some preliterate tribes who can vary their garb by donning masks and costumes for feasts and rites are better off than we are.

Of course, I do not mean to suggest that the new canon of Veblenism lacks liberating features—or that it is permanent: even now, there is rebellion in many places against the de rigeur drabness of blue-jeans, though at present it is hard to detect any rebellion of consequence against the "law of diminishing consumption" as a family gets thoroughly accustomed to wealth.* Undoubtedly, dress is now more comfortable and in that sense more workmanlike for both men and women, and there is somewhat more freedom of movement between class lines—the *Middletown* sort of tragedy is rarer today. At the same time, we must not overlook the new constrictions that non-conspicuous nonconsumption brings in its train, in making individuals afraid of the very consumer displays for which they would once have sold their souls: the fear of being envied has for many replaced the fear of envying others. And there is the further constriction that many educated people now tend to examine all their purchases from a *Consumers' Research* point of view, seeking not only to eliminate waste and the influence of advertising, but also to eliminate all peacock-like motives in their own behavior: Veblen, like Freud, provides an arsenal of self-criticism which is relentless. In sum, spontaneity can be lost quite as much from fear that one is showing a leisure-class motive as from fear of failure in reputability in the older mode. And this fact is further evidence of the ideological and individualistic influences on consumption intertwined with the more blatantly economic and invidious ones that Veblen stressed.

Indeed, when I observe women on the beach or in the backyard suffering from sun, sand, and insects in order to become appropriately tanned, I sometimes wonder whether the management of corsets was more uncomfortable than that of bare skin now. The cult of nature, as Veblen partly realized, is itself an artifice, and can be a very strenuous one. Moreover, the cult of the suntan can serve to remind us that Veblen left entirely out of

* In a wise and witty article, "Veblen Revised in the Light of Counter-Snobbery," Robert L. Steiner and Joseph Weiss make the excellent point that an old, somewhat impoverished elite defends itself against the parvenu by "inverse exhibitionism"; the parvenu, who has just attained the wherewithal for exuberant display, can scarcely inhibit his long-held yearnings for show in spite of the disapproval of his new associates: it takes him a while to learn to control himself in accordance with the snobbery of anti-snobbery. However, the authors anticipate, just as I do, that as millions become accustomed to such restraint, new elite mores will emerge to mock the now widely distributed fashion of "plainery." The current highbrow revolt against functionalism in architecture and decor may be an illustration. See *Journal of Aesthetics & Art Criticism,* vol. 9, pp. 263–268 (1951).

account the role of sexuality as consumption and in consumption. While he places great and justifiable stress on the use of women as display-objects for men, he does not recognize that women's dress also symbolizes the prevalent attitudes towards female sexuality. For instance, the present off-the-shoulder fashion for women, in constricting their arm movements, symbolizes a partial defeat of feminism and a pose reminiscent of Veblen's day, of sexual dependence and helplessness in women. But also it symbolizes their sexual availability so openly as to be aggressive.

To be sure, once a fashion is set it will be accepted, often reluctantly, by women for whom it does not have these meanings; or it may sometimes be resisted—a possibility Veblen ignored— by those whose fashion it is to be out of fashion, or who try to develop an idiosyncratic, unchanging personal style. But in any case it seems clear that we cannot explain the tides of fashion, as Veblen sought to do, as a continuously self-defeating search for workmanlike, unfutile expenditure—a search which, after a time, sees the hollowness of the prevailing fashion and is ready to trade it for another which lays claim (until it is in turn unmasked) to greater beauty, comfort, and serviceability.

For one thing, Veblen, though purporting to make an economic study of leisure, left largely out of account the role of the leisure industries as economic factors in the swings of fashion, as well as in the total productive process—perhaps because he regarded this role as entirely a wasteful and inhibiting one. The possibility that the industries and services catering to leisure would one day be scanned hopefully for the signs of a new product to throw into a Keynesian multiplier as a pump-primer of capital goods expenditure never occurred to him—and who, indeed, could have foreseen the abundance with which America would be showered in the 20th century? The role of the radio, the pleasure car, television, the movies, the beauty parlor in sustaining American income levels has still not been fully grasped, although the Australian economist, Colin Clark, has helped to clarify the place of the "tertiary" or service industries in an advanced economy.

Neither did Veblen foresee that the tiny groups which in the 90s had already turned away from conspicuous consumption to form less avaricious standards would expand into the millions in the following decades. What has happened is that values once confined to a small elite group, or to an elite place within the hearts of many—a kind of Sunday rather than weekday place—have now spread much more widely. Indeed, the race for consumption goods has in part become devalued because "everyone" can get into the act—as the result of the lowering of hours and the rise in real income levels—and hence the tensions and compulsions of gentility may become relaxed. Still, there are certain circles in America where one cannot buy a TV set without being regarded as vulgar, just as there are other circles where the TV set, or some equivalent, serves as a compensation for substandard housing or other inadequacy—much as drink was used among depressed workers in an earlier day. Thus, it would go much too far to say that consumption has lost the symbolic meanings Veblen found in it; these still exist along with other meanings.

One of these latter-day meanings is the increasing need or desire of people in the upper strata to put on display not so much their purchased possessions as their more subtle qualities of "personality" and taste. When I see how psychologically unprotected some people are in modern, sparely-furnished, glass-enclosed homes, I look back on the 19th-century type of fetichism of commodities almost as something of an idyll. As one mansion after another built by our Captains of Industry is torn down or converted into a Catholic college, one may even come to admire the social energies, cruel as these often were in their consequences, that the Captains and their wives exhibited.

FUNCTIONALISM: THE HIGHER PURITANISM

All in all, I think we must conclude that puritanical asceticism, though it has greatly changed its forms, is by no means dead in America. Louis Schneider in his book on Veblen assumes that *The Theory of the Leisure Class* comes out of a post-Calvinist stage in American life, when consumption was no longer restrained by religious motives or by the needs of capital accumulation. In fact, it is surprising that Veblen pays no attention to accumulation but pictures the country as engaged on a consumer binge, with the sky the limit; throughout his writings he disregards savings—for one thing, his view of the illimitable if shady resources of credit and inflation led him to overlook the continuing need for private accumulation. For another, it may be that he felt himself too much a prophet in the wilderness and failed to realize that his own asceticism, disguised as a theory of leisure, would strike responsive chords.

One reason, perhaps, why Veblen felt so utterly out of step is that his thriftiness had peasant roots rather than burgher ones. Unlike the American Puritans who wasted the country's resources while accumulating their own fortunes, he was emancipated from blue-nose moralities and opposed enjoyment only where it was tinctured with exploit and exploitation. It did not occur to him that his own peasant distrust of landholder and city-bred pomp and waste would ever have any relation to the Scotch-Irish Jeffersonian and New England Puritan sources of American asceticism. Yet even the urbanized spendthrift generations from the close of the Civil War to the racoon-coated era of the 1920s did not succeed in extirpating these ingrained attitudes. For instance, when rationing was imposed during World War II, many pronouncements welcomed it, not as a temporary and unpleasant expedient, but as independently desirable: now Americans can be lean and spare again, it was said. Moreover, the reduction of all Americans to a single level of consumption struck many as a good thing: it appeared that all sorts of middle-class guilts were assuaged by mild consumption hardships. Especially as the rationing process did not impair the vogue of hygienic feeding that marked the newer asceticism for many who brought *Consumers' Research* into the kitchen—and Thoreau into camp—and had thus already begun to ration themselves before the War broke out. Unlike Bellamy, who wanted his utopians freely to exercise the arts of consumption choice (though his books show them as practiced within highly genteel limits), Veblen would have had no objection and every reason to welcome a regimen of leisure free of all extravagance, whimsicality, and superfluity.

Even those high-income people, however, who buy, not with an eye on the Joneses but rather with a Veblenian ascetic eye on their own motivations, let themselves go when they are selflessly acting as purchasing agents for their children, and much of American abundance has found its way into the stockings of the young. When I noticed on the financial pages recently that the Lionel Corporation, makers of toy trains, had had sales of more than $12,000,000 in the first six months of 1951, up more than sixfold in a decade, I speculated on what Veblen might have made of this. Very likely, he would have suspected that the growing extravagance of children's toys was an effort to make up for the fact that women today, with servants quite scarce, have to do their own housework and so serve less well as jewel-trays and clothes-horses than in an earlier day—the trains would not only take the place of paid supervision but be a sign of parents' emulative zeal to overtake and surpass one another. Nor would Veblen fail to notice the waste of metals in a time of world stringency, and of the incidental training of the children themselves in emulation and waste. Yet, on the other hand, Veblen might think it a favorable omen that children are playing, not with knights in armor or with fairies or other debilitating archaisms, but with mechanical and electrical realities—useful for indoctrination in the cold, matter-of-fact impersonality of the machine process. But then underneath this, Veblen might find an archaic note, in that trains may be booming as toys just when they are losing their primacy as transport to buses and trucks. And he would ask whether the trains are anthropomorphically conceived (as such children's fare as *Tootle the Engine* might indicate), or in the light of a magical penumbra surrounding the structural toy-materials, rather than with the brutal opacity of science—or, again, whether they are regarded with the snobbery and antiquarianism of Lucius Beebe and other railroad "bugs" whose fondness for trains harks back to the obsolete steam engine and the gaudy elegance of early Pullman cars.

According to report, Veblen's own stepchildren were not allowed any such nostalgias and yearnings. Even before their teens, they were accustomed to criticize conspicuous expenditures, and would walk down Fifth Avenue making caustic comments on the frivolities displayed in the shopwindows. Other parents are said to have pitied these girls, precociously deprived of the fiery joys of possession and aspiration. But today one can find many such children in the educated strata, who are knowing critics of advertising before they are ten and who early learn to look with abhorrence on all non-functional consumption, from lipstick to cupolas. The more prestigeful girls' preparatory and finishing schools are frequently spare and ascetic in their appointments; where uniforms are worn, they are without elegance.

Indeed, I should speak for myself here. When I was in college in the late 20s, President Lowell of Harvard announced the famous Harkness House Plan and put the tradition-minded Boston architectural firm of Coolidge, Shepley, Bulfinch, and Abbott to designing large new buildings that would harmonize with Harvard Georgian. My friends and I on the college paper violently attacked these plans from the standpoint of a Veblenian functionalism, observing for instance how chimneys were put up for show which contained no flues and how windows were spaced to meet pseudo-Georgian canons rather than student needs. Veblen's own text on this issue, though based more on Yale or Chicago Gothic than Harvard Georgian, is worth quoting (*Theory of the Leisure Class*, p. 349):

> The diversion of expenditure to honorific waste in such cases is not uncommon enough to cause surprise or even to raise a smile. An appreciable share of the funds is spent in the construction of an edifice faced with some aesthetically objectionable but expensive stone, covered with grotesque and incongruous details, and designed, in its battlemented walls and turrets and its massive portals and strategic approaches, to suggest certain barbaric methods of warfare. The interior of the structure shows the same pervasive guidance of the canons of conspicuous waste and predatory exploit. The windows, for instance, to go no farther into detail, are placed with a view to impress their pecuniary excellence upon the chance beholder from the outside, rather than with a view to effectiveness for their ostensible end in the convenience or comfort of the beneficiaries within; and the detail of

interior arrangement is required to conform itself as best it may to this alien but imperious requirement of pecuniary beauty.

President Lowell won a pretty easy victory over the young functionalists of the Harvard *Crimson*. But in the course of it he revealed to me a strategy even more self-conscious than the picture here given by Veblen. He wanted to surround young Harvard men with luxurious buildings and appointments in order to make them discontented with less luxurious surroundings later on. They would then, to recapture their undergraduate publicly-provided extravagances, privately proceed to make a lot of money and to get themselves into positions of influence; some of that money and influence would then redound to the further glory of Harvard. A Captain of Erudition, indeed!

However, so far as I know, this was about the last victory of so blatantly leisure-class a complex of motives frozen into architecture: Harvard has since gone "functional." But what we, like many young functionalists, failed to appreciate was that buildings did not design themselves from the inside out, as Veblen thought society and architecture alike could design themselves from the inside out. Functionalism is an aesthetic, too, as Veblen's quoted strictures (at odds with his self-proclaimed aesthetic impartiality) on "aesthetically objectionable . . . stone, covered with grotesque and incongruous details" reveal by negation. It is an aesthetic no less ideological than Lowell's and often no less contemptuous of the comforts (in the larger sense) of the "beneficiaries within," as anyone knows who has observed the ascetic dictatorship many modern architects exercise over their clients. In regarding a house as a "machine for living," a phrase Veblen would have admired, living itself is often made more mechanical and impersonal than liveable. Today, of course, the best architects fully realize this, and "modern design" is no longer synonymous with an expensive and artful lack of art.

Louis Sullivan and Frank Lloyd Wright, with their hatred of architectural cant, make-believe, and European vogues, might have been disciples of *The Theory of the Leisure Class* in their preachments, though of course in their often baroque design they were "originals." However, the fact that functional architecture and design became the "international" style is evidence, if any were needed, that the tendencies we are discussing are much wider and broader than any single book. Very likely, Veblen's step-daughters would have fitted in not too badly with the *Wander-vogel* movement on the Continent, with its contempt for whatever was stamped as bourgeois. Still *The Theory of the Leisure Class* was one of the American books which in this country largely took the place occupied in Europe by anti-bourgeois tendencies originating, from one side, in artistocratic disdain and, from the other, in socialist resentment. That is, we have Veblen in part to thank for the fact that the country which, in the 90s and on through to the Great Depression, was the stronghold of middle-class complacency should turn so quickly and energetically to the extirpation of these once-dominant mores without undergoing either an elite revolution from on top or a labor revolution from below.

Today, if we want to find the old splendiferous joy in conspicuous consumption, we do best to travel to South America or Spain or maybe Lyons, where the blue-jeans revolution has not yet set in.

But indeed, we do not need to leave the country: it is sufficient to go into any social strata of American life, for instance of newly-urbanized Negroes or newly-affluent factory workers, where underprivilege has been financially greatly and rapidly assuaged. In *The Theory of the Leisure Class*, Veblen had some pungent things to say about the effort on the part of social workers to compel the depressed classes to adopt standards of gentility; as he declared (pp. 344–5):

For instance, many of the efforts now in reputable vogue for the amelioration of the indigent population of large cities are of the nature, in great part, of a mission of culture. It is by this means sought to accelerate the rate of speed at which given elements of the upper-class culture find acceptance in the everyday scheme of life of the lower classes. . . . The propaganda of culture is in great part an inculcation of new tastes, or rather of a new schedule of proprieties, which have been adapted to the upper-class scheme of life under the guidance of the leisure-class formulation of the principles of status and pecuniary decency. This new schedule of proprieties is intruded into the lower-class scheme of life from the code elaborated by an element of the population whose life lies outside the industrial process; and this intrusive schedule can scarcely be expected to fit the exigencies of life for these lower classes more adequately than the schedule already in vogue among them, and especially not more adequately than the schedule which they are themselves working out under the stress of modern industrial life.

There is not only wonderful fun here but also a very just appraisal of the unconscious motives and consequences of settlement house work in a day when sociology and social work alike were pre-occupied with acculturation of the poor to the rich rather than, as today, the other way round. But certainly Veblen's assumption that without such class-biased tutelage the workingmen would evolve an economical, sensible, no-nonsense culture of their own is romantic: if a "standard of living" is not obtained from the intrusions of social workers, it will be obtained from the intrusions of advertisers, of mobile family members who have left the class, and of daydreams which, in a democracy, are an inalienable right: I am told workers prefer Poe to Whitman or Thoreau. Such dreams, in fact, can only be repressed by force: by the weight of a feudal culture or an utter deprivation of hope. And where, as in Europe, a "workers' culture" has evolved in conscious contempt for bourgeois forms, it has often meant little more than that workers have their own football, their own sensational press, their own *Volksopern*—sometimes in the most dismal and dated bourgeois taste. Veblen would have been glad to see the American working class, once given affluence, find its way without lag to a "natural" aesthetic, free of invidious elements. But that is asking too much of the oppressed—just as it is asking too much of women to expect they will not adopt all the occupational vagaries of men in their effort at emancipation. The working class has fallen heir to conspicuous consumption, which the leisure class is giving up. Aristocratic and Puritan upper strata have always disapproved of lower-class extravagance; Veblen has now furnished an additional reason for doing so, so that many of us object to Negro workers driving Cadillacs not because they should save their money but because they should spend it less gaudily. We are apt to disapprove of tenement television much as in Veblen's day we disapproved of tenement dirt and promiscuity. Neither Veblen nor his successors have suggested what else the lower strata might do with their money and time—surely, "the stress of modern industrial life" will not answer the question by itself. A better answer would require better private and social invention, and would surely not be the result of a reductionism which substitutes a propaganda of anti-culture for a propaganda of "culture."

Indeed, it seems today that the range of tolerance for clothes and other consumables is widening in the several social strata, as wealth spreads along with communication—a person who dresses as Veblen did at the turn of the century is not subjected to similar adverse criticism. Nor does a person suffer ostracism who lives as Veblen did. It is another question whether the range of tolerance for personality is wider now than then; in some respects it certainly is, but in other respects, as already indicated, our inability to hide behind our clothes and other consumption barriers makes it harder for us to protect our privacy. If Veblen were around now, his friends would almost certainly, with the best will in the world, urge him to consult a psychoanalyst. The consumption of therapeutic intangibles has become a way for academic people, already impecunious, to assure the avoidance of other forms of showier consumption. In such an atmosphere, Veblen would have more difficulty in remaining opaque to himself and others. And yet when we think how much suffering he underwent, and caused, we cannot unequivocally condemn the propaganda of adjustment to which contemporary eccentrics are exposed. Even less can we condemn therapy as an exercise in idle curiosity, a form of consumption not to be forced into the Veblenian canons of explanation.

DEATH OF A SALESMAN

To understand Veblen's influence on these matters of living and taste, we must remind ourselves that his books were an attack not only on spending, but on getting—that he saw the race for conspicuous consumption as supporting the race for acquisition. In fact, in a brilliant passage of *The Theory of the Leisure Class*, he suggested that the leisure class was an inhibiting force in society not only because of its exemption from industrial employments but also because its extravagances resulted in starving and impoverishing the lower classes so that these lacked the energy to conceive of change or carry it out. (In all this, he appears greatly to have exaggerated, in muckraker fashion, the actual consumption take of the wealthy, as against re-investment; as Justice Holmes observed in a famous defense of "waste," the rich man was himself merely a conduit for the social product and was often victimized by the illusion that he was important in his own right.) However, in seeing the Captain of Industry as the predatory successor to the barbarian chief and the feudal lord, Veblen limned the qualities needful for personal success as those that best conserved the archaic predatory traits—and, incidentally, took for granted a lineal connection between earlier ruling classes and the present-day middle or business class, when indeed history shows they have no such connection. Veblen declared that the less the individual has of "the gifts of good-nature, equity, and indiscriminate sympathy," the better off he is; conversely (*The Theory of the Leisure Class*, p. 223):

> Freedom from scruple, from sympathy, honesty and regard for life, may, within fairly wide limits, be said to further the success of the individual in the pecuniary culture.

The American businessman did not feel flattered to be portrayed as staunch in antique prowess and well equipped for survival by dolicho-blond heredity and selective Darwinian adaptation. Perhaps he feared he could not live up to this billing; it is significant that Brooks Adams, writing in the same years, was troubled precisely because he felt that businessmen were soft and sentimental, incompetent to defend and strengthen an imperial America. For him, as for Schumpeter later, America was more a nation of shopkeepers than a nation of tycoons.*

Certainly, the fact must be explained that American business leadership, with few exceptions, turned in the post-Civil War period to developing the mass market within the country and not to imperial adventure. Even today, it is the tough, labor-hating industrialists of the Midwest who are the most fiercely isolationist, quite willing to retire (behind tariff walls) from opportunities abroad. Likewise, whereas the salesman was for Veblen a prime example of a person given over entirely to chicane, it is indicative of the change in mores that salesmen are hard to recruit today. Increasingly, selling is built into an organization scheme, beginning with consumer research, going on through advertising, and ending in a self-service "sale," rather than being built into the characters and careers of energetic, egocentric, free-spending individuals. The play and film, "Death of a Salesman," may have been popular in part because its themes, insofar as they dealt with business and not father-son relations, were already interred with the Victorian age of enterprise. For one thing, the Arthur Miller drama is archaic in presenting the failure of failure rather than, as more avant-garde writing does, the failure of success. And when success is called into question, whether from a Christian basis or some other, then the American social pyramid itself is called into question—it is no longer a pyramid but a sphinx, an asker of questions rather than an answer to them, a touchstone of new values rather than a memorial to old and accepted ones springing, Veblen would say, out of the Barbarian past.

In one respect, at least, Veblen anticipated this development. In his essay on "Christian Morals and the Competitive Sys-

---

* In *Reflections on Violence*, written in 1906, Sorel was already angry with French businessmen for their softness, their willingness to arbitrate labor disputes, and their concern for the good will of the arbitrator and the public behind him. He wanted businessmen to be tough and virile because otherwise he feared labor itself would not develop the Spartan virtues. He seems to have thought American employers were less conciliatory, though today they are, if anything, more so than the French. In my judgment, Sorel had a keener eye than Veblen for the psychology of the businessman.

tem," he linked the early Christians with his imaginary primitives as governed by the two traits of humility (or abnegation) and brotherly love; these traits, which he regarded as going back to the earliest days of the race, survived among the lowly in the Christian era, gradually gaining power even over the high and mighty. Indeed Veblen's Christian, succoring and humble, belongs to his gamut of peaceable types which includes Pueblo Indians, early Icelandic democrats, captive women in all ages, and idly curious and colleaguially-minded savants.

Undoubtedly, such a Christian has a real historical existence, but it is noteworthy that Veblen completely leaves out any Calvinist traits, or any aspects of the Church Militant. This makes it possible for him to argue that Christianity can never be at home in the pecuniary culture but, beyond an anemic "fair play" and "thrifty charity" among absentee owners, is wholly at odds with the competitive system. Veblen concludes that since brotherly love has had thousands of years to become an indefeasible trait of human nature, whereas emulative ethics has had only a hundred and fifty, the future—barring an unlikely reversion to a regime of unadulterated status—must lie with "the ancient racial bias embodied in the Christian principle of brotherhood." *

What seems to be missing here is the very concept of "contamination of instincts" Veblen worked out in other writings. In his naive, quasi-Pavlovian view that the older learnings of the race will outlast the more recent ones, he does not face the possibility of a mixture of motives which might allow the pious, Protestant businessman to have his Christian cake and to eat his competitors—as Mr. Rockefeller did. In regarding business activity at the century's turn as almost purely exploit, with an occasional hypocritical bow to Christian moral trimmings, Veblen did

* It is interesting to see here how Veblen, in defense of his ideals of personality and culture, covertly "pulls rank" by insisting that his ideals are older and hence have more status than the ideals he is combatting. By locating his utopia in a fictitious instinctual base laid down in a quasi-mythological epoch, he retains his pose of detachment along with his avowed Darwinian belief in adaptation to existing conditions, and yet damns current ethics as nouveaux. (I have traced the way Freud similarly uses an imagined past to belittle the present in "Authority and Liberty in the Structure of Freud's Thought," *Psychiatry*, vol. 13, p. 167, 1950.)

not see that businessmen were moved not only by acquisitiveness for the sake of conspicuous display but by a sense—and more than a hortatory sense—of communal serviceability. In my opinion, much of American individualism and egoism has been big talk, not different in import from Veblen's protestations of cold scientific objectivity. In fact, Veblen was always taking other people at face value and asking not to be taken at face value himself.

The matter at issue (like other points dealt with in this chapter) is really one for close empirical study, of a sort we do not have, but my guess is that such a study would show that Christian morals in Veblen's sense had found more of a lodgment in the "pecuniary culture" than, in his hatred and fear of the latter, he was willing to grant. While the 19th century abounded in fabulous financial pirates such as Daniel Drew or Commodore Vanderbilt, we still have to look in Dickens or Balzac for our most perfect villains of pecuniary single-mindedness.

But the mention of a fictional "type" helps to make clear that Veblen should not be offhandedly criticized for "exaggeration." It is largely because, in his picture of the Captain of Industry or of Erudition, he created a type that we remember him: in stripping individuals of unessential features and connecting them with historic predecessors, he held up a magic mirror in which Christian gentlemen could "see" themselves as latter-day pirates substituting chicane for coercion; and in this there was sufficient truth to be clarifying. Had Veblen qualified his picture to include the various shadings we have been making here, his satire would have lost its point, as would a caricature that softened into a likeness. It is only today that Veblen's mirror has lost its magical qualities for those who, before looking into it, already suppose they are monsters— whose self-esteem may indeed partly come from the conviction that they are really tough, not given to a hypocritical pretense of virtue. It is for such people that the distorting quality of the mirror must be stressed, lest a glance in it confirm rather than challenge their complacencies. For Veblen's mirror was a decisive challenge to an age which, having conquered many of the tasks of the production frontier, was turning with energy and enthusiasm to the frontier of consumption; indeed, Veblen's realization of the importance of consumption and leisure—for their own sake and for their indirect bearing on production—showed his uncanny understanding of his country. To the very considerable extent that his country is still our country, what he had to say in *The Theory of the Leisure Class* remains applicable; to the extent that we are living in a new country, we must make new mirrors, new selections, though often based on his models of analysis, to help us understand it.

CONSPICUOUS PRODUCTION

One such selection based on Veblen's work would suggest that we are moving away from conspicuous consumption and towards conspicuous production. That is, as we become less individualistic and less wrapped up in personal display, we "socialize" our abundant wealth by corporate display. Corporations vie with each other to have modern factories, equipped with all manner of personnel services from masseurs to music by Muzak, and their advertisements increasingly sell, not the product, but the company's up-to-dateness in the arts of conspicuous production. The very men who would shrink from being salesmen themselves sublimate in the corporation their wish for esteem and push the company towards extravagances rationalized as necessary for good will—these can be afforded because the competition, which reads the same trade magazines and attends the same meetings, is competing in like extravagances and not in cheapening product cost (this would be termed "unfair" competition). And in their entertaining, corporate officials use the expense account as a rationalization for buying expensive dishes which might excite envy or comment if they were exhibiting their personal rather than their corporate ability to pay.

Conspicuous production as carried on by large organizations in the mid-twentieth century is not at all equivalent to the sabotage of production about which Veblen complained. For he was talking about the milking of industrial processes for the sake of building up private fortunes for private consumption, whereas conspicuous production is in that sense disinterested—indeed, the absentee owners are milked to build up the corporate fortunes for the sake of further and still more conspicuous expansion. In fact, it may not be simply coincidence that the reaction against conspicuous individual consumption has occurred at the same time that saved corporate wealth is no longer rapidly distributed to stockholders but is retained in depreciation funds or other concealment accounts as well as in labeled "reserves"—all this, of course, apart from the operation of the corporate and individual income tax. In what Peter Drucker terms the "employee society," these retained funds are saved or spent by managers, at the behest of the various publics who influence them; the employees at various levels share in the benefits and glories, tangible and otherwise. Hence, I cannot stress too much the way expansion itself or redesign of plants and tooling is today dictated by these subtle pressures for corporate prestige rather than because some operator hopes to make a market killing. But since these motives cannot be openly admitted, all these changes must be rationalized as cost-cutting or other sound business practice—but what else, Veblen might ask, are accountants for?

I do not mean to suggest that conspicuous production is an entirely new device. A brilliant book in the Veblen tradition by John A. Kouwenhoven, *Made in America*, shows how the factories and machine tools of the 19th century were almost invariably influenced by current "beaux arts" attitudes so that they were made more ornate and less "vernacular" than needful by considerations of taste and propriety. At the World's Fair at Philadelphia in 1876, for example, machines of simple, functional design were disregarded in favor of those with the proper curlicues and scroll-work. "Modern design," in fact, had first to become an ideology before we could alter our stylistic perceptions as to what was sound craftsmanship.

But these are the kinds of conspicuous production to which Veblen himself, with his awareness of how the leisure class set standards which made the functional seem vulgar, drew our attention; these tendencies hung together with Victorian attitudes towards the functions of the human body, or towards the metaphor of a piano leg. The new conspicuous production of our own day has somewhat different roots—less in archaic standards of genteel "good taste" than in the rise of the corporation as the channel for our more socialized allegiances. I myself am old-fashioned enough to prefer the older egotism of conspicuous consumption, which is individual and not always compulsory, to conspicuous production, in which individuals have a share only as members of a corporate group and are in fact bound to the group by what it does for them in this particular.

And this brings me back to the point made earlier, in connection with Veblen's *Imperial Germany*, that by far the most important conspicuous production is that of armaments, in which a jet bomber becomes a symbol of national emulative propensity —and here, indeed, the sky is the limit. Some years ago I suggested, with all the seriousness of satire, that the United States undertake to bring down the Soviet Union without war by an uninterrupted bombing of its people with consumer goods, from nylons to refrigerators, canned goods, and jeeps; I thought the Russians might bomb us back with caviar and furs and Stalin's collected works; and that in a race to apply the Keynesian multiplier in reverse the United States would surely be the winner and production in the Soviet Union entirely disrupted by too much plenty in the midst of want. I proposed that by turning our production to conspicuous account in this way we could take advantage of the Soviets in the area where we were still in the lead rather than waiting until, by Veblen's law, they had caught up with us and forced us to fight in the traditional military manner. And only in some such way, I am inclined to believe, will our production be used for the sake of consumption, at least by someone, and not for its own sake. For the "instinct of workmanship" still seems to be strong enough to make us want to spend eight hours a day at the factory or office, keeping ourselves busy in the rituals of conspicuous production.

CHAPTER NINE

CEDRO, HANNIBAL, AND DEARBORN

> Although Veblen was aloof, he was not isolated. Historians
> have emphasized his Norwegian inheritance, but Ole Rølvaag
> had a similar inheritance and was not flawed. The environment
> was more important—the Middle Border that produced in his
> generation Lester Ward and Frederick Turner, Vernon Par-
> rington and Charles Beard, Simon Patten and John R. Com-
> mons, and so many others who broke through the neat patterns
> of thought which the wise men of the East had designed for
> them.
>
> Henry Steele Commager, *The American Mind*

A T LEAST since the Romantic movement, the intellectuals of
all the Western world have been been prey to disaffection.
On the Continent, they have not lacked place and power,
but they have bemoaned the lack of stable class and symbolic
identifications or have leaped into factitious identifications with
"the workers" or "the State" or some similar abstraction. Everywhere, as an attempted banner of their own identity, they have
elaborated a stance towards the machine, sometimes to rhapsodize
but more commonly to denigrate. Occasionally, they have looked
beyond the machine to the processes of social organization, viewed
as machine-like—as in Max Weber's image of the West caught in
an "iron cage" of overrationality and overcontrol, to be coped
with only by stoic self-control. In the novels and aphorisms of
Kafka these cumulated attitudes received perhaps their most profound expression.

We may remind ourselves of these attitudes by reference to
what I regard as the most searching criticism that has been published on Veblen: T. W. Adorno's "Veblen's Attack on Culture,"

an article which makes the point that Veblen, for all his splenetic rage, was too much the prisoner of the norms of American culture, such as efficiency and hard-headed practicality, to render an adequate account of it. Adorno writes (*Studies in Philosophy and Social Science*, vol. 9, 1941, pp. 392, 401):

"As the mass production of identical goods and their monopolistic distribution advances and as the framework of highly industrialized life permits less and less the genuine individuation of a *hic et nunc*, the pretension of the *hic et nunc* to escape universal fungibility becomes more illusory. It is as if each thing's claim to be something special were mocking at a situation in which everyone and everything is incessantly subject to a perennial sameness. Veblen cannot stand this mockery. His rebellion actually lies in his obstinate insistence that this world present itself with that abstract sameness of its commodities which is prescribed by its economical and technological condition. . . . To him, the false castle [modern Gothic and Baroque] is nothing but a reversion. He knows nothing of its intrinsic modernity and visualizes the illusionary images of uniqueness in the era of mass production as mere vestiges instead of 'responses' to capitalistic mechanization which betrays something of the latter's essence." *

The wave of avant-garde pessimism about industrial (or "mass") society hit America late, and spottily. But, just as America had developed its own brand of economic interpretation of history prior to the importation of Marx—many of the Federalist papers are good examples—so a number of mid-19th-century observers such as Hawthorne, Thoreau, Melville, had found their

* These excerpts should of course not be taken as representing the total animus of the Adorno essay, with its intense and ramified scrutiny of *The Theory of the Leisure Class*. For instance, Adorno has a sense of the mindlessness implicit in Veblen's debunking attitude—Veblen blaming angels for the "industrially unproductive rehearsal" which occupies them is an example of his hatred for all mediation, whether that of the priest, the decorator, the trader, or at times even the thinker. Adorno relates this outlook to "the zealotry of Scandinavian Protestantism which does not tolerate any intermediary between God and inwardness."

way to a pessimistic and sardonic view of their society—indeed, of human society in general. By the end of the century the native stream, with roots in seaboard provincialism, frontier loneliness, and, often, more or less secularized Calvinistic strains, had merged with the older and richer Continental tradition of pessimism and disenchantment. The nineties were not gay for Brooks and Henry Adams, for O. W. Holmes, Jr. (in his public role), Mark Twain, Henry James, the "new" Howells, Veblen. (Note that I do not include here the reformers and the muckrakers—such writers as Lloyd and Bellamy: these people were not deeply disaffected: for them the world was real; it made sense, or could readily do so provided such and such were done; their very protest related them to what was going on.)

Some of these men, it is true, were not so much impatient with the Western world as a whole as with the figure cut in that world by the United States. Brooks Adams much of the time was angry with his country for being crass, not strong and brave: he despised commerce and admired war. Henry Adams wavered between being cross with his country for not making more prominent use of him and his cadre and being in despair about the world of the dynamo where, as Walter Lippmann later put it, translating Aeschylus, "Whirl is king, having driven out Zeus." Henry James wanted to see America more cultured and civilized, an attitude common to many sensitive expatriates whether or not they left home; at the same time, like Brooks Adams, he had small hope even for the commercial culture of Britain.

In comparison with these men whose disenchantment with the world or with America was sophisticated, there is something jejune about Veblen, as also about the only literary man of stature who recognized him, namely Howells. Howells and Veblen, like Mark Twain, were Midwesterners and, though each in his way was educated in the East and in close touch with its thought and values, they were never socially secure enough to afford the kind of ennui-pessimism of the Eastern patricians. As a result, it is not surprising that avant-garde literary fashion in our day has left them pretty much out of account. And with a certain justice, I think. It is hard not to be impatient with Mark Twain when we read his remark about Henry James' *The Bostonians* (when it appeared in the same *Century* magazine with *Huckleberry Finn*): he'd "rather be damned to John Bunyan's heaven than read that" —a remark more in keeping with Paul Bunyan's America than John's heaven. If Veblen ever read *The Bostonians*, in this writer's judgment one of the finest novels ever written about America, his biographers give no sign of it, but they speak of his liking the verse of Edward Carpenter. Though himself one of the few social scientists to become a master of literary craft, he was incapable of identifying himself with the literary world—a not uncommon experience of American writers then and since. When he read Ibsen we can be pretty sure it was for the great Norwegian's iconoclasm rather than for his dramatic art.

By the same token, however, Veblen, Twain, and Howells partially escaped those currents of attitude towards America that engulfed men and women whose tastes were formed on European standards. In fact Veblen, like Mark Twain, was something of a Philistine, but he was not so provincial as to judge his country from the eyes of a foreign capital. He did not want anything for America that he did not also want for Europe. By making himself at home (true, with all the discomforts of home) in the international field of economics, he avoided petty transatlantic arguments. In his erudition, he is more cosmopolitan than Mark Twain or Henry Ford, both men with whom I wish now to compare him.

VEBLEN AND MARK TWAIN

Veblen and Mark Twain have been linked in my own mind as men whose irony at once expressed and concealed a raging bitterness against all in the Gilded Age (Mark Twain's term) that was shoddy, effete, or pretentious. Both men grew less benign as they aged, and more willing to reveal their rancor. Both were instinctively on the side of the downtrodden—the Negroes, the ne'er-do-wells, the impious in the case of Mark Twain. Both viewed the Middle Ages in a similar Voltairean light, as a regimen of brutal lords and swindling priests. Indeed, *A Connecticut Yankee at King Arthur's Court* takes a view as rosy as Veblen's towards the machine process, and manifests as little nostalgia for the peasant and handicraft era. Both the *Connecticut Yankee* and *The Theory of the Leisure Class* have only ridicule for archaism, mystery and priestcraft: both are the books of freethinkers who keep hoping the better man, the matter-of-fact man with slide-rule, will win in the end. Bernard DeVoto writes (in *Mark Twain's America*, p. 274) that "The nineteenth century, which 'turns automata into men,' is vindicated and the Utopia of Mark's imagination is seen to be an affecting blend of Hannibal's small farms and the Colt's Arms culture of Hartford." Mark Twain urges the oppressed to take matters into their own hands but, like Veblen, he has little faith that they will: the book is full of pain at the way "this oppressed community had turned their cruel hands against their own class in the interest of a common oppressor." The book closes with the revolution defeated in a pool of blood.

What is striking in both men is that they believe in progress and yet doubt it. They are harbingers of doom and corruption while still sharing, with hardly an exception, the beliefs of the Enlightenment as transplanted to the American Midwest. They are against the corporations and against high tariffs, against chivalry and the genteel tradition, against all vested interests and for the common man. But they see the common man as easily duped; hence their despair. For one thing, both lack self-confidence: common men themselves, they feel vulnerable and pull or disguise their punches. Mark Twain submitted to editing by his refined wife and by refined editors such as Gilder and (to a degree) Howells, much as Veblen was persuaded to tone down *The Higher Learning.*

In Mark Twain the despair takes the form of seeing the pre-Gold Rush Midwest and pre-pubertal boyhood as idyllic: in his work as in his life, he could not come to terms with post-Civil War America, or with adults whom he tended to make either into saints like Joan of Arc or sinners like the corrupted men of Hadleyburg. Veblen describes his own similar difficulties projectively when, in *The Theory of the Leisure Class,* he discusses the character and aptitudes of his concededly somewhat mythical savage (pp. 223–4):

"As seen from the point of view of life under modern civilised conditions in an enlightened community of the Western culture, the primitive, ante-predatory savage . . . was not a great success. Even for the purposes of that hypothetical culture to which his type of human nature owes what stability it has—even for the ends of the peaceable savage group—this primitive man has quite as many and as conspicuous economic failings as he has economic virtues,—as should be plain to any one whose sense of the case is not biassed by leniency born of a fellow-feeling. At his best he is 'a clever, good-for-nothing fellow.' The shortcomings of this presumptively primitive type of character are weakness, inefficiency, lack of initiative and ingenuity and a yielding and indolent amiability, together with a lively but inconsequential animistic sense. Along with these traits go certain others which have some value for the collective life process, in the sense that they further the facility of life in the group. These traits are truthfulness, peaceableness, good-will, and a non-emulative, non-invidious interest in men and things."

Even if his fellow-men had followed Veblen's injunction not to write any biographies of him, this passage would serve as an amiable, non-invidious description of him. He might cavil only at the statement that he possessed an animistic sense, since so much of his life was spent attacking animism, but I am inclined to think (and can find supporting passages in Veblen himself) that hardly anyone gets through life without some animism—certainly, few scientists do. However that may be, the passage expresses Veblen's lack of self-confidence and his feeling, which he shared with Mark Twain, of vulnerability in the modern market-place. While Veblen disguised his feelings of inadequacy by silence and withdrawal in company, Mark Twain disguised his by joking and occasional truculence, but when this was ill-received as in the famous dinner for the elder Holmes, Twain would beg apologies abjectly. This is not unlike Veblen's method of repeated disclaimer that he means no ill in his books, and we must recall in this connection his abject reply to Cummings.

These similarities led me to wonder whether Mark Twain, like Veblen, had suffered from an intimidating father coupled with a weak but whimsical mother. Dixon Wecter's book, *Sam Clemens of Hannibal*, offers some fairly convincing evidence on this. Mark Twain described his father as "a stern, unsmiling man" —"My father and I were always on the most distant terms when I was a boy—a sort of armed neutrality, so to speak" (Wecter, p. 67). The father "never demonstrated affection for wife or child." Sam Clemens, like Veblen, was a silent rebel, a prankish nonconformist. Wecter quotes an autobiographical note: "Campbellite revival. All converted but me. All sinners again in a week." (p. 88). Mark Twain's mother, like Veblen's, was more whimsical than the father and less orderly, given to fairy tales and fond of the Bible.

Mark Twain's *Mysterious Stranger*, in an unpublished version, "thinks well of the cat because she is the only independent; says there is no such thing as an independent human being—all are slaves. . . ." The Stranger "often said he would not give a penny for human company when he could get better. . . . He said that the natural man, the savage, had no prejudices about smells, and no shame for his God-made nakedness. . . . The wild creatures trooped in from everywhere, and climbed all over Satan, and sat on his shoulder and his head; and rummaged his pockets and made themselves at home. . . ."

This mood vis-à-vis the animal kingdom, it seems to me, strikingly resembles Veblen's—recall his defense of cats whom he praised as against the servility of dogs in *The Theory of the Leisure Class*. Duffus describes Veblen at Cedro as getting on better with animals than with men. A skunk would brush against him, and animals would wander in and out of his house without Veblen moving a muscle. "He had no sentimental love for nature," Duffus writes; "What he had was a kind of amused tolerance."

Shortly before he died, Veblen wrote a characteristically self-effacing note (quoted by Dorfman, p. 504):

"It is also my wish, in case of death, to be cremated, if it can conveniently be done, as expeditiously and inexpensively as may be, without ritual or ceremony of any kind; that my ashes be thrown loose into the sea [he was in Stanford at the time], or into some sizable stream running to the sea; that no tombstone, slab, epitaph, effigy, tablet, inscription, or monument of any name or nature, be set up in my memory or name in any place or at any time; that no obituary, memorial, portrait, or biography of me, nor any letters written to or by me be printed or published, or in any way reproduced, copied or circulated."

There are of course many ironies in Veblen's use here (as in other writings) of the language of legal chicane that had cost his father so dear—as if to prove he could handle the English language as badly as any man of native stock. But what is more striking is how closely Veblen's attitude here, too, resembles that of Mark Twain who wrote to a friend (Wecter, p. 119):

"If Henry and my father feel as I would feel under their circumstances, they want no prominent or expensive lot, or luxurious entertainment in the new cemetery. As for a monument—well, if you remember my father, you are aware that he would rise up and demolish it the first night. He was a modest man and would not be able to sleep under a monument."

Yet, concealed in such casual attitudes towards the bodies of the dead, are bitter aggressions against the sentiments of the living.

To be sure, Mark Twain, who ended up an unhappy celebrity, did not order his papers destroyed; he handled the problem of post mortem scrutiny quite differently. Life forced and aided him to overcome his tendencies to withdrawal; although like Veblen he seems never to have come to terms with his own sexuality either in his life or in his work, he himself became something of a businessman and promoter, following in this in the footsteps of Tom Sawyer. Veblen's picture of the American businessman was much more steadily relentless, and his critique of course far more searching. What nevertheless links the two men beyond the details of biography and theme are the courage and the limitations of their satire. For both, satire served as a mask of detachment from the world's brutalities. Neither, however, could maintain a consistent tone: in both, irony sometimes barely rises above mere description, sometimes verges on burlesque. Even their best books proceed by association from one thing to another: both were too much, for good and ill, at the mercy of their material to impose plot and ordered structure upon it. Both repeat themselves end-lessly—possibly, satire cannot escape monotone since it compels only a one-eyed view of its subject, and Gulliver's voyages fade into one another as do Mark Twain's and as do Veblen's sallies against the sporting men and the "kept classes," the Yahoos of his day. But every limitation for a writer is also an opportunity, and in both Veblen and Mark Twain it is satire that saves them from the dreariness of muckraking and the pieties of the genteel tradi-tion in literature and scholarship.

VEBLEN AND FORD

If Veblen as an artist bears comparison with Mark Twain, Veblenism as a set of attitudes bears comparison with Fordism. When my colleague, Reuel Denney, called the Model-T, and its successors among the hot-rods, "Veblenian vehicles," he meant that the stripped-down, matter-of-fact car could be taken as repre-senting a protest against the plushy, yacht-like cars of 1915 and the chrome-spangled parlor sofa which has become the Detroit merchandising staple today. Staughton Lynd, who assisted me in this book, has pointed out the personal and ideological resem-blances of Ford and Veblen. Ford, indeed, may be seen as the archetype of the Veblenian engineer, waging relentless war on behalf of industry against business (with its subsidiary chicaneries of banking, law, and politics), and against conspicuous consump-tion and leisure-class values generally.

Garet Garrett says of Ford in *The Wild Wheel* that he "dis-covered familiar things with the innocence of first-seeing" (p. 19). Money, he never wearied of pointing out, had not built the Ford Motor Company but hard work, coupled with the skills embodied in machinery. Like Veblen, Ford did not believe that work went on in the office. It is a twice-told tale how he was always either firing white-collar workers or forcing them into overalls—he himself never used his office in the Administration Building which had somehow risen in spite of him, and he was happiest on the factory floor. Once he discovered a group of men who told him they comprised the Statistical Department. He told his production boss Sorensen he could have the space, and the latter moved in with crowbars and demolished the Department.

Fearing constraint and formal rules much as Veblen and Mark Twain did, Ford refused to allow any titles to develop in his organization. Hating absentee ownership and the "money power," it is well known how he chivvied his stockholders, refusing to pay them more than trivial dividends until compelled by a court order, and finally managing by a series of ruses to buy them out. It is ironical that the freedom from Wall Street and stockholder control that he fought for so bitterly is now available to most large corporations, quite differently managed, because they have disfranchised their stockholders by wide ownership dispersion and have consequently been able to retain profits (and heavy depreciation reserves) as a source of expansion without the need periodically to consult the money market. All his life, Ford inveighed against the profit motive and was in favor of the industrial motive of "providing goods for all" (*The Wild Wheel*, pp. 17–18); in the stockholder suit he testified (*ibid.*, p. 117):

> "The money is not mine to do with as I please. The men who work with me have helped to create it. After they have had their wages and a share of the profits, it is my duty to take what remains and put it back into the industry to create more work for more men at higher wages."

When he set up his tractor business he proclaimed there would be "no stockholders, no directors, no absentee owners" and no more "parasites" (Keith Sward, *The Legend of Henry Ford*, p. 69). At the same time, he insisted no less emphatically than Veblen that he was "not a reformer" (*ibid.*, p. 79), and he refused to commit himself permanently to any party or group inside or outside his plant.

On the side of production, then, Ford shared Veblen's awareness of the enormous productive possibilities of American industry, though the latter seems to have lacked Ford's recognition that mass production depends on mass consumption. The sense they had in the early 1900s of what "miracles" technology could accomplish was prophetic, and their belief that it was the business-law-banking fetters that held engineering genius down, though an oversimplification, receives some measure of support from Ford's own struggle to expand and lower costs rather than pay dividends. For Ford and for Veblen, price policy was no problem: the problem was to get rid of the legalistic stratagems which hampered and obfuscated the "obvious" engineering solutions to the tasks at hand. (In Ford's case, literally at hand: according to Garrett, he thought with his fingers.) It is a grand Veblenian irony that Ford was finally defeated by consumption tastes of the leisure class rather than by the wiles of bankers. He nearly bankrupted the company (and did bankrupt many dealers and employees) before he consented to abandon the workmanlike Model-T for a model more suited to genteel suburban life. Partly, he gave in to the insistence of his son Edsel, whose moving to Grosse Point, the Detroit "society" suburb, seemed to his father an invitation to betrayal and ruin at the hands of dilettantes, wastrels, and snobs.

For all the polite, smooth ways of modern business enterprise and modern social intercourse both Ford and Veblen had nothing but contempt. True, Veblen did not say as Ford did that "history is bunk," but much else of the classical, gentlemanly culture he did think to be bunk; like Ford and Mark Twain, he regarded religion as bunk;* and certainly he rated any pre-Darwinian science not much higher. Both Ford and Veblen distrusted the received realities, though of course Veblen went about his subversion in a more roundabout way. The War had a similarly up-

---

* Persons close to Ford have told me that late in life he became interested in the cult of the "Pyramid Inch," a pseudo-religion and pseudo-key to history.

rooting effect on both, leading Veblen into the Washington adventures already discussed and Ford into the fabulous foray of the Peace Ship.

No less striking than these similarities are the more deeply personal ones. Both men had a romantic sympathy for the insubordinate underdog—in fact, their attack on the received realities may be viewed as a defense of the unreceived ones. Veblen admired the Wobblies and their precursors throughout history —he admired the Vikings while regarding them as a bunch of crooks—whereas Ford (see Harry Bennett's *We Never Called Him Henry*) was drawn to criminals and the underworld. Even Ford's anti-Semitism had pro-underdog roots; he was going to be for Hitler and Gerald K. Smith since all the good people in his circle seemed to be down on them (Veblen, the friend of Jacques Loeb and admirer of Marx, never made the fatal Populist identification of Jews with Wall Street bankers and Washington financiers). Stories of Ford's dress—his insistence on wearing cheap socks despite his wife's entreaties—could easily be matched by Veblen's economies in dress.

Both men, moreover, were shy, sly and evasive. Ford enjoyed slipping out the back door of Harry Bennett's office to avoid a distinguished visitor much as Veblen slipped out of the paperwork requirements of academic administration. Harry Bennett tells the story of how Ford, walking one day on the roadbed of his Detroit, Toledo and Ironton Railway, saw slag from the Rouge plant being dumped which contained visible traces of iron ore; he ordered it to be sent back and re-smelted—a costly procedure for an infinitesimal return. To avoid this, Sorensen improved his recovery of ore, but was curious why Ford had not told him directly to do so; apparently, it was Ford's ironical way of controlling waste, which he hated with a passion akin to Veblen's. Ford's irony, of course, was not literary, but it sprang from a similar delight in indirection, a country boy's way of being sharp.

Ford, like Veblen, grew up hating farm work; as he wrote (Garrett, p. 192):

"What a waste it is for a human being to spend hours and days behind a slowly moving team of horses when in the same time a tractor could do six times as much work!"

When he went back to the farm as a rich man, it was with tractors; he boasted: "Our dairy farm is managed exactly like a factory." Yet, like Veblen with his sagas, foot-races with Icelandic friends, and Baltic antiquities, he was prey to fabulously inconsistent nostalgias, going in late in life for folk-dances, fiddlers and American antiques—and foot-races.

Needless to say, there were great differences as well as similarities between Ford and Veblen. Ford, active and successful man that he was, dominated his son and the men around him in ways utterly alien to Veblen's softer and more resigned temperament. Moreover, one can hardly emphasize enough Veblen's marginality as a second-generation Norwegian, put off and alienated from the parents' parochial culture but without the ability fully to assimilate and accept the available forms of Americanism— indeed, already anticipating in his loving translation of the Laxdaela Saga the third-generation nostalgia (to whose literary forms Marcus Hansen has called attention). This marginality drove Veblen into the Bohemian fringes of society, as it also drove there many other second-generation internal exiles in the period from 1890 to 1930; Ford, by contrast, while eccentric, was never in the least Bohemian.

Thus, rather than pushing too far the similarities in outlook and disposition between Veblen and Ford, it is important to study Ford as a living embodiment of Veblen's ideal engineer, whose eye was on the industrial arts, not the business ones, and who, far from despoiling industry for the sake of his own emulative consumption, lived sparely and simply, using technological advance and a widening market to cut production costs (not only in his own plants but also, by enforced economies, in his suppliers' and the railroads that served him), raise wages, and rebuild obsolescent plants. To be sure, Veblen never mentions Ford by name, but then he seldom cited his sources, either of person or print. And in *The Engineers and the Price System*, written after Ford had gained national celebrity, Veblen makes what is for him an unusual admission. After once more setting forth his shibboleth of the conflict between engineer and financier, he declares that there exist (p. 10):

> "exceptional, sporadic, and spectacular episodes in business where business men have now and again successfully gone out of the safe and sane highway of conservative business enterprise that is hedged about by conscientious withdrawal of efficiency, and have endeavored to regulate the output by increasing the productive capacity of the industrial system at one point or another."

Later on, he makes the even more startling admission, inconceivable to Marx or the earlier Veblen, that business could actually make more profit by quantity production at low prices than by restricted production at high prices. Scattered throughout the book, moreover, one encounters types intermediate between the angelic engineer and Satanic financier: the investment banker, less speculative than the old corporate financier because more bureaucratic in his procedure and more closely in touch with the technological experts; the "consulting engineer" who advises the investment banker not only as to the commercial but also as to the industrial soundness of any enterprise that is to be underwritten; the captain of industry who, even in this later day, is more interested in production than the absentee owner and comes into conflict with the latter.

These, however, are mere hints, which are undeveloped in the book; they are quite lost amid the usual raillery at "one-eyed captains of industry," and the "unearned increment" gained by chicane-minded men capable only of sitting tight at the expense of the gullible common man. For Veblen, such men as Ford were relics of a more heroic age, not—short of revolution sparked by the aroused engineers—part of the American future.

Yet Ford marches on around the world. His impatience with the human, noneconomic costs of the machine process is duplicated by the Soviets and their satellites for whom Ford was becoming a hero just about the time Americans were taking a more critical look at him. American emissaries, no longer welcome at home with their gospel of hard work and industrial progress, compete with Communist intellectuals in bringing Fordism to "backward" countries. Meanwhile advertising men, sharing Veblen's belief that they belong to the kept classes and Ford's belief that cars aren't built with words, seek to expiate their guilts by government service, work with their hands on their country places, and the use of their media to sell intangible values like tolerance and the American Way. It would, in fact, take an ironist of Veblen's skeptical and disenchanted power to crack open the deadly seriousness with which all these activities, influenced by attitudes to which he gave currency, are conducted. We will not find this in the heavy portentousness or hardly less heavy humor characteristic of most American talk and writing in our own day no less than in his.

Whatever our debt to the theories Veblen developed, I think we are all in his debt for his way of seeing. Irreverent and catty to the very end, he avoided becoming a substantial citizen, which he defined as one who owns much property. He died insolvent. But the intangible assets that have come down to us, his books and his personal style, have still the power over us that Veblen was all too inclined to disparage: the power of ideas and of personality.

CHRONOLOGY OF
THORSTEIN VEBLEN'S LIFE

1857	Born on Wisconsin farm
1874	Entered Carleton College (B.A., 1880)
1880	Taught one year, Monona Academy, Madison, Wisconsin
1881	Entered Johns Hopkins, one semester
1881	Entered Yale University (Ph.D., 1884)
1888	Married Ellen Rolfe
1891	Entered Cornell
1892	Joined faculty, University of Chicago
1895	Promoted to instructor
1896	Visited William Morris in Europe
1899	*The Theory of the Leisure Class* published
1900	Promoted to assistant professor
1906–09	Faculty, Stanford University, associate professor
1911–18	Faculty, University of Missouri
1911	Divorced by Ellen Rolfe
1914	Married Anne Fessenden Bradley
1918	Employee of Food Administration, Washington, D.C.
1918	An editor of *The Dial,* New York City
1919	Joined faculty of New School for Social Research, New York City
1926	Returned to California
1929	Died

A LIST OF VEBLEN'S BOOKS
PUBLISHED BY TRANSACTION

The Engineers and the Price System
With a new introduction by Daniel Bell

The Higher Learning in America
With a new introduction by Ivan Berg

Imperial Germany and the Industrial Revolution
With a new introduction by Otto G. Mayer

*The Instinct of Workmanship
and the State of the Industrial Arts*
With a new introduction by Murray G. Murphey

The Place of Science in Modern Civilization
With a new introduction by Warren J. Samuels

The Theory of Business Enterprise
With a new introduction by Douglas Dowd

The Theory of the Leisure Class
With an introduction by C. Wright Mills

SELECTIVE BIBLIOGRAPHY

An excellent short bibliography appears in Max Lerner's *The Portable Veblen* (N. Y., Viking Press, 1950), pp. 630–632; Lerner's introduction to this volume is one of the best sympathetic statements on Veblen to be found, and his selection, like that of Wesley C. Mitchell in *What Veblen Taught* (N. Y., Viking Press, 1947), is a good place to begin the study of Veblen. Repeated reference has been made in the foregoing pages to Joseph Dorfman's *Thorstein Veblen and His America* (N. Y., Viking Press, 1934), which contains not only the full, detailed, and authoritative account of Veblen's life and a digest of his writings (including a complete bibliography of them) but also an effort to place Veblen in his epoch and to relate him to currents of American thought. In "The 'Satire' of Thorstein Veblen's *Theory of the Leisure Class,*" *Political Science Quarterly*, XLVII (1932), pp. 363–409, Professor Dorfman ingeniously shows how greatly Veblen's evolutionary theory was influenced by Herbert Spencer's dichotomy between "military" and "industrial" societies, with Veblen turning the tables on Spencer by insisting on the military and feudal aspects of modern capitalism. (In the writings of W. J. Ghent, such as *Our Benevolent Feudalism,* Macmillan, 1902, a view similar to Veblen's is taken: Ghent saw the captains of industry as the new, if chastened, overlords.)

Richard V. Teggart has written a monograph—"Thorstein Veblen: A Chapter in American Economic Thought," *Univ. of California Publications in Economics,* XI (1932), pp. 1–124— which is a critical investigation of the sources and implications of Veblen's thought. Perhaps Teggart's lack of sympathy with Veblen is partly responsible for the relative neglect of his fine

211

study, which is to be contrasted with the clear but superficial *Veblen* (London, Chapman & Hall, 1936) by the English economist and publicist, John A. Hobson.

In *The Innocents at Cedro: A Memoir of Thorstein Veblen and Some Others* (N. Y., Macmillan, 1944), R. L. Duffus describes, from the perspective of a student who worked for him, Veblen's "domestic economy" during his Stanford University days. A searching portrait of Veblen as artist and thinker appears in Alfred Kazin's *On Native Grounds* (N.Y., Reynal & Hitchcock, 1942), pp. 130–142; this is one of many surveys which contain material on Veblen—others are Henry Steele Commager, *The American Mind* (New Haven, Conn., Yale Univ. Press, 1950), pp. 235–243; Daniel Aaron, *Men of Good Hope* (N. Y., Oxford Univ. Press, 1951), pp. 210–233; Charles A. Madison, *Critics and Crusaders* (N. Y., Henry Holt, 1947), pp. 308–339; all these books discuss Veblen's contribution to the intellectual climate of American progressivism. John Dos Passos' eloquent, staccato portrait of Veblen in *The Big Money* (N. Y., Harcourt, Brace, 1936), pp. 93 ff., can remind us of the effect Veblen had on young radicals in the 1920s and 30s; see also the discussion of Veblen in relation to Randolph Bourne in Max Lerner's *Ideas for the Ice Age* (N. Y., Viking Press, 1942), pp. 135, 147.

T. W. Adorno's "Veblen's Attack on Culture," *Studies in Philosophy and Social Science*, IX (1941), pp. 405–433, compresses into a few pages a most penetrating grasp of Veblen's hatred for many middle-class values, and a rare understanding of his functionalist aesthetic. It should be read in connection with Robert L. Steiner and Joseph Weiss, "Veblen Revised in the Light of Counter-Snobbery," *Journal of Aesthetics and Art Criticism*, IX (1951), pp. 263–268.

Veblen is treated more specifically as an economist in John R. Commons, *Institutional Economics* (N. Y., The Macmillan Co., 1934), pp. 649–680; Philip C. Newman, *The Development of Economic Thought* (N. Y., Prentice-Hall, 1952), pp. 344–361; and John S. Gambs, *Man, Money and Goods* (N. Y., Columbia Univ. Press, 1952), pp. 154–174; Gambs' *Beyond Supply and Demand: A Reappraisal of Institutional Economics* (N. Y., Columbia Univ. Press, 1946) deals also with Veblen's methodology. This latter theme is capably treated in Morton G. White's *Social Thought in America: The Revolt Against Formalism* (N. Y., Viking Press, 1949), chapter vi; this book relates Veblen to other contemporary iconoclasts such as Dewey, Holmes, and Beard; a quite technical treatment, relating Veblen to Kant, is Stanley Matthews Daugert's *The Philosophy of Thorstein Veblen* (N. Y., King's Crown Press, 1950); while Louis Schneider's *The Freudian Psychology and Veblen's Social Theory* (N. Y., King's Crown Press, 1948) includes at once a restatement of much of Veblen's work and a thoughtful critique of his social psychology.

Veblen and institutional economics are treated judiciously in Paul T. Homan's chapter on Veblen in *American Masters of Social Science* (Howard W. Odum, ed., N. Y., Henry Holt, 1927), pp. 229–270 (further developed in Homan's *Contemporary Economic Thought*, N. Y., Harper & Bro., 1928); and both are sharply criticized by Abram L. Harris, "Veblen and the Social Phenomenon of Capitalism," *Am. Economic Review*, XLI (1951), pp. 66–77, as well as in a forthcoming monograph, "Toward a Soviet of Technicians: A Reappraisal of Veblen," to appear in *Ethics* for April, 1953. D. R. Scott insists that Veblen should be regarded primarily as an apostle of science in "Veblen Not an Institutional Economist," *Am. Economic Review*, XXIII (1933), pp. 274–277. Veblen's relation to economic history is briefly noted in Harold A. Innis, "A Bibliography of Thorstein Veblen," *Southwestern Political and Social Science Quarterly*, X (1929), pp. 1–13.

Arthur K. Davis' doctoral dissertation (*Thorstein Veblen's Social Theory*, Harvard University Library, 1941), already referred to, is a critical examination of Veblen from the standpoint of modern "structural-functional" sociology; three articles drawn from the thesis have been published: "Veblen's Study of Modern Germany," *Am. Sociological Review*, VIII (1944), pp. 603–

609; "Veblen on the Decline of the Protestant Ethic," *Social Forces,* XXII (1944), pp. 282–286; and "Sociological Elements in Veblen's Economic Theory," *Journal of Political Economy,* LIII (1945), pp. 132–149—the last-named article follows up and develops Professor Abram L. Harris' early insistence on normative elements in Veblen in his two articles, "Types of Institutionalism," and "Economic Evolution: Dialectical and Darwinian," *Journal of Political Economy,* XL (1932), pp. 721–749, and XLII (1934), pp. 34–79.

Much more sympathetic to Veblen than either Davis or Harris, and emphasizing the importance of *The Higher Learning in America,* is Bernard Rosenberg's doctoral dissertation, done in 1949 at the New School for Social Research. Another recent publication reveals one of the early collisions of Veblen with the higher learning, when he was turned down for a teaching job in natural science at St. Olaf's College because the President did not think him able to "bring our youth nearer to Christ," in view of his critical view of the Bible and of Lutheranism: "Thorstein Veblen and St. Olaf's College: A Group of Letters by Thorbjørn N. Mohn [1890]," edited by Kenneth Bjork, *Norwegian-American Studies and Records,* XV (1949), pp. 122–130.

Karl L. Anderson's article, "The Unity of Veblen's Theoretical System," *Quarterly Journal of Economics,* XLVII (1933), pp. 598–626, has been mentioned above; the discussion of Veblen and Keynes in chapter seven draws on Rutledge Vining, "Suggestions of Keynes in the Writings of Veblen," *Journal of Political Economy,* XLVII (1939), pp. 692–714. See also Allen Gruchy, *Modern Economic Thought* (N. Y., Prentice-Hall, 1947), pp. 31–135.

The novels of Rølvaag are of course a prime source for the attitudes of the Norwegian pioneers in America, and the picture of second-generation rebellion is especially fine in the Christmas party scene in *Their Fathers' God* (N. Y., Harper & Bro., 1931).

A lucid summary of Veblen's life and influence appears in *Fortune* (December 1947), p. 132.

SELECTIVE INDEX

215